Hollywood's Italian American Filmmakers

Hollywood's Italian American Filmmakers

CAPRA, SCORSESE, SAVOCA,
COPPOLA, AND TARANTINO

Jonathan J. Cavallero

University of Illinois Press

URBANA, CHICAGO, AND SPRINGFIELD

Library of Congress Cataloging-in-Publication Data
Cavallero, Jonathan J.
Hollywood's Italian American filmmakers : Capra, Scorsese,
Savoca, Coppola, and Tarantino / Jonathan J. Cavallero.
p.   cm.
Includes bibliographical references and index.
ISBN 978-0-252-03614-9 (cloth)
ISBN 978-0-252-07807-1 (pbk.)
1. Italian Americans in motion pictures.
2. Ethnicity in motion pictures.
3. Motion picture producers and directors—United States.
4. Italian Americans in the motion picture industry.
I. Title.
PN1995.9.I73.C38   2011
791.43'08951073—dc22   2011008424

*To my ancestors, whose sacrifices have made
my opportunities possible*

Contents

Acknowledgments

This book would not have been possible without the help of family, friends, filmmaking professionals, and others who have supported it. It began as a dissertation, and so I am especially grateful to the members of my dissertation committee at Indiana University. James Naremore served as my dissertation adviser and became a role model in more ways than one. Working with Jim has been one of the great honors of my life. Peter Bondanella graciously supported my work with his vast knowledge of Italian and Italian American cinema and even helped me to craft arguments that disagreed with his own ideas. Gregory Waller suggested a number of readings including those on postclassical Hollywood cinema that became instrumental in shaping my understanding of the works of Scorsese and Coppola, and Yeidy Rivero's understanding and awareness of ethnicity and media expanded the implications of this project beyond Italian Americans.

I was also supported by a number of filmmakers and archivists who have provided me with experiences that I will be talking about for years. Nancy Savoca agreed to a three-hour interview about her life and her films. Melville Shavelson, Hal Kanter, Angela Lansbury, and Jane Wyatt each spoke with me about working with Frank Capra. Francis Ford Coppola generously granted me access to the *Godfather Notebook* and other production materials at the American Zoetrope Research Library, and Patricia Prestinary, the American Zoetrope Research Librarian, not only helped me to gather relevant documents but also went through *The Godfather, Part III* production materials when my time was running short. Fellow Penn State graduate and Hollywood producer-executive Tom Ortenberg provided scripts related to my research on Quentin Tarantino. Joan Miller, head librarian at the Wesleyan Cinema Archives, helped me to navigate the vast holdings of the Frank Capra Collection, and the staff in the Motion Picture Reading Room at the Library of Congress granted me access to some of Capra's earliest and most elusive films.

Fred L. Gardaphé and Anthony J. Tamburri have discussed this project with me—offering ideas, suggestions, encouragement, and contacts. They are world-class scholars and leaders in the field of Italian American studies, and they believe strongly in assisting less experienced writers interested in Italian Americana. I am grateful to have them as mentors and friends. Frank P. Tomasulo provided detailed feedback on various manuscript drafts and pushed me to prove my assertions. His close readings have vastly improved the overall quality of my work. I have also received helpful suggestions and feedback on early Italian American cinema from Giorgio Bertellini, on Scorsese from Aaron Baker, and on Scorsese, issues of whiteness, and the White Ethnic Revival from Laura Cook-Kenna.

Early in my undergraduate career, Carol Kent helped me to see film as a possible career path. While I was a master's student at Penn State, Kevin Hagopian worked tirelessly to develop my knowledge of film history, and Chris Jordan spent countless hours directing my master's thesis. Thomas W. Benson, M. Heather Hartley, and Alan R. Perry were generous with their time and ideas. Each offered readings and discussions that exposed me to new approaches to the cinema. Penn State also offered generous financial support for some of my research and travel expenses. Thank you to Deans Richard L. Barton, Douglas Anderson, John Nichols, Robert D. Richards, and Anne Hoag and department head Anthony Olorunnisola for always finding the resources to support this project.

A number of faculty members and graduate students have discussed this book with me, and their comments have shaped its content. My thanks go to Brian Amsden, Patricia Andrews, Chad Beck, Jeff Bennett, Barbara Bird, Shelley Bradfield, Matthew Broussard, Cara Buckley, Michael Butterworth, Ed Chamberlain, Robert Clift, David Coon, Eric Covil, Lauren De Carvalho, Darrel Enck-Wanzer, Suzanne Enck-Wanzer, Charles Frederick, Seth Friedman, Matt Guschwan, Torunn Haaland, Michel Haigh, Mark Hain, Joan Hawkins, Dorn Hetzel, Matthew F. Jordan, Jim Kendrick, G. S. "Soon" Khoo, Barbara Klinger, Ryan Lizardi, John Lucaites, Matt McAllister, David Moscowitz, Jeff Motter, Dave Naze, Jonathan Nichols-Pethick, James Paasche, Phaedra Pezzullo, Natasha Ritsma, Michelle Rodino-Colocino, Zak Roman, Shira Segal, Sarah E. S. Sinwell, Jacob Smith, Jason Sperb, Ted Striphas, Robert Terrill, and Isaac West. Additionally, a number of my undergraduate students have asked repeatedly about the book's progress and its ideas. My sincere gratitude goes to Drew Anderson, Matt Antonelli, Matt Avedesian, Courtney Bentz, Tommy Camaano, Chris Carlantonio, Ryan Coutu, Jason Derck, Adam Eshelman, Frank Giannetto, Joy Grant, Jason Hellerman, Andrew Karasik, Danielle Knittle, Ryan Kroboth, Jacob Lasher, Tony Lloret, Ben Ogrodnik, Chris O'Konski, Jason Oshman, Ryan Quinn, and Kyle Vinansky.

My colleagues at the University of Arkansas, including Tom Frentz, Frank Scheide, Myria Allen, Patricia Amason, Laurie Brady, Robert Brady, Lisa Corrigan, Stephanie Schulte, Stephen Smith, Kasey Walker, Ron Warren, Lynne Webb, and Rob Wicks, have provided valuable feedback on this and other projects. I feel honored to be surrounded by such generous and intelligent teacher-scholars. Thanks also to Hershel Hartford for our frequent conversations about *The Godfather* and Scorsese and to Brenda McCrory for helping with the administrative tasks associated with this project.

The Department of Italian at Gettysburg College invited me to present a selection from my chapter on Coppola. Portions of chapter 1, "Frank Capra: Ethnic Denial and Its Impossibility," appeared in modified versions as articles. The section of the chapter that deals with the "Why We Fight" films first appeared in *Italian Americana* (University of Rhode Island) (Spring 2004); the portion that deals with Capra's 1920s films originally appeared in *MELUS: The Journal for the Study of Multi-Ethnic Literatures of the United States* 29, no. 2 (2004): 27–53, and is reprinted by permission of the journal. I am grateful to the editors of both of these publications—Carol Bonomo Albright at *Italian Americana* and Martha J. Cutter at *MELUS*—for their generosity and valuable suggestions. Additionally, Veronica Makowsky, former editor of *MELUS,* went over my essay with a fine-tooth comb, and I am a better writer because of it.

At the University of Illinois Press, Joan Catapano has been a responsive and insightful editor, and Annette Wenda's suggestions have cleaned up the manuscript and made it more readable.

I am also lucky to have several friends outside of academia who have contributed to the completion of this book. Russell Lofgren read multiple drafts of this and other projects. His suggestions have improved the overall readability of my writing. Ben Helwig and Chris Koebbe have been good friends through the years and have helped me to keep things in perspective, and Lisa Vicens saw potential in this project when it was just an idea. My aunts and uncles—Judy Ramakers, Paul DuBois, Betty and Don Holloway, Linda Dorr, and Paul Dorr Jr.—my cousin Bethany, and my sister, Kim, have attended various presentations of this and other material. Their love and support are something for which I am exceedingly grateful. Members of the McGill family—Dan, Debbie, Jessica, Amy and Kevin Miller, Sean, and

Patrick—have brought other films of which I was unaware to my attention. And my parents, Mary Dorr Cavallero and Jim Cavallero, have encouraged me to follow my dreams even when they were seemingly unattainable.

Finally, Kathryn McGill has lived with this project on a daily basis. She has loved and supported me through the stress associated with deadlines and the long hours of research and writing. She has been exceptionally understanding when our vacations have been planned around the locations of conferences or archives. She has been honest in her assessment of my ideas and writing. She (along with our five cats—Haley, Rescue, Oliver, Isabelle, and Oreo—and one dog—Sofia) has truly been my partner throughout this process. This book, like a great many other things in my life, would not have been possible without her. I love her dearly, and every day I feel very thankful for the life we have together.

Introduction

"Team!" That is what that olive-skinned, tuxedo-clad man muttered just before the wooden baseball bat cracked the back of his skull. He fell forward onto a white cloth that shrouded a massive oval-shaped dining table. Again, the bat cracked the back of the man's head, and the guests at this luxurious dinner party mumbled "Jesus" as Al Capone's repeated blows spawned a pool of blood that stained the white tablecloth and the mind of this impressionable eleven-year-old viewer.

Brian De Palma's film *The Untouchables* (1987), an R-rated movie that I got to see in the theater because my dad was able to convince my mom that it would be okay, was my first introduction to Italian Americans in the movies, or at least the first image of cinematic Italian Americans that I can remember. I did not know who this De Niro guy was, but Al Capone was a name I had heard (fig. 1). He was the guy whose vault had been opened on national television the year before. The vault was empty, except for a few bottles, but Capone was still the "great" gangster. He was the man who went to prison on Alcatraz and a man who was an Italian American . . . like me. I knew Capone. I took pride in Capone. I remember my best friend, Ahmad, making some comment about Capone being a murderer and my response that Capone was an Italian who demanded loyalty. I was demonstrating mine by defending this gangster. For this young kid, claiming his white ethnicity meant Capone was a man of his word, and I felt some kind of connection to him based on ethnic ties.

Of course, I was not very ethnic. I grew up in predominantly white middle-to upper-middle-class suburbs. My skin was always among the palest in my classes, and my red hair made others think I was Irish, not Italian. I did not

Figure 1. Robert De Niro as Al Capone in Brian De Palma's film *The Untouchables.*

have any Italian American friends, because there were few to be had, and if they existed, they were not marked as such. I did not learn to speak Italian; did not speak English with an accent; did not come home to a house that blasted Frank Sinatra, Dean Martin, or Tony Bennett; and was not even Catholic. Outside the family, my Italian ethnicity was relegated to a nice story to tell in my elementary school classes on the one day each year that our teacher decided to ask, "What countries did your relatives come from?"

Within the family, markers of Italianness were also elusive. The iconography we associate with Italian Americans—corpulent mothers; dark-skinned, dark-haired Latin lovers; excessively large extended families that meet each Sunday for family dinners; excessively emotional, violent criminal types; impeccably dressed crooners—all seemed to be absent from my American ethnic experience. I later learned that some of these stereotypes were applicable to my relatives, but as a child, they did not seem to be. Nonetheless, when the family (not just my immediate family, but my aunt, her family, and my grandparents) would congregate for holidays and other special occasions, the get-together would take on a clearly ethnic tone. The food served, the short colloquial Italian phrases that would creep their way into the conversation, even my grandfather's darker skin tone introduced an Italian element to the gathering.

Ethnicity runs deeper than surface-level experience. The ways my family communicates, the ways we see the world, the structures that govern family dynamics all fall into this category, but they became so ingrained in our everyday experience that they were no longer viewed as ethnic. They became the way things were done, and without the anti-Italian prejudice that characterized my great-grandparents' and grandparents' generations, the assumption was that we were the same as everybody else—that all families, or at least the white ones, did things this way, and that the ethnic gatherings we so enjoyed were a nostalgic throwback to a different time. It was not who we were now. Italian ethnicity was where we came from, but it was not where we were going.

Nonetheless, it was a part of my past of which I was aware, and one I would grow to embrace for two reasons. First, having early-childhood friends like Ahmad who were ethnically different encouraged me to embrace the otherness in myself. Second, I had a close relationship with my Italian American grandfather. As a child, I knew that he was a World War II veteran, that he was always laughing and smiling when he was around his grandchildren, and that he was Italian. Our family photo albums include images of us clowning around with him and putting on his officer's jacket. I loved being around him, and I suspect that embracing our shared ethnic heritage allowed me to feel closer to him. My grandfather died just weeks before Geraldo Rivera opened Capone's vault, and I guess Capone became a kind of stand-in for my grandfather. In being loyal to Capone, I was being loyal to my family, to my people.

As I was losing my clearest connection to my ethnic past, I began turning to the movies and television to find my ethnic roots and come to a better understanding of my ethnic culture. I was not conscious of it at the time, but in finding "role models" like Capone, I was building an "imagined community" in which I could stress the character traits I found most acceptable (Capone's power and the respect and loyalty that he commanded) and rationalize those that were objectionable (the murderous and criminal means by which he acquired and sustained his power, loyalty, and respect).

I was not the first Italian American to look to the media for a sense of cultural definition. Italian American scholar Peter Bondanella writes, "What ethnic roots I profess from Sicily are those I learned about from the movies—strictly Hollywood Italian origins, not authentically Italian American ones" (10). Bondanella's experience and my own are not unusual. Throughout the twentieth century and into the twenty-first, many Italian Americans came to better understand their ethnic backgrounds by watching movies and television shows that were about or created by Italian Americans.[1] This is due in part to the fact that late-nineteenth- and early-twentieth-century Italian immigrants left a land defined largely by fragmented regional and local communities and entered a country that encouraged a more national perspective.[2] From labor unions to political parties to Census Bureau statistics, U.S. institutions privileged nationality over other regional identities, and the media contributed to this perspective. Italian-language newspapers spoke to a readership defined by its country of origin (Italy) as much as its geographic position in the United States.[3] The movies presented Italian American characters who came to represent Italian Americans as a whole, and Hollywood's Italian American filmmakers became figures around which market demands, widespread prejudice, historical contexts, and personal identities circulated.

This book about Italian American directors mainly discusses the films of Frank Capra, Martin Scorsese, Nancy Savoca, Francis Ford Coppola, and Quentin Tarantino. Noticeably absent from this list are respected filmmakers like Gregory LaCava, Vincente Minnelli, Ida Lupino, Michael Cimino, Brian De Palma, Abel Ferrara, Penny Marshall, Michael Corrente, and Sofia Coppola. Time and space limitations, rather than a lack of interest, prevent their inclusion. Each offers a unique take on Italian ethnicity, and the book makes occasional references to their work. However, while the specifics of their films may differ, their general perspectives toward Italian ethnicity are often similar to one or more of the directors treated in detail. For instance, De Palma has worked at the same historical moment as Scorsese and Francis Ford Coppola, but his approach to Italian ethnicity might be more closely aligned with Capra.

*   *   *

Throughout the time period in question, Italian Americans' standing in the U.S. social hierarchy varied greatly. By 1930, more than 4.5 million Italians had immigrated to the United States (Mangione and Morreale 33). Viewed as a cheap source of labor during an era of industrialization, Italians (and other immigrant groups) were treated as a necessary evil. "To put it simply," Stephen Steinberg writes, "America needed the immigrant at least as much as the immigrant needed America" (37). Still, the relation between the two groups remained tenuous. Stereotypical caricatures plagued Italians, and in 1891, the largest lynching in American history claimed the lives of eleven Italians in New Orleans.[4] In 1921, Nicola Sacco and Bartolomeo Vanzetti, two Italian immigrants, were arrested for a double murder. Many suspected their Italian ethnicity coupled with widespread anti-Italian prejudice led not only to their arrest and conviction but also to their execution in 1927. Between 1929 and 1941, Italians and other immigrant groups were blamed for the Great Depression. "Nativists" in Congress argued for the deportation of six million aliens as a way to quickly and easily solve the economic ills that the United States faced.[5] World War II brought travel restrictions, curfews, and even internment.[6] In the postwar years, thousands of Italian American veterans took advantage of the G.I. Bill and federal housing loans that allowed them to move out of their urban ethnic enclaves and into the suburbs of assimilated America. By the late 1960s, a historical era known as the White Ethnic Revival encouraged Italian Americans (and other white ethnics) to embrace their ethnicity. This mitigated white ethnics' complicity in race-based prejudice. They were no longer white Americans but Italian Americans, Greek Americans, Jewish Americans, or "other" Americans who had overcome prejudice. Today, Italian Americans have largely assimilated, but for many, cultural background remains an important aspect of their identities.

The general move within Italian America from a population of lower-class immigrants to a more assimilated group with increased wealth and power is in some ways sociologically correct. But it is also fraught with oversimplifications that lead to historically inaccurate conclusions. For one, Italian Americans were never as marginalized as this general history implies. As Thomas A. Guglielmo has shown, Italians were recognized as "white" from the moment they arrived in the United States, and this whiteness "was their single most powerful asset in the 'New World'; it gave them countless advantages over 'nonwhites' in housing, jobs, schools, politics, and virtually every other meaningful area of life" (12). That said, in national media outlets, particularly in the early years of the twentieth century, Italian Americans were often a group that was spoken for rather than being a group that spoke for itself. Italian opera may have enjoyed a degree of notoriety in the American cultural landscape, but there were only a handful of published Italian American writers (Mangione and Morreale 353–63) and no significant Italian American filmmakers at that time.

However, by as early as the 1930s, Italian Americans had secured a relatively comfortable position in Hollywood's directors' chairs, and they have maintained that position ever since. Throughout the past nine decades, at least one of Hollywood's most respected directors has been of Italian heritage. Their films sometimes represent Italian American characters, neighborhoods, and concerns explicitly. Other times, material with ethnic or immigrant undertones has been smuggled into their movies. But ultimately, despite the "silencing" that occurred within the dominant culture, Italian Americans have almost always had a voice in Hollywood and hence American culture at large. The study of their films has the potential to serve as a kind of alternate history.

This cultural reality challenges the assertions of theorists like Roland Barthes who argue that the "author" is "dead." At the end of "What Is an Author?" Michel Foucault (quoting Samuel Beckett) poses the now famous question, "What matter who's speaking?" (138). In response, Janet Staiger has argued, who is speaking matters "especially to those in non-dominant positions in which asserting even a partial agency may seem to be important for day-to-day survival or where locating moments of alternative practice takes away the naturalized privileges of normativity" (27). Similarly, James Naremore asserts, "Marginalized social groups can declare solidarity and create a collective identity by adopting authors as culture heroes—names that signify complex, coded meanings" ("Authorship and Cultural Politics" 21). For both Staiger and Naremore, issues of authorship, especially as they relate to marginalized communities, carry a political potential wherein groups whose histories have been quashed by the social power structure might have their voices heard.

This book treats the directors in question as distinct historical actors confronting their historical moment and as members of a larger ethnic culture contributing to a collective experience. In so doing, it hopes to marry classical film studies approaches to authorship with a cultural studies perspective. Cultural studies and authorship studies are often thought of as antithetical. Cultural studies scholars argue that authorship studies fetishize the author and the text, making it easier for institutional and corporate entities to exploit these products commercially. Classical film studies scholars contend that a cultural studies position ignores the artistry of films and filmmakers in favor of an audience- or commercially centered view (or both) that seems more akin to sociology or economics. Drawing on the valid insights of both perspectives allows for a model that stresses these directors' authorship (which recognizes the historical, institutional, social, and economic contexts of a production) rather than their auteurism (which tends toward the ahistorical and oftentimes favors the author over the text) (Naremore, "Cultural Politics"). Further, recognizing the compromises that these directors made and still make exposes the ways in which their representations of Italian American ethnicity catered to and challenged the dominant culture's view of Italian Americans.

Focusing on individuals also challenges the idea that Italian Americans are a relatively homogeneous group. This myth has been proffered by studies that perpetuate past stereotypes by assuming that *Italian American* means acting a certain way, being from an urban area (usually New York), and having a working-class background. For instance, one Italian American scholar describes Scorsese's *Mean Streets* (1973) as "the first American film to present Italian-Americans as they really lived" (LoBrutto 135). *Mean Streets* presents a unique representation of Italian Americans, but this statement offers a totalizing view of the Italian American community. Not all Italian Americans (including people like myself) lived like this.

Each of the filmmakers investigated here has a unique background. Capra was a Sicilian immigrant whose family settled in Los Angeles. Scorsese is a Sicilian American who grew up in Queens and Manhattan. Savoca is of mixed

Argentine and Italian heritage and grew up in racially diverse, working-class communities in the Bronx. Coppola was born in Detroit, comes from a middle-class family, and has lived in the New York area and California. Tarantino has Irish, Cherokee, and Italian blood and was raised in Tennessee and Los Angeles. Highlighting not just the similarities between these filmmakers but also their differences works against essentialized notions of Italian American culture and exposes some of the diversity that exists within the community. Ultimately, we should not be talking about "*the* Italian American experience" but rather "Italian American experienc*es*."

* * *

Much of the scholarly attention devoted to Italian Americans' presence in Hollywood has centered on cinematic characters. The overarching concern of writers like Carlos Cortés and Daniel Sembroff Golden has been the degree to which various representations conform to Italian American stereotypes. Unfortunately, such analyses rely on the creation of an equally damaging and limiting "positive stereotype" as a barometer of accuracy. Ella Shohat and Robert Stam endorse a more discursive approach to stereotype analysis that attempts to minimize an individual critic's hypotheses on "proper representation" by linking analyses to the larger social, historical, and ideological climate surrounding the creation or reception of individual characters (180–81, 198–204). Although this approach has useful possibilities, its attempt to essentially evacuate stereotype analyses of *any* value judgments is not only impossible but also undesirable. As Jacqueline Stewart has shown, multiple discourses surround the creation of images, and both the discourses privileged and the interpretation of the historical moment surrounding the creation or reception of these images are necessarily and justifiably laden with value judgments (30–38).

Not judging the relative worth of a representation allows culture to stagnate. In discussing *Raging Bull* (Scorsese, 1980), Vincent LoBrutto writes, "Scorsese's seemingly unannounced violence in this and other films is rarely a shock for the Italian American viewer who understands the dynamics of high temperature personalities and the flashpoints" (232). Absent from this once again homogeneous image of Italian Americans is any indication that these perceived cultural dynamics need to be questioned. Instead, LoBrutto delights in a kind of insider knowledge that validates the less progressive practices of the past while disregarding larger concerns about desirable and undesirable behaviors and thought patterns. If one's cultural background insulates them from the shock of Jake LaMotta's (Robert De Niro) violent outbursts—his beating of his wife, his assault on his brother—then the norms of that cultural background (or the author's understanding of that background) need to be interrogated.

Some scholars have combined studies of Italian American characters with analyses of Italian American filmmakers. Bondanella's *Hollywood Italians,* for instance, offers chapters on specific stereotypes while also including discussions of how individual Italian American filmmakers have mobilized, nuanced, and questioned these stereotypes. Ultimately, he argues that Italian Americans have maintained a prominent position "not by claiming the status of victim . . . but by believing in the American Dream: that hard work and education would ultimately result in progress, and economic betterment, and a place at the table so to speak" (11). Despite Bondanella's debatable equation of Italian American experiences with African American and other ethnic experiences, his study provides a useful and developed history.

Both Fred Gardaphé and Robert Casillo suggest that the presence of an Italian American filmmaker carries significant implications for a work, particularly if that work makes use of Italian American characters or stereotypes.[7] Both limit their studies mostly to the films of Scorsese and Coppola. Casillo suggests that they represent "Italian-American cinema in its highest form" and dismisses Minnelli and Capra because their works do not center on Italian American characters. Sylvester Stallone, De Palma, and Cimino are of less interest, because their movies are artistically inferior by comparison ("Moments" 394–95). Many of these same filmmakers fall outside the purview of Gardaphé's study, because he narrows his focus to the ways Italian American artists represent gangster characters. Both Casillo and Gardaphé have valid reasons for privileging Scorsese and Coppola, but focusing so intently on just two filmmakers (who consistently offer gangster narratives) risks presenting a homogenous view of Italian Americana and Italian American cinematic production.

Pellegrino D'Acierno's book-length essay complements these studies by including a consideration of "Old Hollywood" filmmakers like Capra, Minnelli, and Lupino. D'Acierno suggests that directors like Coppola and Scorsese contest and disturb "the stereotyping discourse" of Hollywood, while the ethnicity of "Old Hollywood" filmmakers "is 'spoken' through a series of repressions, negations, displacements, distortions, and above all, through the strategy of 'passing' itself, which involves the use of genre as a mask" ("Cinema Paradiso" 607–9). D'Acierno's paradigm moves toward embracing the diversity that exists within Italian America, but the strategies used by individual filmmakers to engage their ethnic background cannot be reduced to two broad categories.

At first glance, Lee Lourdeaux's *Irish and Italian Filmmakers in America* seems to provide an alternative. Lourdeaux attempts to discern the ways that individual filmmakers engage their ethnic identity, and he devotes entire chapters to Capra, Scorsese, and Coppola. Unfortunately, his study often bases its arguments on stereotypes while equating Irish and Italian identity with Catholicism. Catholicism is an important aspect of both cultures, but it is not the religion of *all* Irish or Italian Americans.

Finally, some scholars have argued for the existence of an "Italian American cinema." Casillo, for instance, maintains that "Italian American cinema" refers to "works by Italian-American directors who treat Italian-American subjects" ("Moments" 394).[8] However, although Italian American ethnicity is an important aspect of these filmmakers' work, the creation of a specifically Italian American cinema has never been necessary.[9] Unlike black filmmakers, Italian Americans were never systematically excluded from directorial positions, nor was there a need for Italian Americans to establish their own independent film industry.[10] Further, drawing boundaries around what is and what is not Italian American cinema leads to the same essentialized notions of Italian American identity and culture that this book hopes to counter.

*   *   *

In the media-saturated environment of the twenty-first century, cinema and television continue to consolidate cultural identities for group members while also defining groups for a more general American audience. Specific historical contexts and ethnic experiences need to be respected, but similarities between Italian American experiences and those of other ethnic groups do exist. This book, then, is interested in recognizing not just the difference that exists within ethnic groups but also the sameness that exists between them.

I have divided this study into five chapters. Chapter 1 examines the films of Frank Capra and presents him as a filmmaker whose work is inextricably linked with his immigrant experience. Throughout his career, Capra consistently sought to undermine Hollywood's usual Italian and Italian American stereotypes while also incorporating an immigrant narrative that he sometimes explicitly and sometimes implicitly presented. Martin Scorsese, a filmmaker who sees Italian American ethnicity as both a defining and a confining identity, is the subject of chapter 2. Scorsese's closed ethnic neighborhoods grant his characters a secure community and sense of identity but limit their available opportunities, threaten their personal happiness, and sometimes signal their self-destruction. Chapter 3 investigates the cinema of Nancy Savoca, whose movies are particularly adept at recognizing the ways ethnic, gender, and class identities overlap. As a filmmaker of mixed ethnic heritage, Savoca also seems especially aware of and sensitive to the similarities between ethnic groups. Francis Ford Coppola's nostalgic treatment of Italian American ethnicity in the *Godfather* films is the focus of chapter 4. Coppola's trilogy offers a far more nuanced representation of Italian ethnicity than previous gangster films, but it also tends to embrace Old World culture without sufficiently interrogating some of its less progressive aspects. Finally, chapter 5 considers the movies of Quentin Tarantino, a writer-director whose ties to an ethnic Italian background are limited. Nonetheless, Tarantino's thematic interest in performance and his copious quotations of Italian American filmmakers represent a playfully postmodern engagement with Italian American ethnicity, and his quotations of blaxploitation films and Asian cinemas carry the potential to undo some of the racist practices of the past by exposing present-day Hollywood audiences to the cinema of marginalized others.

These five filmmakers represent their Italian American ethnicity in different manners, but each contributes to our collective understanding of the ways Italian American ethnicity functions socially, culturally, and historically. By mapping their various treatments of ethnicity, we might better appreciate the interactions among ethnic identity, social prejudice, historical context, and individual experience. Ultimately, the work of each director becomes a case study where an individual historical actor negotiates a strategy to first comprehend and then represent an important social identity within the context of the commercial medium of American motion pictures. In doing so, the directors solidify that identity not just for themselves but for Italian Americans and non-Italian Americans alike. Given the continued importance of ethnic identities today, this is an increasingly valuable object of study. It allows us to better appreciate the role ethnicity has played in shaping our collective understanding of American identity, and it carries the potential to form alliances between those groups who endured prejudice in the past and those who continue to endure prejudice today.

1 Frank Capra

Ethnic Denial and Its Impossibility

In 1978, Dominic Candeloro wrote to Frank Capra asking him to be a speaker in the Italian American program at the University of Illinois at Chicago. Capra denied Candeloro's request in a lengthy letter, writing:

> Many times intellectual people ask me if my Italian heritage had anything to do with my work. And frankly, I don't know what the hell they're talking about. The word heritage evokes memories and spiritual experiences with the cultured heroes of the past. I never had such experiences. I am very proud to have been born an Italian, very proud of all the great men that Italy has produced in the arts and the sciences, very proud of the giant Italian intellects that created the Renaissance. But only as history, and as great men who contributed to making history. I admire Shakespeare and Tolstoi and Dante with equal reverence.

In that same letter, Capra described himself as a "10–90 Italian-American," saying that he immigrated to the United States at such an early age that he had little memory of the land he left.[1] Such remarks would seem to place Capra, who arrived in America at the age of six, firmly within the tradition of what Werner Sollors labels "consent" (4–6). By effectively denying his "descent" identity as an Italian, Capra consented to a new identity as an American.

Joseph McBride agrees with Capra's self-assessment, arguing that the immigrant filmmaker, in an attempt to distance himself from his working-class, ethnic, immigrant origins, made films about "white" Americans (not ethnic others or immigrants) as a way of assimilating into American culture. Such a perspective reduces the impact of Capra's ethnicity to something the director wished to deny, repress, or transcend. Lee Lourdeaux counters McBride's (and Capra's) claims by offering the first extended analysis of the ethnic elements of Capra's films. By arguing that Capra was significantly affected by his ethnic immigrant origins, Lourdeaux lends credence to Michael Novak's contention that our "emotions, instincts, memory, imagination, passions, and ways of perceiving are passed onto us in ways we do not choose, and in ways so thick with life that they lie far beyond the power of consciousness (let alone of analytic or verbal reason) thoroughly to master, totally to alter" (xvi).

More recently, Robert Sklar and John Paul Russo have investigated the ethnic themes in Capra. Sklar focuses his essay on *For the Love of Mike* (1927), a lost film, and *The Younger Generation* (1929).[2] Russo includes a noteworthy analysis of *For the Love of Mike* while also providing the first serious consideration of Capra's 1959 film, *A Hole in the Head,* the only Capra-directed work to take Italian Americans as its main characters. By arguing that these two ethnically focused films, separated by thirty-two years, share similar themes, Russo implicitly contends that an ethnic vein is present in select films throughout Capra's career. Sklar, Russo, and Lourdeaux frame Capra as a "*descent*" artist and may open up similar avenues of research on other filmmakers who disavow their ethnic identity or have not been treated as ethnic artists.

Nonetheless, Sklar and Russo perpetuate the idea that ethnicity is a somewhat minor consideration when it comes to Capra. Lester D. Friedman implies a different view by suggesting that ethnicity is a vital consideration in the analysis of any director: "As a female director does not stop being a woman even when her film is not about overtly feminist issues, so one's ethnic identity and sensibility do not disappear when he or she makes a film about non-ethnic issues. . . . Films, like other art forms, spring from the minds, hearts, and souls of men and women who speak in the language and partake in the activities of their world, even if their participation takes the form of denial, avoidance, and repudiation. Their culture shapes their daily experiences and artistic perceptions" (31, 33). This view is especially important when studying Capra, a filmmaker who worked during a period in American history when Italian ethnicity was heavily scrutinized. As Sklar has suggested, even if Capra attempted to "cancel" his ethnic identity, he still had a "very clear identity" for 1930s audiences ("Leap" 47). Sklar's point is validated by the many interviews and personality profiles that noted Capra's Italian identity, which were particularly prominent between the director's rise to commercial and critical stardom in the mid-1930s and his return to Hollywood in the immediate post–World War II years.[3] Usually, these references are made in passing, oftentimes simultaneously lauding the ability of this immigrant to succeed in America and U.S. exceptionalism for allowing immigrants such an opportunity. Other times, the director's ethnic ties are given a more stereotypical treatment. In the February 24, 1940, issue of the *New Yorker,* for instance, Capra's doctor attributed his childhood survival of a burst appendix to "the fact that Sicilians, conditioned by generations of knifings, have very hardy interiors" (Hellman 7). Thus, Capra was painted as an individual who was simultaneously able to benefit from an undesirable past while rising above it.

If Capra's ethnicity was an issue for the public at large, it was also an is-sue for Italian Americans. In "The Master of the Human Touch," published in *Motion Picture* in July 1935, Capra stated, "Every time the name of my birthplace appears in print, I get hundreds of letters from the hometowners who want me to read their scenarios or put their children into pictures. If I tried to answer half of them, I could make up my mind to shut up shop, and devote the rest of my life to correspondence" (Harrison 16). Capra's comments suggest that some Italian Americans looked to Capra as a kind of culture hero similar to other prominent figures such as Joe DiMaggio, Fiorella La Guardia, and Frank Sinatra.[4]

Whether he felt influenced by his roots or not, Capra was viewed by many as a representative (if exceptional) Italian American, and it is surprising that scholarly work on Capra has largely marginalized the director's ethnic identity. As we shall see, Capra introduced an ethnic aspect into a Hollywood cinema that often tried to erase ethnic difference.[5] Rather than being of minor interest in a few Capra films, these ethnic immigrant concerns are a major aspect of his filmography, appearing in every phase of his nearly forty-year career. They are evident in his 1920s films, where Belgian, Irish, and Jewish immigrant characters struggle with conflicting American values like indi-vidualism and community or equality and capitalism. *The Strong Man* (1926), *For the Love of Mike,* and *The Younger Generation* argue for the necessity of immigrants' inclusion and acceptance in American society while explicitly exploring various ethnic (though not Italian) immigrant experiences of the United States. In the 1930s, Capra's 1920s explicitly immigrant protagonists are replaced by WASP Americans who migrate not to different countries but to different regions of America where they effectively undergo an im-migrant experience, confronting the prejudice of entrenched interests and balancing the competing value structures of their previous lives with those of a new culture. On the surface, these films offer a traditional Hollywood narrative pattern, but when viewed in the context of Capra's earlier films and his biography, they become stories of geographic relocation that double as allegories of immigration. Finally, in the early to mid-1940s, Capra's involve-ment with wartime documentary production led to the "Why We Fight" films (1942–45), a series that attempts to counter Hollywood's stereotyping of Italian Americans, even as it validates stereotypes of the Japanese and Germans. Ultimately, Capra's life history and his work further our understanding of what it meant to be an Italian American immigrant in the first half of the twentieth century. By exposing the complex negotiation that he was forced to undertake as a Hollywood and governmental filmmaker, we gain a greater appreciation for the sometimes perilous and always complicated existence that ethnic Americans live.

Capra in the 1920s:
The Explicit Immigration Tale

Capra's filmmaking career began in the 1920s, a tumultuous decade for Italian Americans. Despite the prominence of baseball Hall of Famer Tony Lazzeri, banker Amadeo Pietro (A. P.) Giannini, and screen icon Rudolf Valentino, the decade was characterized by pervasive anti-Italian prejudice that at times became official governmental policy. The Immigration Acts of 1921 and 1924, prompted by widespread anti-immigrant sentiments, severely restricted the number of Italians (and other ethnics) that could immigrate to the United States. Meanwhile, within Italian American communities Mussolini's rise to power led to deadly altercations between fascists and antifascists (Mangione and Morreale 318–20).

However, it was the seven-year ordeal of Nicola Sacco and Bartolomeo Vanzetti that crystallized popular opinions about Italian Americans. Avowed anarchists and atheists who were accused of a double murder, Sacco and Vanzetti were globally recognized by the time of their execution in 1927. Many were convinced of their innocence or at least their right to a retrial, while others were equally convinced of their guilt. Their case became a cause célèbre, with figures such as H. G. Wells, John Dos Passos, Upton Sinclair, Eugene V. Debs, and Emma Goldman coming to their defense. Helen Keller and Charlie Chaplin "took a vocal interest in the plight of the two political prisoners" (Davis 8), and protests attracted thousands throughout the United States and Europe.[6] In a June 29, 1927, *New Republic* article, Bruce Bliven reported that the atmosphere in Boston was so contentious that the support of Harvard University faculty for Sacco and Vanzetti had adversely affected the annual fund drive and that schoolchildren were forbidden from discussing the case (67–68). Sacco and Vanzetti's politics may not have helped their situation, but neither did their ethnic identities as immigrant Italians. As Jerre Mangione and Ben Morreale suggest, the Sacco and Vanzetti case indicates that the relationship between "those early immigrants and the rest of America" was a contentious one, characterized by prejudice, resentment, and sometimes violence (299).

Neither Capra nor any of his biographers have discussed how the Sacco and Vanzetti case affected him personally or professionally, but McBride's meticulous research shows that Capra's ethnicity was consistently an issue in his personal and professional relationships; in the 1920s, however, Capra's public profile was not high enough for the Sacco and Vanzetti case to be a factor in his success. Nonetheless, the projects he undertook during the decade betray a consistent concern with the place of (non-Italian) immigrants in American society. So, while Capra's ethnic identity as an Italian American is of vital importance (and would become more important later in his career), it might be more productive to approach his 1920s films from a perspective that stresses his more general identity as an immigrant.

Such a move expands the scope of the existing literature and reveals a degree of consistency not just between *For the Love of Mike* and *The Younger Generation,* as Sklar has suggested, but also between those films and Capra's first feature, *The Strong Man.* These films take immigrants and immigrant families as their subject and feature main characters that have ethnic ties, immigrant identities, or both. This "otherness" complicates the characters' lives, forcing them to negotiate between their ancestral roots and their professional and social aspirations. The American immigrant experience becomes the general subject of these films, but the specific conflicts of each narrative confront a different aspect of that experience. Throughout the decade, Capra's criticism of the American establishment becomes more muted as his films instead focus on the right and wrong choices that individual ethnic immigrants and their children make. This minimizes institutional pressures and prejudices while assuming a degree of free choice on the part of the immigrant that might be best described as fantasy.

The Strong Man follows Paul Bergot (Harry Langdon), a childlike innocent who serves as a Belgian soldier during World War I.[7] Even though combat surrounds him, Bergot becomes absorbed in a letter from his American pen pal, Mary Brown (Priscilla Bonner). While Bergot reads Brown's letter, a burly German soldier named Zandow sneaks up on the Belgian and takes him prisoner.[8] After the war, Zandow immigrates to America, bringing Bergot as his assistant. Zandow hopes his strongman act will bring him wealth and fame, but Bergot's dream is to find Brown, with whom he has fallen in love. Impeding Bergot's quest is a series of Americans who try to take advantage of him. After accidentally assaulting a laborer, Bergot flees Ellis Island (or what the film labels "the funnel of America") with Zandow in tow. As he runs through the main hall, he unintentionally knocks down all of the pews on one side of the room, offering a not so subtle jab at Ellis Island's dehumanizing immigrant processing routines. Eventually, our hero and Zandow arrive in Cloverdale, a border town that used to be a peaceful place and also, amazingly, the hometown of Mary Brown.[9] Zandow's love of alcohol and women renders him unable to perform his act, so the physically meager Bergot is forced onstage, where he performs his "feats" of strength for a raucous crowd. When the crowd insults Mary Brown, Bergot becomes her defender, eventually clearing the hall with a cannon that was supposed to hurl him through the air. Order and decency are restored; Bergot and Brown are coupled, and Bergot is granted the official position and the social standing of the town's sheriff.

At the heart of *The Strong Man* is a conflict between "Old World" and "New World" values. The Old World, typified by Bergot and Brown, values family and romantic love over materialism (that is, American capitalism and the rise to success). Zandow counters this view by falling prey to New World values, which favor selfishness, greed, materialism, and vice. The film reaches its climax when these competing values come into direct conflict, and the audience is encouraged to side with the Old World characters. Nevertheless, being loyal to Old World values cultivates a form of naïveté. Here the casting of Harry Langdon becomes important. Langdon made a career of playing childlike innocents, and while Chaplin, Keaton, and Lloyd also constructed characters whose innocence endeared them to audiences and allowed them to triumph over foes, Langdon seems even less aware of the treachery that surrounds him.[10] Capra's work consistently returns to this kind of innocence, revealing a connection between immigrant characters like Bergot and later characters like Jefferson Smith.

In *The Strong Man*, Bergot's innocence is closely connected to his immigrant standing, and both make him vulnerable initially. The film's form works to emphasize this vulnerability and highlight the newly arrived immigrant's precarious standing. Throughout the narrative, Capra shoots Bergot in mostly long and extreme long shots, which emphasize the enormity of Bergot's new environment and his own smallness. Long shots of Bergot in Ellis Island place him among stacks of luggage and work to dehumanize him (fig. 2). When he ventures onto the streets of New York City to find Mary Brown, many of the Americans Bergot encounters "other" him. A woman yells at him, insisting that she is not Mary Brown, and Capra again uses long shots to emphasize Bergot's bewilderment, showing masses of people filing by and gawking at the newly arrived immigrant (fig. 3). Soon after, a doorman (whom Bergot mistakes for a military commander) lies to Bergot, telling him that Mary walks by the nearby corner every day. This pattern continues

Figure 2. Belgian immigrant Paul Bergot (Harry Langdon) is reduced to another piece of luggage in this shot from Frank Capra's film *The Strong Man*.

Figure 3. Americans offer Bergot a cold welcome to the land of opportunity in *The Strong Man*. Capra uses the reflection in the store window to entirely surround Bergot.

when a prostitute-flapper, Lily of Broadway (Gertrude Astor), uses Bergot to avoid the police and then attempts to seduce him in order to retrieve the money she has, unbeknownst to him, hidden in his jacket.

Bergot's innocence makes him an easy target. Nonetheless, like many of the Capra heroes who will follow, Bergot simultaneously benefits from his naïveté.[11] As Peter Bogdanovich has argued, the character "comes up against hard reality yet manages not only to keep his illusions but to triumph with them" (quoted in Scherle and Levy 13). Ultimately, Bergot's optimism fosters his continued belief in American myths. As a result, he is in one sense the most American of heroes. Most of *The Strong Man*'s other Americans are cynical and jaded and care only for themselves.[12] United by a kind, virtuous nature that teaches them to care for other people, Brown and Bergot subsume their self-interest and help *The Strong Man* to reduce the contradictory dynamics of American ideology to a conflict between moderation and excess—with an innocent immigrant character framed as the ideal American.

This is not to suggest that Capra inaugurated a new kind of American film with *The Strong Man*. As Robert Ray argues, Hollywood films tend to convert "all political, sociological, and economic dilemmas into personal melodramas" (57). Further, Bergot's construction as a reluctant defender-hero who pursues love and responds with violence only when provoked aligns him closely with another classical Hollywood paradigm.[13] According to Ray, Hollywood characters work to resolve the contradictions of American mythologies by reifying the idea that making choices between competing values not only is unnecessary but also violates "the national spirit" (67). Ray describes a series of characters culminating in *Casablanca*'s Rick Blaine who enter conflicts but do so only on their own terms. Rick accepts communal "responsibilities without forfeiting autonomy" (110). Whereas Bergot more closely resembles Ray's "official hero" (as opposed to Rick's "outlaw hero"), he still fits nicely within the tradition of reluctance, thus working to construct the myth that a choice between the ideologies of community and individualism is unnecessary.[14]

What makes Bergot (and Capra's other 1920s heroes) different is his immigrant status. Bergot becomes Cloverdale's savior and the quintessential American hero. Following the plotline of many westerns, Bergot is an unknown man who descends upon a rowdy town, bringing law and order and restoring humane values in the process. However, unlike many of the western heroes who will follow, Bergot does not ride off into the sunset once order is restored. Instead, the citizens of Cloverdale entrust their future to this resident alien, making him a permanent and prominent fixture in their community. Not only does this naive, innocent immigrant pose less of a threat to

American ideals and institutions than many of the American citizens who surround him, but he is also able to redeem American institutions like the church and the government (represented by the police). Bergot need not assimilate completely (although he does seem to speak English effectively, a point that the film emphasizes when in her first letter to Bergot, Brown comments that his English is improving). Instead, it seems imperative that he maintain the values he has espoused since the beginning of the narrative.

* * *

A year after *The Strong Man,* Capra directed *For the Love of Mike,* which unfortunately, survives only as a plot synopsis available at the Library of Congress. The film tells the story of a baby boy who is abandoned at the landing of a Hell's Kitchen tenement. Herman Schultz, Abie Katz, and Patrick O'Malley adopt the boy, naming him Mike.[15] After completing high school, Mike (Ben Lyons) wants to enter the workforce, but his fathers and Mary (Claudette Colbert), "a pretty Italian neighbor," persuade him to attend Yale (Wolfe, *Frank Capra* 45). At Yale, Mike excels socially and athletically, and on his twenty-first birthday, his fathers organize a dinner in his honor, inviting local political and business leaders and hoping to secure a job offer for their "son." Mike, however, becomes distracted by the vices that his status as an assimilated and "successful" American offers him. An "amorous girl" lures him to a cocktail party where he becomes inebriated (Wolfe, *Frank Capra* 45). He arrives at the dinner late and insults the guests, at which point O'Malley knocks him unconscious. The next day, tensions persist, and Mike returns to Yale dejected. He falls in with a gambler and sinks into debt. By the time of the Yale-Harvard crew race, he owes so much money that the gambler threatens to send him to jail if he will not intentionally row his team to defeat. Luckily for Mike, his fathers and Mary arrive on the scene and bet on the Mike-captained team. Yale wins the race, earning the fathers and Mary enough money to pay off the gambler (whom they throw into the river) and securing for Mike Yale's esteem, his fathers' forgiveness, and Mary's love.

Like *The Strong Man, For the Love of Mike* features an "Old World versus New World" conflict, but rather than having the fate of a town hanging in the balance, it is a young American with ties to both worlds whose future is in jeopardy. In addition, the prominent role that ethnicity plays is new. Here, an Irishman, a Jew, a German, and an Italian outsmart the New World materialism of the gambler and rescue Mike from a path that would replace the Old World values of community and family with New World values that favor myopic individualism and greed. By grouping ethnic Americans together, *Mike* suggests that individuals with a shared experience of immigration can form multiethnic communities and alliances. Having an Italian in the mix would have resonated personally with Capra and forwards an argument of ethnic tolerance (especially since the film was released in the same year that Sacco and Vanzetti were executed); once again, it is immigrant characters (this time ethnic characters with immigrant pasts) who preserve American ideals.[16]

Mike's ethnicity is unknown, but, as Sklar suggests, he struggles to reconcile his assimilated college personality with his family upbringing. Mike, Sklar says, gains "entry into the upper classes" and retains "his earlier allegiances" but "only after those who love him also cross the social barriers and assist him on the new territory" ("Leap" 51–52). Of this assessment, Russo asks, "How could those who love him, themselves still in the ghetto, join him in crossing the social barriers? And how could they assist him?" (294). In real life, the answer might not be clear, but, in this film, the supporting players seem to perform the same function that Bergot did in *The Strong Man:* they seek to better their community by bringing together the best of the immigrants with the best of American institutions. By securing Mike a job in the establishment, they hope to bring the two worlds together, synthesize "descent" with "consent," better America, and improve their child.[17] Total assimilation is not their goal, nor do they want it to be Mike's. Instead, the film suggests that including (ethnic) immigrants within the American mosaic can redeem a specific kind of American Dream and specific American ideals—ones that balance the attainment of wealth and status with family and community.

* * *

Released in 1929, *The Younger Generation* explores what happens when Old World and New World values are not balanced. The film follows the Goldfishes, a Jewish family with an immigrant past who live on New York's Lower East Side. Julius/Papa (Jean Hersholt) and Tilda/Mama (Rosa Rosanova) have two children, Birdie (Lina Basquette) and Morris (Ricardo Cortez).[18] To the delight of Mama, Morris is an aspiring businessman, while Birdie, a tomboy, is the apple of her father's eye. As Morris becomes more successful, he rises from the ethnic tenement to a Fifth Avenue penthouse, bringing his family along with him. However, his desire for an assimilated, nonethnic identity causes him to impose his "New World values" on his Old World family, which strains familial ties.

Morris is countered by Birdie's love interest, Eddie Lesser (Rex Lease). Unlike Morris, Lesser remains true to his "Old World values," maintaining a close relationship with his mother and allowing his passion for songwriting and his love for Birdie to determine his career choices and life decisions.

Even when he decides to take part in a jewelry store robbery (in order to free Birdie from the prison of Morris's apartment), Lesser is pursuing his interest in music by performing one of his songs to distract the public. Lesser goes to prison for his part in the heist, but he marries Birdie, continues to work on his songwriting, and is eventually rewarded with a happy marriage, a child, and a successful small business. He becomes a representation of the Puritan ethic, pursuing his goals through hard work and showing love and respect for the well-being of others. By the end of the film, Lesser is the one who has secured happiness, while Morris ends up alone in the cold, vacuous surroundings of his extravagant lifestyle.

Once again, an Old World versus New World conflict lies at the heart of an early Capra film, but *The Younger Generation* offers characters who have differing views of wealth and assimilation despite sharing ethnic, class, generational, and even familial backgrounds. Here, the divide between Old and New is clearly one of choice, with Birdie and Papa on the side of the Old and Morris and Mama (the only first-generation immigrant character in these Capra films who is not consistently loyal to "Old World values") on the side of the New. Early in the film, an exchange between Papa and Mama makes their differences clear. To Mama's chiding, "Someday, papa [sic], Morris will be a big businessman ~ ~ like you ain't!" Papa responds, "Money ain't good for nothing, mama [sic] ~ ~ if it don't buy happiness."

As Robin Wood has shown, the idea that money cannot buy happiness is one of the dominant Hollywood myths, directly contradicted by Horatio Alger stories about the rise to success ("Ideology" 669, 673–74). In Capra's cinema, admirable yet naive characters like Papa repeatedly encounter wealthy yet contemptible characters like Morris. Papa garners audience sympathy and forwards the film's thematic concerns by living his life as if money is of minimal importance; the film's romanticized depiction of the ethnic enclave further bolsters these ideas. The old neighborhood may be crowded, but it is relatively free from crime, disease, and disaster. Capra's exterior shots emphasize a sense of togetherness, with peddlers lining the streets and friends and family surrounding the main characters. As Giuliana Muscio has shown, the old neighborhood may minimize privacy, but it only results in a closer community ("Lower East Side"). In addition, Capra's use of mobile camera shots in the Delancey Street location reinforces the sense that life in the ethnic ghetto is vibrant and dynamic.[19] These formal choices are contrasted by his envisioning of the Fifth Avenue setting, where exterior shots and mobile framings are exceedingly rare. Through its form, *The Younger Generation* suggests that Delancey Street offers more freedom than the staid rigidity of upper-class life.[20]

The film's stylistics are complemented by its narrative, which essentially grafts an Old World versus New World conflict onto Hollywood's traditional "money can't buy happiness" mythology. Morris's commitment to and blind and selfish pursuit of a life of opulence lead to a life of restriction and constraint. Wealth becomes his only goal, and throughout the narrative, Morris is willing to sacrifice everything, including family, to achieve it. Worse, he readily imposes the same choices on others. Papa and Birdie are uncomfortable with the norms of Morris's upper-class life, but Morris demands their assimilation, believing that he knows what is best for them. To Morris, daily bathing and formal clothing remove the stain of ethnicity and make "real people out of [them]," but the film sees Morris's actions as undemocratic and therefore un-American.

For Morris, ethnic identity is not a source of strength but an obstacle to success, and, so, he tries to efface any signs of his Jewish heritage. As his business becomes increasingly successful, the storefront signage becomes more opulent, but each successive sign also demonstrates Morris's lack of gratitude toward his father's contributions since the visual presence of his ethnic surname is increasingly minimized.[21] Morris believes that wealth can erase his Jewishness, so he sets out to create the illusion of an assimilated, nonethnic American. His snobbishness and pretension work toward his assimilation but isolate him. To make certain that his identity cannot be connected with the ethnic neighborhood, he rejects all of the family's friends, and this leads to his destruction. As Leland Poague notes, "It is not just being a capitalist that is significant, but the kind of capitalist you are" (*Cinema* 37). Capra does not believe in wealth for wealth's sake. He thinks that the pursuit of financial wealth needs to be balanced with family and community.

Morris differs from characters like Zandow and Mike, because he never succumbs to New World vices like gambling and alcohol. He does, however, forgo romantic love in pursuit of a seemingly distant and cold woman from the upper-class Kahn family. In contrast, Birdie is so motivated by love that she marries Lesser even though Morris forbids it. Morris responds by evicting Birdie from the apartment and blocking any communication between her and her parents. This action, along with Morris's decision to temporarily disown his parents in order to maintain the illusion of an assimilated identity later in the film, ensures his self-destruction.[22] In the film's last scene, Mama leaves the penthouse to live with Birdie, Eddie, and their young son on the Lower East Side while Morris enters a huge, ornate, but empty room, wraps himself in a blanket, and shivers as the shades of the apartment are drawn and the shadows envelop him. An extreme long shot emphasizes the character's loneliness as Morris turns his back to the camera and the film fades to black.

In addition to endorsing Hollywood's "money can't buy happiness" theme, *The Younger Generation* leaves the impression that the American Dream is somewhat easy to achieve. Capra does not show us an ethnic other who fails in that pursuit. This is a far cry from the reality of both Capra's own biography and immigrant life in the early twentieth century.[23] *The Younger Generation*, like *The Jazz Singer* (Alan Crosland, 1927), promotes the idea that the ethnic viewer can have both New World success and Old World ties (Rogin 86), thereby idealizing the choices available to immigrants. By focusing on the agreeable aspects of immigrant life without confronting the poverty, the film softens class conflicts and avoids a deeper criticism of American capitalism.

* * *

In each of these films, Old World values and the characters who espouse them, regardless of their immigrant standing, become fundamentally "American" by castigating an overly selfish and materialistic American Dream.[24] In doing so, they maintain their immigrant innocence, ethnic status, or both and reinvigorate the mythic ideal of equality that drew so many to the United States. However, this wish-fulfillment plot hides a contradiction. The goal of the immigrant community is materialistic, and the immigrants see material wealth as a way to better their lives. Nonetheless, the idea that an individual's worth and potential in the United States are determined not by ethnicity but rather by a combination of assimilation and communal values represents a dissenting voice on the ways immigrants were perceived by the population at large in the 1920s.

The perspective in Capra's films is significantly different from what we find in other famous films of the era. In *The Jazz Singer,* for instance, the patriarchal figure represents "defeated Old World provincialism and not New World power" (Rogin 69), but in Capra's film, the older generation is a source of strength and the patriarch serves as a model. Nonetheless, Capra's dissent is increasingly muted throughout the 1920s. By the end of the decade, he largely ignores the social power structures that encourage assimilation, and his narratives have shifted from a laudatory endorsement of an innocent immigrant and a critique of the treachery of native-born Americans (in *The Strong Man*) to one that ignores nonethnic populations and targets a second-generation character for making the wrong choices.

This desire to mute the proimmigrant, anti-American theme was probably a response to real social conditions. Throughout the 1920s, the dangers of being an ethnic American became increasingly apparent as restrictive quotas on some immigrant groups morphed into state executions of individuals whose guilt was at least partially substantiated by ethnic prejudice. Meanwhile,

Capra's stardom was on the rise. He was now the top filmmaker at Columbia Studios, a Poverty Row outfit to be sure, but one that was garnering more attention and one that offered Capra increasingly prominent opportunities.

Capra in the 1930s:
The Implicit Immigration Tale

The 1930s were characterized by the rise of individual Italian American heroes and the continued denigration of Italians as a group by the Anglo-Saxon majority. The decade also produced two types of Italian celebrities. Angelo Rossi became mayor of San Francisco in the same year that Al Capone was convicted on tax evasion charges. Between 1933 and 1939, Fiorello La Guardia served as New York City's mayor, Russ Columbo rivaled Bing Crosby as the most popular singer of his time, Frank Sinatra began his singing career, and as part of their effort to secure and expand their fan base by signing players of Italian descent, the New York Yankees welcomed Joe DiMaggio to the "House That Ruth Built" (Cramer 66–67). Meanwhile, infamous mobster Lucky Luciano was arrested on prostitution charges, Italy's invasion of Ethiopia sparked tensions between Italian Americans and African Americans (LaGumina 250–52), and "nativists" argued for the deportation of Italians and other aliens as a way to quickly and easily solve the Great Depression ("Drive for Law"). This "bad press" tended to be applied to Italians generally, while the "good press" treated the Italian American heroes as exceptional. In 1939, for instance, *Life* wrote of DiMaggio, "Although he learned Italian first Joe, now 24, speaks English without an accent and is otherwise well adapted to most US mores. Instead of olive oil or smelly bear grease he keeps his hair slick with water. He never reeks of garlic and prefers chicken chow mein to spaghetti" (Busch 69).

Within the Italian American community, the rise of Mussolini and fascism in Italy had divisive effects; some vehemently opposed his regime, while others supported it by sending money and even wedding bands to Italy (Mangione and Morreale 319). As many sons and daughters of immigrants came of age, they shunned their parents' cultural norms, preferring English to Italian and dating outside of their ethnic group (Gambino, *Blood* 199–200). This generational conflict was further exacerbated by the second generation's willingness to fight the prejudices and injustices that their parents had accepted (Gardaphé, *Italian Signs* 57). Such conflicts, coupled with cultural intolerance, isolated Italians from mainstream American society and left many feeling alienated even within their neighborhoods and families. Fears of Italian hoods sparked wide-scale prejudice against average Italians, an attitude that persisted as the Depression continued and war with Italy seemed inevitable. According to Gardaphé, "If the Italian was not seen as a gangster or a knife-wielding, mustachioed foreigner who had taken away American jobs from the earlier immigrants, then he was depicted as 'a restless, roving creature who dislikes the confinement and restraint of mill and factory,' 'very slow to take to American ways,' 'volatile, and incapable of effective team work'" (*Italian Signs* 56).

The 1930s was also the decade during which Capra rose to prominence, becoming a major player in Hollywood and a nationally recognized Italian American. Throughout the decade, he served as the president of the Screen Directors Guild *and* the Academy of Motion Picture Arts and Sciences. He paired with writer Robert Riskin to create some of the decade's most memorable and profitable movies, including *It Happened One Night, Mr. Deeds Goes to Town,* and *You Can't Take It with You.*[25] He took home three Best Director Academy Awards and, in 1938, appeared on the cover of *Time.* With his celebrity status came a dramatic increase in the number of his published interviews and personality profiles. *American Cinematographer, Variety,* the *Los Angeles Times,* the *New York Herald-Tribune,* and the *Christian Science Monitor* all published pieces on Capra, and many referenced his Italian American heritage.

Like DiMaggio, Capra was often treated as an exceptional Italian American, though he conformed to a series of Italian American stereotypes in a way that DiMaggio did not. "Despite a good deal of economic difficulty," this Italian immigrant was able to succeed in the United States (Daugherty 20). Authors wrote, half in admiration, half in disbelief, "He is short, 5 feet 4 inches; dark, with a mop of black hair, terse-speaking, with a grim grin" (Scheuer 12), and described his face as "olive-skinned, vigorously moulded, quiet on the surface, [with] a vibrant quality that made it seem more alive, even in repose, than does the average face in animation" (Harrison 15). In 1935, *Collier's* published a personality profile titled "Fine Italian Hand." In it, John Stuart lauded Capra as a father, a husband, and a filmmaker but consistently linked the director's identity to Italian stereotypes. Capra was said to have barely escaped a life of crime and snarled like a gangster when he played bridge. The piece drew Capra's ire, and according to McBride prompted him to launch "an intensified campaign to upgrade his image" (332).

The *Collier's* article was widely quoted and became a persistent thorn in Capra's side. When David Bush was researching a 1935 radio biography of Capra, he sent the director a rough draft of the program. Bush wrote, "He had the usual ups and downs of the immigrant boy. . . . One little misstep or one bad companion, or one bad break at the [wrong] psychological time might have made a racketeer out of the great producer." Capra replied, "While I appreciate the message you are trying to get over in your proposed radio talk, I object to the use of my name in any connection with 'gangsterism.' That portion of the article in *Collier's* from which you got your information is definitely untrue" (Frank Capra Collection, Box 1).

While Capra's ethnic identity was becoming more well known, the ethnic aspects of his cinema seemed to fade away. Characters with names like Longfellow Deeds and Jefferson Smith replace the immigrants of *The Strong Man, For the Love of Mike,* and *The Younger Generation.* Completely devoid of any ethnic or immigrant signifiers, these WASP American characters do not speak with accents, and they do not journey to different countries. However, their stories involve the same ideological conflicts as in the earlier films, and the characters themselves undergo experiences that closely parallel those of many ethnic immigrants. For instance, *Platinum Blonde's* (1931) Stew Smith and *Mr. Smith Goes to Washington's* (1939) Jefferson Smith travel between different geographic and social settings, and those journeys introduce them to a new way of life and impel them to interact with a new culture.[26] The experience of immigrants and immigrant families is thus treated implicitly rather than explicitly, with each movie becoming an allegory for American immigration. The endings of these pictures, however, like those of previous films such as *The Strong Man* and *For the Love of Mike,* provide fantasy resolutions. Stew and Jeff Smith reject the comforts and anonymity of assimilation for the idealism of resistance. Assimilation is not a necessity for them, only an option, and it is never accepted or chosen. Instead, as Ray Carney suggests, Capra exploits America's cult of individualism in an effort to reframe his immigrant characters not as swarthy foreigners but rather as mythical (assimilated) Americans who fight the system, maintain their integrity, and win.

The displaced theme of immigration appears in every decade of Capra's career. In the late 1920s and early 1930s, *That Certain Thing* (1928) and *Ladies of Leisure* (1930), two early features at Columbia Pictures, focus on middle- to working-class female characters who fall in love with male characters from wealthy families. In each case, the wealthy family shuns the female character because of her economic background, and so she and her beau are forced to overcome a cultural conflict predicated on economic standing and social status. *Broadway Bill* (1934) and Capra's remake of that film, *Riding High* (1950), feature a similar story line. *Lady for a Day* (1933) and *Pocketful of Miracles* (1961) focus on a New York bag lady named Apple Annie who must assimilate into high society if her daughter's impending marriage to a Spanish nobleman is to be saved.[27] Even films like *Forbidden* (1932), *It's a Wonderful Life* (1946), and *State of the Union* (1948) feature elements that conform to this general story structure.[28] In many of these films, ethnicity seems to be a nonissue, but in Capra's life, as in the lives of many immigrants, ethnicity and class were intertwined, and both led to intolerance and discrimination.

Ray Carney, Giuliana Muscio, Stephen Handzo, Leland Poague, Charles J. Maland, Charles Wolfe, and Vito Zagarrio have thoroughly investigated the story structure of Capra's films, but none has sufficiently targeted the ways in which a redesigned immigrant theme links the narratives of his 1930s films with those of his 1920s work. Carney focuses on the ways in which the individual operates within the system, a theme that is vitally important to understanding the ways in which Capra camouflaged his immigrant concerns and a trend already apparent in *The Younger Generation*. Poague argues for a degree of consistency between the Langdon features and Capra's later work at Columbia while offering a description of the generic Capra narrative that sounds like but is never identified as being rooted in immigrant experiences. Poague writes, "The Capra story, we might say, often begins with some form of social rupture—a death, a revolution of some kind—that has the effect of transporting the Capra hero from a familiar role or position into a foreign environment, often epitomized by a palatial house of some sort, usually empty and cavernous except for 'native' servants who do their best to indoctrinate the main character into his or her new (social) role" (*Another* 128). Muscio offers a description that could easily be applied to a number of American immigrant groups. "When [the Capra heroes] 'go to the city,' they carry with themselves the values and the ethical resources with which they have grown up," she writes. "Initially these values constitute a cumbersome baggage among the throng of a city that is ready to deride these attitudes, which it considers naive and out of date" ("Roosevelt" 173).

Viewing characters like Jefferson Smith as the WASP descendants of Bergot, Mike, and the Goldfishes reveals the ways in which an ethnic perspective, conscious or not, shaped Frank Capra's cinematic vision. It also shows the ways in which immigrant groups like Italians and Jews were able to claim an assimilated "whiteness" through the Hollywood films they helped to create. Despite the minor ethnic characters that appear in his films throughout the 1930s and beyond, Capra consistently asserted his assimilated whiteness by placing his immigrant characters in "whiteface."[29] Names like Smith and Deeds masked the immigrant origins of the Capra narrative and served for Capra the same function that Rogin argues blackface performed for Jewish actors. By "blacking up," performers like Al Jolson demonstrated that they were white and not black, assuming a position where they could speak for both races. For Capra, though, whiteness was only one step, if a major one, in the march toward assimilation. In his films, he sought nothing less than to prove that the immigrant was if not the, then at least among the, most American of (white) Americans.

In Capra's 1930s films, class prejudice replaces ethnic prejudice. *Platinum Blonde*'s Stew Smith (Robert Williams), for instance, marries into an upper-class family, thinking that money will bring him happiness, only to find that it pressures him to conform to a series of formalities that he finds confining. Throughout the film, Capra's visual aesthetics show that from the outside, a life of wealth seems to offer greater freedom. At multiple points, long tracking shots emphasize the enormity of the Schuyler mansion and the seemingly limitless potential for movement. Following one such shot, Smith asks Anne Schuyler (Jean Harlow) for carfare back to the front door. Nonetheless, Capra includes cagelike metalwork in the mise-en-scène of the mansion to communicate the idea of a prison, and he also incorporates long shots to emphasize the loneliness and emptiness of life. In perhaps the film's most famous shot, Capra shoots Smith in an extreme long shot from a high angle as our hero plays hopscotch on the tiled foyer floor (fig. 4). Ultimately, Smith divorces his wife and escapes the prison of wealth. As the decade progressed, however,

Figure 4. Robert Williams as Stew Smith is completely out of place in the Schuyler mansion and resorts to playing hopscotch on the tiled foyer floor in *Platinum Blonde*.

the Capra hero's ability to overcome prejudice weakened. For Jefferson Smith, resisting the dominant idea of success is more treacherous. His problems are not only personal but also institutional, where economically and politically powerful groups fight to protect their interests.

Jeff Smith is relocated from his humble, small-town life and transported to Washington, D.C., where an elite group surrounds him and seeks to manipulate him.[30] As Carney writes of Smith, *Mr. Deeds Goes to Town*'s (1936) eponymous hero, and *Meet John Doe*'s (1941) Long John Willoughby, "Each is uprooted from his old world background and identity and suddenly set adrift in a new world of uncharted paths and relationships" (297). Initially, Smith's small-town innocence and naïveté make him an easy target for the entrenched and powerful. At his first press conference, Jeff thinks he is entertaining a group of new friends and demonstrates a series of animal calls. He is shocked the following morning when ridiculous pictures of him are run on the front pages of several important newspapers. Smith responds in frontier style; he hunts down the reporters responsible for these fabrications and sends each of them reeling with a single punch to the jaw. Such scenes develop what Andrew Sarris has labeled "a somber Christian parable of idealism betrayed and innocence humiliated," but they also rely on the myth that a good-hearted individual can overcome systemic evils (88). In later scenes, *Mr. Smith* showcases the power of American political institutions to repair themselves, but in moments like this, the film seems to favor a kind of vigilantism. Yet, again, Capra resists making a clear choice by offering the impression that there is a place for both choices. Vigilantism and institutional deliberation can coexist without any tension.

Like Bergot, Smith encounters assimilated characters who take advantage of his innocence and genuine love of others. Eventually, he recognizes the corrupt power of Taylor and Paine and, realizing how powerful they are, considers fleeing D.C. However, his willingness to forgo the privileges of political clout for the comforts of middle-class anonymity are short-lived. Smith may not fit into the new culture that surrounds him, but the stakes are higher than *his* desires and interests. He becomes the defender of American democracy and communalism while also embodying American individualism. Smith has long been seen as a champion of the common man (Maland, *Frank Capra* 93), but he might also be viewed as a champion of the immigrant. Since migrating to Washington, he has been an outsider. Elites have scorned and mocked him, and at one point, he longs to return to a community where he was surrounded by friends and accepted.

Throughout the film, these cross-cultural encounters take on an ethnic or immigrant tinge that bolsters the film's immigrant allegory. For instance,

Smith struggles with the rules (which is to say the culture) of the Senate when a senator from the opposing party objects to his appointment. Jeff tries to defend himself, but is told that only senators have a voice in the chamber; since he has not been sworn in, he cannot speak. Smith also struggles with a language barrier when he is forced to learn new words like *quorum*.[31] Nonetheless, our hero's lack of knowledge does not disconnect him from the principles he seeks to defend and that American democratic institutions are supposed to uphold. Smith may not understand specific words or phrases, but his understanding of the Senate's intent surpasses that of his fellow senators. His new colleagues are more familiar with the institution's language and rules but less knowledgeable about its history and purpose.

Finally, after trying to assimilate, our hero becomes somewhat disillusioned, and he begins to consider how acculturation and assimilation may be obtained and reconciled with his humble beginnings and his ideas of America.[32] Each of these experiences parallels those of many American immigrants and would have resonated with Capra personally. Further, throughout the narrative, Capra lionizes the allegorical immigrant and his values. He shoots Smith, almost exclusively, from a low angle, forcing the audience to literally look up to and at the idealistic and innocent senator. And Capra's casting of James Stewart encourages a similar view. Smith towers over his colleagues, especially the diminutive Senator Paine (Claude Raines).

Interestingly, the social capital and freedom typically associated with wealth and political power do not work in Smith's favor. Instead, they make him a target and intensify the pressure on him to conform. Smith responds like Bergot, becoming a heroic individual who fights for the values of equality, communalism, and moderation. His refusal to assimilate becomes a metaphor for the tensions within American society and exposes the dangers of the social and political elite's fascist tendencies.[33] But while Jeff rebels, he also conforms. He rejects one aspect of American culture—plutocratic capitalism—while embracing the values of democracy and community. As a result, the film simultaneously endorses the assimilative pressures of America *and* the individual's supposed ability to resist assimilation. *Mr. Smith* argues for a certain kind of assimilation while offering audiences the visual pleasure and spectacle of nonconformity.

At the end of the film, Paine has been disgraced, but Smith's fate with his constituents remains unresolved. He may have convinced those in the Senate of his innocence and, more important, the superiority of his "American values" to those of the other senators, but what he realizes is that freedom is contingent upon one's willingness to conform, one's ability to influence the masses, or both. Resistance to the will of the ruling class must be justified to the populace, even in a country that touts individual freedom.

Throughout the 1930s, Capra's heroes confronted increasingly powerful, entrenched, institutional foes, and this led to progressively more fantastical endings. Stew Smith's decision to resist the upper-class culture and return to his roots is somewhat believable, but Paine's suicide attempt at the end of *Mr. Smith* leaves even the staunchest Capra defenders admitting that the ending seems forced (Saltzman 116).[34] After all, Jefferson Smith not only escapes assimilation into the culture of elite Washington but also forces that culture to bow to his norms. In some ways, the individual overpowers the system, and while this kind of individualism is romantic, it is also highly improbable. To save our heroes from a tragic end, to allow for the choice of nonassimilation, and to praise American institutions, Capra's films allow the individual to create a new community through individual action.

If Capra's 1920s films establish him as a "descent" artist, then those of the 1930s extend that tradition while complicating it. Rogin has argued that Sollors's consent-descent model may place too much emphasis on the individual and not enough on the social forces that compelled (or compel) him or her to conform. Rogin's point extends Ray's argument by recognizing films not just as discursive sites around which competing value structures and ideological contradictions are mutually embraced but also as entities that work to establish the represented culture as the culture itself. This is particularly important to consider in a mass medium like film, where producers and studios often see filmmaking as a business venture. Capra's refusal to choose between the competing values of individual success and family or communal solidarity gives him a wide audience but also leaves fundamental contradictions unresolved. By focusing on an individual who saves the people, he preserves basic Hollywood myths.[35]

Capra's artistic choices in the 1930s are particularly interesting when one considers the social, cultural, and political climate that Italian Americans faced during the Great Depression. With prominent politicians arguing that the deportation of immigrants could quickly solve the country's economic ills, it is easy to see why Capra and Columbia would wish to feature WASP characters rather than immigrants. Given Capra's own ethnic background and the increased media attention he received throughout the 1930s, a move away from immigrant and ethnic characters was even more imperative and dovetailed nicely with his desire to distance himself from his ethnic upbringing. By fusing a WASP character with an immigrant narrative, Capra asserted his own assimilated "whiteness"; by claiming Capra as one of their own, other

Italian Americans attempted to obtain that social standing. During World War II, Capra would use the political events of the time to further advance this argument.

Capra in the 1940s:
Stereotypes and Documentaries

On March 23, 1941, Capra appeared on the Justice Department's *I'm an American!* radio program to proclaim his patriotism. With the threat of war looming, the Department of Justice thought it advisable to ask "distinguished naturalized citizens" (McBride 437) to pledge their allegiance to the United States—thus attempting to redirect the assumed mixed loyalties of foreign-born citizens.[36] In a fifteen-minute interview, Capra professed his love for the United States, at one point stating, "Once people come to America, the great majority stop being anything else but Americans. As far as I'm concerned, although I came here as a baby, I feel I was born here. And spiritually, I've been here since 1776." At the conclusion of the interview, the narrator remarked, "Your faith in America is an inspiration to all Americans—those who count their ancestry from the *Mayflower* and those who came by way of Ellis Island."[37] After again proving himself to be a loyal American, the foreign-born Capra returned to his career as a filmmaker.

Less than nine months later, the Japanese attacked Pearl Harbor, and America entered World War II. Italy was now an official enemy of the United States, and Italian Americans were being subjected to increased discrimination and suspicion. National identity cards were issued to 600,000 Italian Americans, and about 10,000 Italian immigrants were forced to relocate (Di Stasi xviii). Rose D. Scherini states that "by June 1942, the number of Italians who had been arrested for such reasons as contraband, curfew, or travel violation[s] reached 1,500" (16), and Lawrence Di Stasi points out that approximately 250 Italians, some of whom were the parents of American soldiers, were interned in military camps for several months or even years (3).[38]

Capra's position did not isolate him from the ethnocentrism and fear that pervaded American society and seemed to motivate *una storia segreta*—literally, "a secret history" and the term given to the discrimination that Italians and Italian Americans faced within the United States during World War II. As America went to war with Italy, Capra, a World War I veteran, reenlisted, but federal authorities targeted his sister Ann as an enemy alien.[39] Despite her famous army major brother, Ann was subjected to the same travel and curfew restrictions as other Italians in the United States. Eventually, Capra's fame and position allowed Ann to be exempted from such treatment, but, clearly, the director was aware of the discrimination that many Italians were confronting (McBride 450).

As Ann endured discrimination, Capra began his work on the "Why We Fight" films, a series meant to educate U.S. soldiers about the reasons for U.S. involvement in World War II. The army could have delegated this project to another enlisted Hollywood filmmaker like John Huston or John Ford or even a documentarian like Pare Lorentz, but instead they chose a naturalized Italian. Certainly, Capra's prior credits played a role in his selection, but it also seems that his well-publicized ethnic background was an important factor.[40] Here was an Italian by birth telling Americans why his new homeland was the right country to back in a confrontation with his former homeland.[41]

Capra's supervision of the project allowed him to define the enemy and their people. Like him, many of the individuals who worked on "Why We Fight" had prior experience in Hollywood, and this background influenced their work. Hollywood films have traditionally relied on stereotypes to define entire ethnic and racial groups; the "Why We Fight" films conformed to this strategy. However, despite its use of Italian and Italian American stereotypes, the film series tends to treat Italians more benignly than the other Axis powers.

This point has been lost on scholars who tend to focus on the series' stylistic and rhetorical techniques rather than the historical implications of individual films or the ways in which they advance our understanding of ethnicity during the war years. Generally, all seven films are discussed collectively, ignoring the specific historical context surrounding the production and release date of individual films;[42] with few exceptions, critics neglect any sense of cultural or ethnic specificity by discussing the German, Italian, and Japanese people as if they were represented as a single enemy.[43]

However, John W. Dower's and William J. Blakefield's analyses of the production of *Know Your Enemy: Japan,* a particularly racist government film whose production Capra oversaw, are sensitive to these issues. Both authors reveal the vehement, behind-the-scenes debates surrounding the representation of the Japanese and thus demonstrate that ethnic representation was a major concern of wartime policy makers and filmmakers. Dower writes, "Capra as well as the military authorities responsible for approving the script supported [focusing on the Japanese people], while some of the scriptwriters were more inclined to emphasize the role of Japan's militaristic leaders, among whom they included the emperor. To the project's more liberal contributors, the attitude promoted by the Army and Frank Capra seemed to border at times on sheer racism" (18). Blakefield's essay offers a comparative analysis of *Know Your Enemy: Japan* and *Here Is Germany* (132). However, since both of these films were produced in 1945—more than a year after Italy's surrender—they are without their Italian counterpart.

In comparing wartime governmental and Hollywood representations of African Americans, Thomas Cripps suggests that a relationship, even an alliance, existed between the two cinemas. A similar comparison can be drawn between Hollywood's and Washington's representations of Italian Americans. The two entities were not always in agreement, but their films offer ideological and thematic similarities.[44] For instance, the portrayal of Italians in Capra's "Why We Fight" films mobilized many of Hollywood's Italian American stereotypes from the 1930s. Stereotypes are consistently repeated representations of groups of individuals (ethnic, regional, class, gender, sexual, and so forth) that "hard[en] attitudes" by offering little if any variation from previous representations (Linn 16). They have the potential to rob group members of their individuality, because discursively they flatten diversity within the group and may help to create an expectation and resultant prejudgment of group members.

Unfortunately, many scholarly studies become preoccupied with the "sameness" of stereotypes rather than their differences. As Shohat and Stam suggest, "This essentialism generates in its wake a certain *ahistoricism;* the analysis tends to be static, not allowing for mutations, metamorphoses, changes of valence, altered function; it ignores the historical instability of the stereotype and even of language" (199). In short, stereotypes and their meanings change depending on historical moment, text, and subgroup. For instance, the representation and significance of the Italian American gangster has fluctuated. Gardaphé writes, "Early films often portrayed gangsters as degenerate and overly feminized men losing their independence in the new capitalist society, but later films recast them as men who wielded power through sexuality and guns" (*Wiseguys* 4). The meaning of the gangster also transforms when the character is "authored" by Italian Americans.[45] Gardaphé writes that the gangster becomes "a telling figure in the tale of American race, gender, and ethnicity, a figure that reflects the autobiography of an immigrant group just as it reflects the fantasy of a native population" (*Wiseguys* xiv).[46]

Throughout the 1930s, Hollywood films reduced the Italian to a set of readily identifiable traits that limited the possibilities of Italian representation and contributed to their marginalization. Gangster films like Mervyn LeRoy's *Little Caesar* (1931) and Howard Hawks and Richard Rossen's *Scarface: The Shame of the Nation* (1932) rendered Italian social clubs as mobster hangouts and offered characters who forsook loyalty, elegance, and social tact for a boyish fascination with guns and a Machiavellian drive for power. But other stereotypes plagued Depression-era Italians as well. Films like the

Fred Astaire and Ginger Rogers musicals *The Gay Divorcee* (Mark Sandrich, 1934) and *Top Hat* (Mark Sandrich, 1935) perpetuated the Italian fool—a character who was completely ignorant of the modern world around him and one who was consistently mocked. In *Horse Feathers* (Norman McLeod, 1932) and *A Night at the Opera* (Sam Wood, 1935), Chico Marx developed the Italian trickster. Marx's characters took on as little responsibility and did as little work as possible; nevertheless, they succeeded in the films' chaotic worlds and empowered Italians by cleverly and benignly manipulating the system to their advantage. *Winterset* (Alfred Santell, 1936) mobilized the Italian radical, a character who attempted to mend the guilty conscience of an American public that had lived through the execution of Sacco and Vanzetti. The gangster, the fool, the trickster, and the radical reduced the complicated experience of being Italian in Depression-era America to a set of character traits that helped to define ethnic Italians.

In "Why We Fight," Capra uses these stereotypes to define not Italians in general but *one* Italian and sometimes that one Italian's followers. The films argue that Mussolini is an anomaly, not the "average Italian." In fact, average Italians are his victims. Almost immediately, *Prelude to War* (1942) represents Il Duce as a trickster. But whereas Chico Marx's tricksters were rather benign, only impairing the plans of unsympathetic characters, Mussolini is "an ambitious rabble-rouser" who has betrayed the Italian people. Taking advantage of their economic hardship, the Italian leader has conned Italians into making a "tragic mistake" by offering an easy solution to a complicated problem. When the ineffectiveness of his policies becomes apparent, Mussolini invades another country to distract the Italian populace. Now, because of this situation, "the march of history was reversing itself" in Italy.

Mussolini is also portrayed as a fool. When his conquest of Ethiopia is discussed in *Prelude,* the film's narrator (Walter Huston) tells viewers, "Mussolini beat his chest like Tarzan." Late in *Divide and Conquer* (1943), a film that greatly ignores Italy, a circuslike score accompanies a sequence of images of Mussolini, and in *The Battle of Britain* (1943), Mussolini is labeled "Hitler's stooge."[47] Mussolini's foolishness is partially to blame for his ineptitude as a leader.[48] When Mussolini (not Italy) tries to conquer Greece, he is shown to be a clownish supporting player in Germany's quest for world domination. So inept is Mussolini that he first fails to conquer Greece and then loses part of Albania (a country he had previously conquered) in the process. Irate and realizing that he cannot trust Mussolini with what are viewed as relatively menial conquests, Hitler sends his own army to conquer Greece and save Mussolini. Germany and Japan had stronger militaries than Italy, but even Hitler sees Mussolini's leadership as that of an inept fool.[49] And in a remarkable framing of the Allied-Axis conflict, Mussolini borders on becoming a source of comic relief.[50]

Despite his ineptitudes, Mussolini has managed to seize and maintain power in Italy, and the films must account for his ability to do so. For this task, "Why We Fight" relies on the trickster stereotype, while also invoking the gangster. In *Prelude to War,* each nation or culture is shown to have its own unique way of silencing dissenters. The German Gestapo break into a dissenter's office, push aside a maid, and gun down their uniformed target while he speaks on the telephone. The Japanese follow a similar course of action; however, their target is wearing pajamas and getting out of bed. "In Italy, they did it different," intones the narrator, and as one might suspect, this difference centers on Mussolini's reliance on the techniques of mob warfare. Black cars careen down a dirt road, while a hail of bullets silences those who disagree with Il Duce. The sequence, which includes three superimposed images—the speeding car, a firing pistol, and a newspaper headline about the assassination of one of Mussolini's political adversaries—features high production values, and parts of it may come directly out of a Hollywood feature.[51] Ultimately, the end result is that Italians had lost democratic choice and freedom of speech because of the gangster-fool-trickster-radical who was their leader.

In *Little Caesar* and *Scarface,* Italian characters who opposed the gangsters were rare, thus offering the idiotic suggestion that most Italians and Italian Americans supported gangsterism.[52] However, while *Prelude to War* includes images of Italian people chanting "Duce! Duce!" it and other "Why We Fight" films are rather forgiving of the Italian populace. Il Duce's coercive techniques, his unprovoked invasion of foreign nations, his withdrawal of Italian ambassadors to the League of Nations, his assassination of political adversaries, and his coalition with other radicals hardly guarantee his legitimacy.[53] He is not an Italian leader in the tradition of Garibaldi, an individual who is mentioned alongside Washington, Jefferson, and Lincoln in the opening moments of Capra's *Prelude to War.*

The same cannot be said of the series' representation of the Germans and Japanese. Capra treats these enemies as genetically predisposed to their current leaders and their authoritarian regimes. Hitler and Hirohito are German and Japanese cultures incarnate, and their individual personalities are indicative of their constituents' national character. As *Prelude to War* tells viewers, the Germans have an "in-born national love of regimentation and harsh discipline," while the Japanese fanatically worship their emperor as God. Thus, while Mussolini must concoct schemes to distract temporarily illogical Italians, Hitler and Hirohito seem to enjoy the full and knowing support of the German and Japanese people. This makes the Germans and Japanese seem more inanimate and mechanical, while the Italians are granted the individualism that democracies like the United States hold so sacred (Ewing 85–88, 95–97). Such rhetoric nearly blocked the films' domestic distribution. Peter Rollins writes, "Office of War Information guidelines required filmmakers to focus blame on the political elites in the Axis countries. . . . Until FDR stepped in to demand a clearance for ["Why We Fight"], the Office of War Information imposed a ban on domestic distribution of the series because of these slurs, warning that stirring up hatred would, in the long run, cause more harm than good" ("Our American Dream" 83).

The genetic predisposition of the Germans to authoritarianism also spurs their attraction to world domination. Early on in *The Nazis Strike* (1943), an intertitle informs viewers that "German ambitions for world conquest go back a long way." Photographs of Otto Von Bismarck, Kaiser Wilhelm II, and Adolf Hitler are interspersed with the dates that their regimes took power or waged war. Emphasizing the point, the narrator declares, "The symbols and the leaders changed, but Germany's maniacal urge to impose its will upon others continues from generation to generation." Lacking the historical evidence to support similar claims about the Japanese, the "Why We Fight" films rely instead upon Japan's current plans for world domination (Blakefield 133). The Tanaka Memorial, which Blakefield notes "was (and is) regarded by most historians as a fraudulent document," was thought to be a detailed, step-by-step strategy for Japanese conquest of Asia, the Pacific, and eventually the United States (133). This plan becomes one of the cornerstones of *The Battle of China* (1944), a film that details Japan's attempted conquest of China (purportedly the first step in the Tanaka Memorial).

In some ways, the decision to paint *both* the Germans and the Japanese as genetically abhorrent is unique. Providing numerous artifacts to account for his arguments, Dower finds that the vehemence and hatred directed toward the Japanese during the war far exceeded those directed toward the other Axis powers. Further, media accounts of Japanese atrocities far outnumbered references to Germany's extermination of the Jews (35). ("Why We Fight" neglects to mention the Holocaust directly.) Wartime public opinion polls showed that 10 to 13 percent of American respondents "consistently supported the 'annihilation' or 'extermination' of the Japanese as a people" (53).[54] Hearst newspapers declared Japan a "racial menace" and suggested that if they prevailed, a "perpetual war between Oriental ideals and Occidental" would rage (quoted in Dower 7). Media outlets regularly reported on Allied troops taking body parts from Japanese dead as war trophies and sometimes sending them home to friends and relatives. "It is virtually inconceivable,"

Dower writes, "that teeth, ears, and skulls could have been collected from German or Italian war dead and publicized in the Anglo-American countries without provoking an uproar" (66). The popular sendoff "Good luck and good hunting," "which moviegoers learned from the 1944 Hollywood film *Destination Tokyo*" (90), further dehumanized the Japanese, and the common practice of referring to the German enemy as the Nazis revealed the racist assumptions of wartime rhetoric. The Germans could be either good Germans or bad Nazis, but the Japanese were almost always referred to as "Japs," something that became "practically canonized" in wartime Hollywood productions (Dower 78–79). "This mode of expression," Dower concludes, "was virtually *de rigueur* whenever the Japanese and Germans were discussed together in American or British writings: the Germans were bad, but the Japanese were worse; the Germans were compulsive, but the Japanese were the most compulsive people in the world; the Germans had regressed to a phallic stage, while the Japanese never came out of it; the Germans, as in this case, had lapsed from a standard the Japanese never knew" (140).[55]

While the Japanese receive a stereotypical representation in Capra's "Why We Fight" films, the similarly racist portrait of the Germans is outside the norm. Wartime Hollywood films like *Sahara* (Zoltan Korda, 1943) and *At the Front in North Africa* (Darryl F. Zanuck, 1943) had made the Fascist Italians look like "hapless understudies who possessed none of the threatening élan and menacing aptitude of the Teutonic Nazis" (Doherty 131), but "Why We Fight"'s especially stereotypical and racist representation of the Germans made the Italians seem even less ominous. According to *Prelude to War,* Mussolini seeks only to "restore the glory that is Rome." Japan and Germany wish to conquer the world. Japanese leaders are quoted as saying, "The Pacific is ours." Germany's rulers say, "Today we rule Germany. Tomorrow the world." These words are reinforced visually when a map designed by Walt Disney animators shows that the Roman Empire included parts of Europe, Africa, and the Middle East. Similar maps, used to demonstrate the ambitions of the Germans and the Japanese, cover the entire globe and include all of North and South Americas. After conquering his half of the globe, the narrator tells us, Hitler would leave "Benito Mussolini a share of the loot if he behaved himself." Mussolini is a minor threat, if he is a threat at all. The real enemies are Germany and Japan.

After all, Italy was an American ally in World War I, while the German Army and through them the German people (according to *Prelude to War*) had never acknowledged defeat in the same war. In the current conflict, the Italians have made a tragic mistake. The Germans and the Japanese have not made a mistake, and they are not being duped. Instead, they are ethnically and racially predisposed to authoritarian regimes. In Italy, then, the current state is a temporary problem; in Germany and Japan, it is the result of cultural forces that will drive conflicts as long as the nations can arm themselves. In Italy, the problem is Mussolini; in Germany and Japan, it is national identity.

By November 1943, Mussolini was no longer in power, the Italian people had been liberated, and Italy was a U.S. ally (Scherini 15). These historical events altered the depiction of Italy in Capra's "Why We Fight" series. *The Battle of Britain*, the fourth film in the series (1943), makes no mention of Italy. *The Battle of Russia*, the fifth film in the series (1943), mentions Italy only to discuss Germany's conquest of Greece, and the only reference to Italy in *The Battle of China*, the sixth film in the series (1944), is a newspaper headline that reads "Mussolini [not Italy] into Ethiopia." Initially, it seems that Italy's defeat allowed Capra's propaganda films to focus their attention on the other Axis enemies.

However, the film that concludes the series deals extensively with both Mussolini and the Italians. According to Capra, *War Comes to America* (1945) "dealt with who, what, where, why and how we came to be the U.S.A. . . . [It] was, and still is, one of the most graphic visual histories of the United States ever made" (*Name* 336). *War Comes to America* answers the "why we fight" question by depicting what the United States stood to lose should it *not* fight. This rhetorical strategy allowed a production crew overseen by an Italian immigrant to define what the United States was and who Americans were.

Not surprisingly, *War Comes to America* states that the United States is a country "where the sweat of men [*sic*] of all nations built America." Early in the film, dozens of ethnic immigrant groups are listed along with one of their specific contributions to the United States.[56] The film even references the Germans and the Italians. Viewers are told that Italian sulfur miners in Louisiana and "the German and his technical skills" have greatly advanced the economic and cultural development of America and influenced its identity.[57] Interestingly, after lauding the contributions of Italian immigrants to the United States, there is a noticeable shift in rhetoric toward Italians living in Italy. Whereas previous films had placed most of the blame on Mussolini, *War Comes to America*'s references to Il Duce are balanced with references to the Italian people. For instance, Mussolini still attacks Ethiopia, but *Italian air forces* enter Spain and Italian soldiers are shown gunning down innocent Ethiopians. Mussolini declares war against the democratic world (an anonymous narrator reads a translation of his words), but a headline declares that *Italy* is attacking Albania. Images of Italian war ships reveal a significant number of Italian military personnel, and "Rome cheered" when Italy, Japan, and Germany signed the Pact of Berlin, a "far-reaching alliance" among the three nations. In the past, "Why We Fight" instilled confidence by treating Mussolini as a foolish, manipulative, and radical gangster. Now, as the United States began its fifth year at war against Germany and Japan, Capra's series instilled confidence by seeing the defeated Italians as a unified people led by Mussolini.

Nonetheless, Capra's film continues to treat Italy and the Italians more benignly than the other Axis powers. References to great German Americans in *Prelude to War* and references to the "technical skills" of Germans in *War Comes to America* cannot counteract the rhetoric of the series as a whole: the Germans have an "in-born national love of regimentation and harsh discipline." The Japanese, or, in the films' terms, "the Japs," whether living in Japan or the United States, are Hitler's "bucktooth pals" who fanatically worship their emperor as if he were God.[58] Italians are never referred to as "wops" or "dagoes." They are not said to have greasy hair or hairy chests (although Mussolini does beat his chest like Tarzan). They do not have an inborn national love of laziness, sex, opera singing, or overeating. In fact, the visual images the films offer are far removed from the stereotypical image of an Italian that was proffered in American films prior to the war. These Italians do not have mustaches, are not overweight, and do not sing uncontrollably. Those characteristics apply to Mussolini, not average Italians. In his wartime series, Capra works to establish a greater respect for the Italian community in the United States by undermining 1930s Italian stereotypes and showing that America went to war with Germany, Japan, and Mussolini, not Germany, Japan, and Italy.

* * *

Thomas Doherty has written, "For the first- and second-generation Americans who ran the studios, the foreign-born directors who spoke with thick accents, and the actors whose real names did not end in Anglo-Saxon suffixes, celebrity stature and financial success did not necessarily dispel feelings of cultural marginality" (44–45). Such was the case with Frank Capra. Try as he might to assimilate into (white) American society, he was never able to disavow his ethnic ties. From *The Strong Man* to "Why We Fight," ethnic identity had an influence on his work. We see it in his 1920s and 1930s films when he looks to immigrant and allegorical immigrant characters to redeem American values not corrupted by greed and materialism, and we see it in "Why We Fight" when he consistently uses the series to defend the everyday Italians against the radical and decidedly "un-Italian" Mussolini.

While Capra's work routinely lauded immigrant and immigrant-like characters, it also cast a derisive eye toward the ruling elite and some kinds of

American assimilation. Sollors has written, "Through social criticism new-comers get ethnicized and Americanized at the same time" (147). Capra's work and his biography have come to signify the ultimate American success story, but that same work and that same biography are filled with criticisms of the "American way." Particularly in the first half of his career, Capra worked in a historical climate that did not welcome Italians. The nativist pressures that Rogin writes of and that Capra faced were particularly salient in the 1920s. By 1924, "nativists" had succeeded in framing the public image of most immigrants, including those from southern and eastern Europe, in terms of eugenics. They were no longer seen as a cheap source of labor but as the parents of future Americans (Jacobson, *Whiteness* 82–83), and so their desirability was significantly questioned. The passage of the Immigration Act of 1924 indicated the great disdain for them. Samuel L. Bailey has writ-ten, "The message was clear. Italians and the other southern and eastern European immigrants were not wanted in the United States" (89). We see such sentiments in the public fervor over the star persona of Valentino and the ordeal of Sacco and Vanzetti.[59] Yet the films made during this time by a young Italian immigrant director offered a dissenting cultural voice within the larger public discourse.

By directing movies like *The Strong Man, For the Love of Mike,* and *The Younger Generation,* Capra acknowledged what Rogin has labeled "the pull of Old World ties" (131), while using those same ties to question the con-struction of an American identity, the importance of critically evaluating the pressures and decisions to assimilate, and the validity of American ideals like individualism, capitalism, communalism, and equality. In doing so, Capra redrew the line between American and un-American—not along ethnic lines but rather along the lines of personal value judgments. This strategy was meant to challenge audiences, which surely included nativists who sup-ported restricting immigration, to rethink their positions and sympathize with (fictional) immigrants who were represented as Americans whose very existence became the battleground of two competing cultures and who were sometimes destroyed by the conflicts that raged within and around them.

Capra's 1920s films are the key to unlocking the ethnic elements of his work in the 1930s. Movies like *Mr. Smith Goes to Washington* continued Capra's criticisms of America's assimilative impulses, even as Capra himself worked to assimilate. Rather than depicting the way things are, the fantastical endings showcase a mythical vision of America and highlight the disparity between real-ity and fantasy. Here, in Capra's tales of immigrant wish fulfillment, the often marginalized immigrant gives (to quote Deeds) his "two cents' worth" while forcing the culture that demands his assimilation to conform to his norms.

Some have argued that the narratives found in *Mr. Smith* and other Capra films present "a familiar narrative motif in American popular culture: the journey of an innocent protagonist from the country to the city, where he or she is subject to mockery or exploitation" (Wolfe, *"Mr. Smith"* 200). However, Capra's ethnic immigrant origins, as well as the immigrant origins of his characters, make these works more than a simple retelling of a typical American story. Certainly, a country-versus-city (as well as a pious-versus-impious) conflict is present in many of these films, but it is also true that the immigrant identity of *The Strong Man's* Bergot, and the origins of many of the characters who come after him, is crucial to their innocence and naïveté. It allows them to steadfastly believe in the promise of America, but it also serves to criticize the treatment that real-life immigrants received upon their arrival in the United States.[60]

During World War II, Capra continued to argue for cultural and ethnic acceptance. By challenging Hollywood's Italian stereotypes, Capra not only worked to establish a degree of tolerance toward Italian Americans but also helped to (re)define the imagined community of Italian America. Some Italian Americans (and non-Italian Americans), after all, looked to Capra to understand their identities. And so Capra could not control the ethnic aspects of his identity. The cultural climate in which he lived and worked always made his ethnicity an issue for someone, even if he refused to see it as an issue for himself. As a result, the strategies Capra used to assimilate often were or became assimilative strategies for Italian Americans at large. When he asserted his assimilated whiteness by making films about WASP Americans, Italian Americans were allowed to follow suit. In "Why We Fight," when he treats the Japanese and the Germans as others, his Italian American audience witnessed an assimilative strategy used repeatedly throughout American history: "othering" another ethnic group in order to establish one's own Americanness.[61] Capra may not have invented these strategies, but he did use many of them, and by using them, he brought them to the attention of a much wider population.

Interestingly, Capra's denial of his ethnic origins was not total or complete, especially after World War II. In *It's a Wonderful Life,* he not only featured Martini (Bill Edmunds), an Italian American character who plays a prominent function throughout the film, but also borrowed the narrative from his ethnic past. In the documentary *Beyond Wiseguys: Italian Americans and the Movies* (Steven Fischler, 2008), Gardaphé suggests Sicilian stories often show that "a man that tries to rise above his culture will drown." We see this narrative not only in *It's a Wonderful Life* but also *The Younger Generation* and other Capra movies. Years later, Capra's film *A Hole in the Head* starred

Sinatra and Edward G. Robinson (a Romanian) as two Italian brothers. Released in 1959, the film stands out not because it includes Italian American characters (they had been appearing in Capra films since at least the 1930s) but because its Italian American characters anchor the narrative and speak openly about their family's immigrant roots. Like most Hollywood films, *A Hole in the Head* perpetuates stereotypes (overly emotional, immature Italian men who gesture with their hands as they speak) even as it challenges them, but, ultimately, it demonstrates a level of comfort with Italian ethnicity that Capra had not shown before. Capra based the film on an Arnold Schulman play about two Jewish brothers, but while he "maintained over half of the original" work, he also inserted cultural norms that are specifically Italian American (Russo 298).[62] In his astute analysis of the film, Russo points out, "Tony gives lengthy advice to his son on the subject of *la bella figura*," an Italian cultural ideal that becomes the focus of Scorsese's cinema (300). Nonetheless, while *A Hole in the Head* is in some ways unique, it also marks a return to the ethnic and immigrant themes of earlier Capra films like *For the Love of Mike* (Russo 294).

In addition to his postwar films, Capra made frequent references to his Italianness and the ways it affected his life in his autobiography. From *The Name above the Title*'s publication in 1971 on, Capra's professional biographies frequently listed him as "President Italo-American Federation of Southern California, 1950–1," and on March 31, 1972, he wrote an extensive remembrance of his Italian American upbringing in the *Philadelphia Daily News*. The piece recounts Sunday dinners, playing bocce for pennies, and old Sicilian folktales of *Lo Lebro* (the Jackrabbit), who imparted the idea that you have to keep working to stay in front and be happy (Frank Capra Collection, Box 1). What had changed was not so much Capra's willingness to accept his ethnicity as the public's (and the studios') level of tolerance for ethnicity in general and Italian ethnicity in particular.

During and after the war, the image of Hollywood's Italians shifted. Numerous war films featured Italians as part of their multiethnic platoons, and films like *Cry of the City* (Robert Siodmak, 1948), *Marty* (Delbert Mann, 1955), *The Rose Tattoo* (Daniel Mann, 1955), and *Full of Life* (Richard Quine, 1956) offered representations that countered the more stereotypical portraits offered in prior films (while perpetuating others like the overly emotional, sometimes dim-witted Italian).[63] Outside of Hollywood, Italians fled their ethnic neighborhoods and moved to the suburbs in large numbers, taking advantage of government housing loans made available to "white" Americans.[64] From their privileged position (as assimilated "white" Americans), Italians were allowed to embrace their ethnic roots and adopt ethnic identities over which they exercised an increasing degree of control. This shifting cultural climate allowed later Italian American filmmakers such as Scorsese, Savoca, and Coppola to use their ethnic identities as marketing strategies that affirmed the realism or nostalgia of their films. But in Capra's time, Italian ethnicity remained something to deny, repress, and transcend, even if it was an inextricable part of one's life experience and artistic vision.

2 Martin Scorsese

Confined and Defined by Ethnicity

Over a pitch-black screen, Martin Scorsese's voice intones, "You don't make up for your sins in church. You do it in the streets. You do it at home. The rest is bullshit, and you know it." Charlie (Harvey Keitel), a twentysomething Italian American, bolts upright from his dream, wipes his eyes, and walks to a mirror. A handheld camera, which mimics documentary techniques and foreshadows the film's interest in the day-to-day lives of its characters, pans to follow him across his tiny room. We watch as, still half asleep, Charlie gazes intently at his reflected visage, trying to make sense of what he sees (fig. 5). He opens his mouth, feels around its edges, and returns to his twin

Figure 5. Charlie (Harvey Keitel) stares questioningly at his own image in Scorsese's *Mean Streets*.

bed. Three quick cuts to successively closer shots establish a degree of intimacy by bringing viewers nearer to the character as his head hits his pillow. Charlie attempts to resume his sleep but is too disturbed by his dream to do so. These are the first sounds and images from Scorsese's *Mean Streets*, a film that catapulted the auteur to widespread visibility and one that establishes several of the motifs he has employed throughout his career. For example, the image of a male character standing before a mirror and gazing at his image questioningly reappears in many Scorsese films, and on some level it serves as an apt metaphor for Scorsese's treatment of his ethnic background.

Unlike Capra, Scorsese critically accepts his ethnic Italianness, only rarely rejecting the label "Italian American" and then only to claim a more specific ethnic identity as a "Sicilian American." References to his ethnic roots characterize many of his films, interviews, and personality profiles, and they have influenced the critical assessment of his work.[1] His Italian American status has granted him a series of experiences that differ from the ones usually proffered by Hollywood cinema, and he continually draws upon and interrogates them in his films.

Despite its visibility, few critics appreciate how deeply Scorsese's ethnic culture grounds his artistic vision and thematic concerns.[2] Robert Casillo's book-length study *Gangster Priest* provides a notable exception. Casillo argues, "Scorsese has gained his popular and critical success not by concealing or denying his ethnicity but by confronting and exploring it" (xi). While commendable for its recognition that Italian American culture is not simply "local colour" or a "pretext for personal nostalgia" (xviii), Casillo's work at times treats Italian American behaviors as fixed and unchanging, rather than recognizing the ways cultural norms are constructed or the role that Scorsese's films play in their construction. He writes, "The failures and successes of this group's immigrant experience form the essential basis by which to comprehend [Scorsese's] ethnicity as it relates to his life and art" (5). Casillo thus imagines a relatively homogeneous group experience where individuals usually "typify their ethnic group" (5).[3]

If Casillo overvalues the group identity of Scorsese's characters, Robert Kolker overestimates their individuality. Scorsese's cinema repeatedly deals with outsiders. Characters like *Taxi Driver*'s (1976) Travis Bickle (Robert De Niro), *King of Comedy*'s (1983) Rupert Pupkin (De Niro), and *The Aviator*'s (2004) Howard Hughes (Leonardo DiCaprio) strive for respectability and acceptance by the establishment.[4] This has led Kolker to proclaim Scorsese's work "a cinema of loneliness." But many of his films that focus on Italian American characters might be more accurately described as "a cinema of group solidarity."[5] While isolated from mainstream society, Charlie and his friend Johnny Boy (De Niro), *Who's That Knocking at My Door*'s (1968) JR (Keitel), and *GoodFellas*' (1990) Henry Hill (Ray Liotta) are not alone; they are members of an ever-present ethnic community that gives them a clear and comfortable, albeit limited, understanding of their backgrounds and their place in the world. In each case, the ethnic community becomes so comfortable that the worst fate that can befall the central character is expulsion or a deliberate journey into mainstream society. However, by isolating themselves within their ethnic enclaves, Scorsese's Italian American characters are marginalized—forced to assimilate to regressive views on race, sexuality, and gender and consequently robbed of the economic and social opportunities that lie beyond the bounds of their neighborhood. In effect, they are torn between a kind of tribal solidarity and a modern world of multicultural assimilation to secular capitalist values.

The White Ethnic Revival, New Hollywood, and Scorsese's Upbringing

Andy Dougan has written, "No American director has been more influenced by his background than Martin Scorsese" (7). He was born in Queens, New York, during World War II, but when his parents fell on difficult financial times, they moved back to Manhattan's Little Italy, where the seven-year-old was surrounded by generations of the Scorsese family. Four overlapping spheres of influence came to characterize the future director's upbringing—the family, the neighborhood, the church, and the movies (Kelly, *Journey* 15–35).[6] Scorsese's personal background has dominated much of the critical commentary on his films, but the larger historical, social, and institutional contexts of his work remain undervalued. Leighton Grist has sought to repair this oversight by investigating the ways in which Scorsese's exposure to European and art-house cinema throughout the 1960s and his postclassical relation to Hollywood have afforded him opportunities that filmmakers like Capra did not have. Following Thomas Schatz and Thomas Elsaesser, Grist argues that Scorsese's cinema, and in particular *Mean Streets*, takes advantage of the loosening of causality and "narrative fragmentation" that characterized many of the "New Hollywood" films of the early and mid-1970s. He thus contextualizes Scorsese's authorship within cinematic trends, but generally avoids other historical and cultural factors that might have influenced Scorsese's work.

In addition to widespread access to international movies, Scorsese was able to create a unique cinematic vision by taking advantage of the opportunities that the White Ethnic Revival made possible. In the 1950s and 1960s, the civil rights and Black Power movements brought racism to the center of national attention. According to Matthew Jacobson, these events "heightened whites' consciousness of their skin privilege, rendering it not only visible but uncomfortable (the more so, perhaps, because it was so hard to disown its chief comforts)" (*Roots* 4). In an effort to mitigate their complicity and investment in segregation and other government-sanctioned racism, descendants of white immigrant groups attempted to mitigate their whiteness by proclaiming their Italianness, Irishness, Jewishness, Greekness, and so forth.[7] In a remarkable move, the same social institutions that in the pre–World War II years had encouraged assimilation now applauded and sanctioned white claims of ethnicity. Genealogical research was suddenly seen as worthy of college credit, politicians hailed ethnic groups and proclaimed their own ethnic identities, and news agencies, trade presses, television networks, and book publishers all rushed to capitalize on the "roots" craze (*Roots* 4). The White Ethnic Revival with the support of the above-mentioned institutions shifted the understanding of race and ethnicity in America. "Normative whiteness," Jacobson suggests, was relocated "from what might be called Plymouth Rock whiteness to Ellis Island whiteness" (*Roots* 7). For Jacobson, the movement "blunted the charges of the Civil Rights and Black Power movements and eased the conscience of a nation that had just barely begun to reckon with the harshest contours of its history forged in white supremacism" (*Roots* 9). Jacobson's understanding of this time period, then, is one in which an interest in white ethnic identities had largely destructive implications for race relations in the United States. By investing too much in their "ethnicness," ethnic groups effectively worked to level racial and ethnic prejudice.

However, Jacobson too easily reduces the White Ethnic Revival to a neoconservative impulse within U.S. politics. As Richard Alba said in his review of *Roots, Too*, "The reference to the post–civil rights era suggests that the ethnicity discourse was solely a creature of racial positioning vis-à-vis blacks and overlooks the extent to which it was aimed not just at the group below but at the one above as well" (237). Alba's recognition of the constructive possibilities of this historical period provides a necessary counterargument to Jacobson. By so intently focusing on the period's destructive potential, Jacobson marginalizes the extent to which it afforded ethnic individuals, including filmmakers like Scorsese, the opportunity to critically explore their ethnicity.

Following the releases of *Who's That Knocking at My Door* and *Boxcar Bertha* (1972), Scorsese began reworking a script that would become *Mean Streets*. When Haig Manoogian, Scorsese's mentor from his film school days at New York University (NYU), received word of this project, he feared it would be too similar to *Who's That Knocking.* "No more pictures about Italians," he reportedly told Scorsese (Kelly, *First* 68). In retrospect, Manoogian's warnings are laughable. Even though *Mean Streets* was not a huge financial success, it granted Scorsese a great deal of cultural capital that would translate into financial capital later in his career. A growing cinephilic culture along with a critical discourse that supported Scorsese's work was invaluable in vaulting him to prominence, but the larger social and cultural trends of post–World War II America, particularly the shifting perception of ethnicity, were also of seminal importance. Previously, Hollywood movies had been hostile to Italian Americans. Throughout the classical period they generally relegated Italians to stereotypical roles. As Mirella J. Affron has shown, when Italians were represented in Hollywood movies between 1918 and 1971, they were usually gangsters or "sentimental hero[es]" (234). Although many of Scorsese's characters, on the surface at least, perpetuate the Italian gangster stereotype, his films are more deeply and critically invested in the lives and identities of Italians.[8] As Leonard Quart and Paul Rabinow recognized in their review of *Mean Streets*, "The films that have dealt with Italian immigrant and second generation life—*Marty, Brothers Rico* [Phil Karlson, 1957], *Pay or Die* [Richard Wilson, 1960], *House of Strangers* [Joseph L. Mankiewicz, 1949]—have been bound to melodramatic conventions or comic stereotypes so broadly drawn that little of the complex concreteness of the culture could seep through" (42).[9]

In contrast, Scorsese's Italians are "individuals . . . not media clichés" (Connelly 158). "Watching *Mean Streets* was a revelation," writes Italian American critic Vincent LoBrutto. "The dark secrets Italian-Americans knew about themselves and their culture were exposed like raw nerves" (xii). LoBrutto's assessment ignores the diversity that exists within Italian American communities, but his suggestion that *Mean Streets* was different from what had come before is worth considering. Like *Raging Bull, GoodFellas,* and other Scorsese films, *Mean Streets* includes Italian gangsters, but it also probes the neighborhoods where these characters live, the circumstances that lead to their life choices, the cultural values that allow them to justify their activities, the spiritual dilemmas they confront, and the ways in which they reconcile their life on the streets with the values they are supposed to uphold. Scorsese's fictional films about Italian Americans do not embrace the Italian American experience in order to level ethnic and racial prejudice. On the contrary, they perform an almost anthropological function.[10] Through them, Scorsese looks critically at Italian American culture, confronting the rigid ways in which it defines men and women while simultaneously imprisoning individuals within a worldview that often robs them of happiness and limits free choice. Although his documentaries seem to embrace Italian American

ethnicity in a way that his fictional work does not, they too see ethnicity as
a complex issue, grounded in family and community but also productive of
narrow, constricting, even imprisoning values. In this way, Scorsese is critical
of Italian American cultural norms in a manner for which Jacobson's model
does not account.

Italian American Cinematic Culture and the Importance of *La Bella Figura*

Critics have been quick to recognize the Scorsese family, Little Italy, and
Roman Catholicism as influences on Scorsese's work, but little attention has
been paid to Italian cinema. Often, the movies Scorsese saw during his childhood are reduced to Hollywood films, negating the equally important foreign
films.[11] Leighton Grist and Pasquale Verdicchio provide notable exceptions to
the rule. Grist emphasizes the profound influence of French New Wave films.
The stylistic innovations of the New Wave, along with *Cahiers du Cinéma*'s
insistence in the 1950s on telling personal stories, were important to Scorsese's
development, but the Italian neorealists were idolized by the French in this
period.[12] Verdicchio recognizes the demonstrably strong, ethnically specific
influence that Italian films have had on Scorsese but suggests that Scorsese's
interpretation of Italian cinema rests on an oversimplified understanding of
Italian history, politics, and culture.[13] This emphasis on the so-called historical accuracy of Scorsese's perception reduces their genuine cultural, artistic,
and personal effect to a historical misconception.[14]

In *Mio viaggio in Italia* (1999), Scorsese's four-hour documentary on Italian
film, the director speaks passionately about the role Italian films have played
in his life: "The fact is I know that if I'd never seen the films I am going to be
talking about here," he says, "I'd be a very different person and of course a
very different filmmaker." In interviews, he has echoed this sentiment, saying,
"In some way Italy is my homeland. I mean, America is, but the subculture
is Italian. . . . I am very close to Italian sensibilities, I think. Italian movies
have been really instrumental in shaping my work" (quoted in Kelly, *Journey*
63).[15] The cultural ties between Italian film and Scorsese suggest a kind of
transatlantic interaction between Italians and Italian Americans that works
to define and redefine Italian American cultural identity.

Furthermore, the environment within which Scorsese first watched Italian
films speaks to the existence of an Italian American cinematic culture. In
1940s and 1950s New York City, the Italian American population was so large
that some television stations broadcast Italian films as regular programming

(Thompson and Christie 4). Scorsese's relatives would often gather to watch the films together. Scorsese recalls, "Some of these images were so moving that I noticed that my grandparents started to cry. I mean they left Sicily in 1909, 1910, they made their way all the way to America, and here they were seeing on television in effect what they had left behind and what had happened to it, what had become of it. When I looked at their faces, I could see that *this* was who my grandparents really were. And that this was the country they called home. And it was overwhelming, because for the first time, I became aware that this was where I came from." Scorsese later offers, "Now, [my grandparents] never set out to teach me where I came from, and I never asked. I learned simply from watching them and the movies about their homeland and so they were the first connection with that ancient land of Sicily" (*Mio viaggio in Italia*). For Scorsese, then, Italian cinema bridged the gap between ethnic and cinematic identity and between the neighborhood, the family, the church, and the movies.

The influence of Italian neorealism on *Who's That Knocking* and *Mean Streets* is profound, and Scorsese's later work with Dante Ferretti (Federico Fellini's longtime production designer) further entwines the two cinematic cultures.[16] The influence is not merely formal but also thematic. The character of Zampanó in *La Strada* (Fellini, 1954) helped to shape the representation of Jake LaMotta in *Raging Bull* ("Martin Scorsese on *La Strada*"), and *Mean Streets* was heavily influenced by Fellini's *I vitelloni* (1953) (literally, "The young bulls" but figuratively "The boys").[17] The twentysomething male groups of both films resist maturing and are surrounded by adults who encourage their arrested development by treating them like children. Fellini and Scorsese imply that this situation is culturally defined and exacerbated by the claustrophobic, constraining ethnic cultures in which the young men live.[18] In essence, the characters are performers of a specific kind of immature masculinity, because that is what their culturally defined environment expects and requires of them. This is not to suggest that young Italian American men are necessarily hypermasculine and irresponsible, but it is a theme to which Scorsese (and others) returns repeatedly.

Performances such as the ones noted above are enormously important in Italian American culture and are commonly grouped under the cultural norm of *la bella figura,* which "designates proper or improper public behavior and thus activates all those protocols that pertain to maintaining and augmenting 'face'" (D'Acierno, "Cultural Lexicon" 708).[19] In both *I vitelloni* and *Mean Streets,* we see characters who sometimes want to resist social norms but are reluctant to do so since it would require such an extreme break with tradition and community. Instead, they make choices that stabilize the culture and lead to lives that are essentially not their own. Italian and Italian American culture is allowed to define them rather than them defining it.

La Bella Figura, Sexism, and the Madonna-Whore Dichotomy

While an appreciation of Scorsese's ethnic background is essential if one is to come to a full understanding of the director's work, his concern with ethnicity is deeply related to a more general interest in gender politics. Gender norms, like ethnic norms, are both challenged and affirmed in Scorsese's cinema, and because these norms are complementary, they need to be discussed in tandem. In *From Wiseguys to Wise Men*, Fred Gardaphé investigates the evolution of the Italian American gangster in American literature, film, and television and suggests that early representations of the gangster figure by non-Italians allowed a stereotype to "co-opt" Italian American masculinity. Italian American artists, he argues, have recuperated the figure by using it to narrate a history of "American race, gender, and ethnicity" while reflecting "the autobiography of an immigrant group" and "the fantasy of a native population" (xvii). For Gardaphé, the evolution of wiseguys to wise men occurs when men are able to achieve a level of emotional intimacy in their relationships. He writes, "This intimacy is achieved only after a man, once conditioned not to acknowledge his feelings so that eventually he has none, becomes aware of his feelings, gains the ability to process them, and then takes the risk of expressing them to others" (209).

This maturation process is complicated by two ethnically specific factors. First, Italian American mass-media artists, in an effort to cater to assimilated American audiences, have significantly altered the gender roles of traditional Italian American culture. This is perhaps most apparent when Gardaphé compares Mario Puzo's second and third novels. *The Fortunate Pilgrim* (1964) tells the story of Lucia Santa, a strong maternal figure who raises her sons in an urban area and steers them to productive lives. The novel received several good reviews but was unsuccessful commercially. Puzo's next novel, the exceedingly popular *The Godfather* (1969), centers on the patriarch Don Vito Corleone, who seems to have been a major factor in the novel's success.[20] This transference of power from the feminine figure to the masculine figure occurs repeatedly in Italian American works, including the films of Martin Scorsese. Almost all of Scorsese's movies conform to the male-centered nature of Hollywood narratives.[21] In films like *Mean Streets* and *GoodFellas*, the maternal characters are offered minimal scenes or reduced to an off-screen presence, while surrogate father figures like Don Giovanni (Cesare Danova) in *Mean Streets* and Paul Cicero (Paul Sorvino) in *GoodFellas* are more thoroughly developed.[22]

The second culturally specific factor that complicates the evolution of wiseguys into wise men is *la bella figura*. In Scorsese's cinema, this pervasive cultural norm encourages male immaturity and demands a level of machismo that oftentimes leads male characters to sacrifice their happiness for the sake of male camaraderie. The sexism (along with the racism and homophobia) of characters like JR and Charlie is so extreme that it isolates them from the women in their lives. Clinging tightly to the rigid cultural ideals of their upbringing, these men are robbed of loving, honest relationships by sexual double standards and inequitable gender norms.

Such issues are most evident in Scorsese's early films. Some critics have marginalized or dismissed these works, because they are not as polished or expensive as the later pictures. Critics suggest that *Who's That Knocking at My Door* "bears too much the stamp of student work to be considered a major film" (Connelly xi) and that it "presents a patchwork of jerky transitions, unintegrated stylistic contrasts and varying standards of cinematography and picture quality" (Grist 31).[23] Such perspectives value the "well-made" slickness of Hollywood over the more raw neorealist or New Wave qualities of these films and ignore the ways they can advance our understanding of Scorsese's later, more universally respected, movies. As Roger Ebert said in his prophetic review of *Knocking*, "It is possible that with more experience and maturity Scorsese will direct more polished, finished films—but this work, completed when he was twenty-five, contains a frankness he may have diluted by then" (Kelly, *First* 159).

It's Not Just You, Murray! is a darkly comic student film that tells the story of a hood who rises to wealth. In the opening shots, Murray (Ira Rubin) shows off his possessions, informing viewers how much each costs. "See this tie?" he asks, as the camera offers us a close-up of Murray's prized possession. After a slight pause, Murray's right hand directs the camera to tilt up. "Twenty dollars," he says now with his face as the subject of the close-up. As the film recounts his rise to success, Murray introduces us to three significant figures in his life. The first is Murray's friend Joe (San De Fazio), whom Murray sees as the source of his success. The two head a successful "syndicate," but early in their career, their illegal gin distillery was raided and Murray went to prison while Joe went unpunished. Joe is contrasted with Murray's mother (Catherine Scorsese), whose black veil and obsession with macaroni convey her Old World values. According to Murray, the only psychological advice he has received from her is "Eat first." Throughout the film, she follows him around feeding him macaroni whenever she can. When Murray introduces us to his wife (Andrea Martin), the third significant person, we surmise that Joe is having an affair with her and is the father of Murray's children.[24] Near the end of the film, Murray seems to get wise to the whole charade, but he dismisses what he calls "misunderstandings" as insignificant, preferring instead to focus on his wealth and success. The film ends with an homage to Fellini's *8½* (1963), with first Murray and then Joe directing all the characters through a megaphone as they dance around Murray's convertible.

Like Charlie in *Mean Streets* and Henry in *GoodFellas,* Murray struggles "to balance the values of family, church, and tradition against the materialism, deception, and violence of the Mafia" (Keyser 16). While such a balancing act is not exclusive to Italian Americans, Scorsese gives an ethnically specific inflection to the conflict, showing how Murray's struggles to rescue a presentable masculine identity from his real status as a buffoon and a cuckold are grounded in the pervasive cultural code of *la bella figura.* As a successful businessman, he presents a good face, but Murray is also a criminal who has gone to prison. As a virile man who has fathered children, he "cuts a good figure," but his apparent offspring are in reality fathered by Joe. As a man with friends, he seems respected, but Murray's best friend takes advantage of him at every turn. His wife looks great, but she is uninterested in him. Near the conclusion of the film, Murray tells the cameraman to cut the sound and confronts Joe. Throughout the narrative, Murray's controlling nature has been communicated by his need to direct the film. Even these efforts have failed to hide his reality from viewers. Now, we see Joe speaking in a calm manner, mostly in low-angle close-ups and medium close-ups, while Murray, mostly in medium two-shots with Joe, drops his head and appears upset. The form frames Joe as more independent—worthy of his own shots—even though Scorsese uses the low-angle close-ups mockingly. Joe is not a man to whom we should look up. Despite Murray's unhappiness, he persists in his attempts to present *la bella figura.* He suppresses his real emotions and masquerades as a success, flaunting his wealth and lying in an effort to salvage his masculinity. His feeble display fools nobody, and he becomes a pathetically comic figure, not because his wife is unfaithful or his friend disloyal but because he accepts their failures as his own.

It's Not Just You, Murray! invites viewers to laugh at the absurdity of Murray's failed masculine performance, and because Murray loses nothing but his pride, viewers oblige. Five years later, *Who's That Knocking at My Door* treats *la bella figura* in a more serious fashion.[25] *Knocking* tells the story of JR, a young Italian American from Little Italy who meets "the girl" (Zina Bethune), a blonde-haired, blue-eyed, college-educated woman. The two begin a relationship, but their class and ethnic differences quickly create tension. When the girl tells JR that a previous boyfriend raped her, JR is crushed—not because he is sorry that the girl had to endure such a traumatic situation, but because he sees women in terms of a Madonna-whore dichotomy (or what he labels "broads and girls") and now must reject her. Most of the film takes place after this rejection, with JR remembering his good times with the girl. One night, a mildly inebriated JR visits the girl's apartment. It looks like they may reconcile until JR says he "forgives" her for the rape and that he is going to marry her "anyway." The girl rejects JR, who calls her a "whore." She tells him to "go home," "leaving J. R." as Grist suggests, "nowhere to go but Little Italy" (25). JR retreats to a church, confesses, and then assures a friend that he will see him tomorrow.

Lawrence S. Friedman has argued that JR's fate is unresolved at the end of the film. He writes, "To read impending desolation and death into *Who's That Knocking at My Door* risks equating adolescent confusion with adult trauma" (30). The film, however, gives no indication that these young men will ever mature or that they want to. On the contrary, *Knocking,* like *Mean Streets,* suggests that the characters are clinging to an adolescent environment. As David Denby has argued, "The punks of *Mean Streets* . . . will never shape up; if they survive, they'll simply become *ageing* punks" (37).

JR allows *la bella figura* to dictate his actions. He must treat "broads" and "girls" within the narrow parameters of his culture, or his masculinity will be questioned. He may love the girl, but he is too weak to move beyond his ethnic environment and the ideals it espouses and has instilled in him. So he capitulates to a misogynistic view of women in favor of the homosocial bonds he has with his friends.[26] He saves face but remains trapped in a confining cultural environment where his superficial masculinity condemns him to a life of repetitive monotony and where his judgmental gender politics make a fulfilling, egalitarian relationship impossible.[27] Scorsese emphasizes this choice with extreme close-ups of doors closing, locks being turned, and car windows being shut.[28] The more JR accepts the views of his neighborhood, the more isolated he becomes. This imprisonment is a source of security for him (although he may not realize it), because his view of women and his sexual insecurities go unquestioned in such a setting. But his commitment to parochial values robs him of the opportunity to become a fully developed person; ultimately, catering to the group's norms makes him unaware of his individual goals and desires. As a result, he is less than honest with himself, let alone with his friends and love interests.

JR's belief in the Madonna-whore dichotomy, what Scorsese has labeled "that whole Italian-American way of thinking," leads to his self-destruction (quoted in DeCurtis 451). But while its prominence in the film may suggest that it is especially prevalent in Italian American cultures, it is worth remembering Casillo's point that such thinking is "partly reinforced by mainstream culture" (172) and Bliss's suggestion that it "reflects the church-influenced attitude toward existence that, along with other elements of their Catholic upbringing, poisons the minds and lives of *Knocking*'s male characters" (*Martin Scorsese* 34).

Grist has argued that *Knocking* and *Murray!* actually espouse such myths of women.[29] In the former film, after telling JR that she was raped, the girl apologizes, and for Grist this apology "tacitly upholds J. R.'s stance on female sexuality; as does her assertion that should she and J. R. have sex 'it'd be the first time'" (42). Scorsese's public comments undermine Grist's interpretation. "I grew up in a certain kind of culture: Sicilian, Roman Catholic," he says. "Women were separate entities; and the Madonna-whore dichotomy encouraged fear of them, distrust, and, because they didn't seem to be like real human beings, difficulty in relating to them" (quoted in Casillo, *Gangster* 90). In *Knocking*, the girl is certainly being sensitive to JR's hang-ups, but such caring attempts to save their relationship do not represent an endorsement of JR's outdated, unreasonable, and inequitable views. The girl may not be challenging such perspectives directly, but viewers are invited to critique them from afar.[30]

In *Mean Streets*, Scorsese becomes even more critical of his young Italian American men, confronting them for the first time with a strong female character.[31] Although she does not fully emerge until fifty minutes into the film, Teresa (Amy Robinson) challenges the chauvinism and masculine posturing of Charlie and his male friends. She longs to escape the neighborhood and wants Charlie to move uptown with her, recognizing that in order for them to have their own lives, they need to escape the confines of their ethnic neighborhood. Charlie is blind to this reality, believing instead that he can negotiate the pressures of *la bella figura* and navigate his way through the complex relationships that rage around him while remaining within the male group.

Teresa, too, believes that she can resist the neighborhood's cultural norms. She is supposed to be off-limits to Charlie because she is an epileptic and Johnny Boy's cousin, but she engages in a relationship with Charlie, refusing to be typed as a Madonna or a whore. Nevertheless, she remains in the neighborhood even though she outwardly desires to escape it. She fights for a degree of independence and free choice, but more often than not, she capitulates to the expected norms. She caters to Charlie's wishes by keeping their relationship secret, and most of the choices she makes are limited by her deference to Charlie. If Charlie refuses to move away from the neighborhood, then she will not, either. If Charlie decides to take Johnny Boy away from the neighborhood, then she can decide to come with him, but she cannot decide where to go. She is forever in a subordinate position, upholding *la bella figura* by deferring to Charlie's masculine performance. Try as she might to break with the culture that surrounds her, Teresa more often than not conforms to it.

Charlie, Teresa, and Johnny Boy seem to escape the neighborhood at the end of the film. As they flee an angry hooligan, they drive out of Manhattan and into Brooklyn. They make wrong turns, miss exits, and are ultimately shot at but not killed by the hooligan's henchman (who is played by Scorsese). The trio's borrowed car careens off the road, strikes a fire hydrant, and crashes into a wall. Bruised and bloodied, punished for escaping the neighborhood, their futures seem unresolved. They may have temporarily broken away from Little Italy, but they have marginalized themselves by flaunting their disregard for the neighborhood's tightly controlled and vigilantly policed cultural norms. Their ability to establish a new life away from their families and friends is as unsure as their ability to be accepted back into Little Italy. Despite this bleak conclusion, when one looks at the progression from *Murray!* to *Knocking* to *Mean Streets,* one sees a director who slowly becomes aware of and begins to interrogate the isolationism and regressive gender norms that were encouraged by his ethnic culture.

Oftentimes, it is difficult to tell when Scorsese's critique of Italian cultural norms ends and his critique of Catholicism begins. The two often overlap and at times become indistinguishable. *La bella figura* may perpetuate an outdated gender politics, but the Madonna-whore dichotomy itself springs from the spiritual upbringing of JR and his friends.[32] In *Mean Streets,* Charlie's Catholic background fosters his prideful belief that he can save Johnny Boy while authorizing his troubling attempts to relegate Teresa to a subordinate status. Their ethnic and spiritual backgrounds define these characters, instilling political perspectives that are more or less uniform and encouraging a set of values that help them to make sense of the world. However, such strong cultural backgrounds saddle the boys with views that marginalize them from mainstream society and trap them within their isolated communities. "The conclusion to be drawn from this schema is clear," Bliss writes. "There is no real future for the next generation in Little Italy, only the promise of the past's repetition. The film's characters must conform to the old ways" (*Martin Scorsese* 75). As viewers, we simultaneously disapprove of their choices and their beliefs while sympathizing with their situations.

La Bella Figura, Racism, and Homophobia

Gloria Nardini writes, "Understanding Italian life is impossible without un-derstanding the intensity with which one must *fare bella figura.*" For Nardini, the term is closely tied to class, gender, and regional identities and is, above all else, a public display. "It's like a Sunday dress almost," says Francesco Nardini, "something you put on to masquerade what you actually are; you try to be part of the group that already has the social status that you are looking for" (quoted in *Che Bella* 10). Historically, in the United States, the social stand-ing of racial and sexual minorities has been lower than that of heterosexual whites. As a result, *la bella figura* often encourages not only an inequitable gender politics but also exclusionary views of race and sexuality. In other words, some Italian Americans try to attain a higher social or economic standing by publicly distancing themselves from "others."

Contentious moments between Italian Americans and black Americans are ubiquitous in American history. Thomas A. Guglielmo's *White on Arrival* and Jennifer Guglielmo and Salvatore Salerno's *Are Italians White?* outline numerous instances when relations between black Americans and Italian Americans resulted in destructive, sometimes violent, outcomes. American history is littered with figures such as Philadelphia mayor Frank Rizzo, who used racial difference to leverage his political power, and Yusuf Hawkins, an African American who was killed at age seventeen by a gang of mostly Italian American teenage boys who thought that Hawkins was in "their" neighborhood to date an Italian American woman (he was there to look at used cars).[33] Of course, there have been moments of relative harmony. Vin-cenza Scarpaci writes of a 1912–13 Brotherhood of Timber Workers strike in Northwest Louisiana where Italians, African Americans, and other racial and ethnic "others" joined together (66). But the tensions between these groups cannot be ignored.

The subtle forms of racism are rarely recognized, partially because mo-ments of extreme violence attract more media attention. Of Bensonhurst, Brooklyn, the site of the Hawkins murder (and an increasingly diverse but still heavily Italian neighborhood), Maria Laurino writes, "Rage has found a secure home under the shingled roofs of Bensonhurst's row houses. To many residents, Bensonhurst's ability to isolate itself and preserve Italian American culture for generations is its major appeal; when threats to the dominant culture arise, the neighborhood reacts, often violently" (130). What Laurino describes is not the heroic preservation of an ethnic culture in the face of assimilative pressures but an effort to maintain clannish solidarity in the name of an idealized vision of a less than ideal past. A (perceived) pristine ethnic culture may be a source of comfort and security, but it limits the group's ability to progress beyond the isolation of the neighborhood and rigidifies the exclusionary politics of the past.[34]

American movies such as *Do the Right Thing* (Lee, 1989) and *A Bronx Tale* (De Niro, 1993) have sometimes recognized these tensions and in doing so become a cultural forum where racial issues can be discussed and negotiated. Scorsese's *Mean Streets* is also deeply troubled by the racial divide and posits *la bella figura* as one of its main causes. Relatively isolated in Little Italy, Charlie and Teresa have only limited contact with black Americans, and racial stereotypes guide their perceptions. This prejudice, coupled with the pressures of *la bella figura* to secure a higher social status, creates Little Italy's rigid, exclusionary views of ethnic difference, which become especially prevalent when non-Italian Americans (blacks, Jews, assimilated suburban teenagers) enter the more or less ethnically homogeneous neighborhood.

Racial stereotypes surface repeatedly throughout the film, sometimes appearing almost inconsequential to the narrative. After an afternoon tryst, Teresa sees an African American hotel maid in the hallway. Once again incorporating documentary aesthetics, Scorsese uses a handheld camera and a series of pans to offer a fly-on-the-wall perspective of this exchange. Teresa says, "Miss, you can make up the room now." The housekeeper, who is already cleaning another room, responds, "I only got two hands!" "Well, use them!" Teresa shoots back as she and an apologetic Charlie walk to the elevator. Teresa's manner of dealing with the maid is dictated by a stereotype that sees African Americans as inferior, lazy, and in need of constant supervision.

When Michael (Richard Romanus) finds out that a girl he is dating was seen kissing a black man, his reaction signals anger and shame; it is not just that the woman has cheated on him but that she cheated with a black man and that Michael's pal Tony (David Proval) says he witnessed this transgression. Michael's *bella figura* has been undermined, and he looks the fool. A scene that began with him touting his masculinity by showing off a picture of his intelligent, beautiful girlfriend ends with his being ridiculed for boasting about a woman who does not respect Little Italy's social hierarchies and cannot be trusted. It hardly matters that Tony seems to be playing a prank on Michael. Charlie has also internalized the racial norms of his environment. He is attracted to Diane (Jeannie Bell), an African American dancer who works at Tony's bar. "But," his voice-over tells us, "she's black. I mean you can see that real plain, right?" Charlie flirts with breaking the cultural norms of his neighborhood by asking Diane to meet him outside of the bar, but he retreats from his transgression and stands her up, preserving *la bella figura*. She is off-limits to Charlie, regardless of her charms or his feelings about her.[35] Both Charlie and Michael sacrifice potential relationships to preserve the racial dynamics of their ethnic group.[36]

But Michael and Charlie also maintain their neighborhood's racial norms to preserve the intense male bond they share. In essence, they reject their potential romantic relationships with women for the attachment they feel toward one another and the other men in their group. Such homosocial feelings are also a threat to their culture; in order to conceal them, the characters embrace a reflexive homophobia. Scorsese makes the situation clear when Benton (Robert Wilder) and Sammy (Ken Sinclair), a flagrantly homosexual couple, join Johnny Boy and Charlie in Michael's car. A medium shot groups Sammy, the more overt of the two, with Charlie and Johnny Boy in the backseat. The film's main characters tell the homosexual men, "Stay on your side!" and "Don't touch me!" As Sammy looks suggestively at Charlie, Johnny Boy advocates throwing the gay couple out of the car.[37] Sammy begins making suggestive comments to random men on the street, who respond with obscene gestures and shouts. Fearing that he will become associated with homosexuality, Michael throws his four passengers out of the car. As the quartet considers their options, Sammy asks Johnny Boy and Charlie, "Hey, fellas, going my way?" They scuffle, with Charlie pulling Johnny Boy away, and then the two male couples go their separate ways (fig. 6). To highlight

Figure 6. In *Mean Streets,* Scorsese draws parallels between Charlie (Keitel) and Johnny Boy (De Niro) and the openly gay couple Benton (Robert Wilder) (*far left*) and Sammy (Ken Sinclair) (*second from left*).

the homosexual tensions between Charlie and Johnny Boy, Scorsese has the two characters wake up next to each other in a twin bed the next morning. The title of the DVD chapter, "Bedmates in the Morning," is accompanied by a screen capture of Charlie and Johnny Boy. As James F. Maxfield writes, "Clearly the relationship between Benton and Sammy is parallel to that of Charlie and Johnny Boy. A reasonable man tries to restrain his irrational and unruly partner but with only minimal success at best" (283).

Johnny Boy and Charlie (and Michael) are so sensitive to suggestions of homosexuality because homosexual feelings lie beneath the surface of their relations with male friends. By treating Benton and Sammy derisively and being outwardly homophobic, they hide their potentially homoerotic feelings for one another. However, throughout the narrative, these feelings are clearly present. In addition to the moments mentioned above, Charlie's insistence that Johnny Boy not find out about his relationship with Teresa reveals his emotions. His masculine posturing is meant to preserve and deepen ties within the male group, but ultimately, it limits his relationships with women.[38] Preserving *la bella figura* erects walls around the characters, quashing the possibility of true honesty between even the best of friends.

In *Mean Streets, Knocking,* and other Scorsese films, the main characters perform in these ways to preserve their ethnic culture and neighborhoods, but the films show that attempts to isolate the community from outsiders are futile. Invariably, the characters interact or come into conflict with other "others." Puerto Ricans fight with JR and his group in *Knocking*. Charlie and his group interact with African Americans and Jewish Americans.[39] The communities are not as contained as the characters would like to think, but this may help the Italian American characters to have a clearer sense of identity. By defining themselves as "not Irish," "not Puerto Rican," "not gay," "not Jewish," "not African American"—that is, in opposition to outsiders—they work to consolidate a group identity. Unfortunately, this also perpetuates an exclusionary perspective that reduces other "others" to stereotypes while creating a narrow understanding of what it means to be "Italian American."

Yet *Mean Streets* maintains its affection for the old neighborhood. Connelly writes, "Scorsese is critical of the prejudices, narrow-mindedness, and violence endemic to these characters. However, the neighborhood, for the most part, is affirmed here, not maligned. There is meanness, but there is also friendship, humor, and warmth" (7). It may trap young men within limited worldviews, demand the suppression of their feelings, compel them to perform an outdated masculinity, and rob them of opportunities for happiness, but it also defines them, and to hate the neighborhood is to hate themselves, their friends, and everything they have known. Their *bella figura* makes it difficult to accept some perspectives while rejecting others. If the maintenance of Old World culture is the primary goal of the group, even to the detriment of individual happiness, then it must be embraced and enforced without exception.[40]

Escaping the Neighborhood in *Raging Bull* and *GoodFellas*

In Scorsese's films, escaping the community is sometimes necessary, but it comes at a cost. Escape removes Scorsese's characters from their past, their friends, and their culture, creating an identity crisis. This is one theme that defines his cinema, and it is not limited to his films about Italian Americans. *The Departed*'s (2006) Billy Costigan (Leonardo DiCaprio) and Colin Sullivan (Matt Damon), *Gangs of New York*'s (2002) Amsterdam Vallon (DiCaprio), *Kundun*'s (1997) Dalai Lama (Tenzin Thuthob Tsarong), *Casino*'s (1995) Sam "Ace" Rothstein (Robert De Niro) and Nicky Santoro (Joe Pesci), and others escape from or deliberately leave an environment where they are comfortable and enter one where they confront the possibilities and pitfalls of their new surroundings. Scorsese's most recent work has investigated the possibility of returning to one's neighborhood, with characters like Costigan, Sullivan, and Vallon fighting to survive their homecomings.

Scorsese's Italian American characters have followed a similar trajectory. Murray and JR linger in their neighborhood. Charlie, Teresa, and Johnny Boy flee Manhattan only to be shot in Brooklyn. *Raging Bull*'s Jake LaMotta and *GoodFellas*' Henry Hill leave not just their isolated environs but also New York City. Freed from the watchful eyes of their neighborhoods, the characters struggle to adapt to their new surroundings. What was once acceptable behavior now carries penalties. In the Bronx, LaMotta can court and engage in questionable behavior with a fifteen-year-old Vickie Thailer (Cathy Moriarty), but he is arrested for comparable actions in Florida. Hill escapes the neighborhood to avoid a prison term, but in the process he enters a life that is uncomfortable, anonymous, and confining. The isolation of Scorsese's ethnic neighborhoods offers a degree of comfort and flexibility, because the neighborhoods police their own cultural norms. The outside world can be just as confining, if not more so, because previous behaviors are no longer acceptable. Saddled with the cultural baggage of their upbringing, the characters can never truly escape; their background always defines them.

In *GoodFellas*, Hill's escape from the neighborhood means his expulsion from the criminal group that provided him with a sort of family. Portrayed as a child who is attracted to the Mob by the promise of wealth and a "need to belong," Hill lauds the Mafia's supposed embrace of Old World values like "loyalty" and "community" (Bliss 96).[41] In fact, *GoodFellas* suggests that the Mob grotesquely parodies and perverts those values, and Hill becomes nothing more than a childish man enamored with the gangster lifestyle. He wants the trappings of wealth without doing any of the work.[42] With this as his foundation, he rats out his colleagues and friends to secure his freedom. Consequently, Hill is expelled from a world where traditional forms of machismo and *la bella figura* could be counted on to provide clear-cut values and hierarchies.[43] He struggles to make sense of his suburban neighborhood and his new life, and he lacks the perspective and maturity to grow up. Like the Italian American characters of *Mean Streets, Knocking,* and *Murray!* his childhood environment defines him, and his exile to mainstream culture makes him an "average nobody."[44]

As Casillo has shown, this stands in direct contrast to the romanticized version of the Mob offered in Coppola's *Godfather* films. In *GoodFellas,* "self-interest conquers honour and loyalty, brutality replaces heroism, and the largely law-abiding, work-oriented, and productive values of everyday society are flouted by the transgressive, parasitic consumerism of its criminal antagonists" (272). Further, Scorsese's picture resists the idea that Hill has been reformed. According to Ebert, the director "uses organized crime as an arena for a story about a man who likes material things so much that he sells his own soul to buy them—compromises his principles, betrays his friends, abandons his family, and finally even loses contact with himself. And the horror of the film is that, at the end, the man's principal regret is that he doesn't have any more soul to sell" (123).

Although the downfall of Jake LaMotta has more to do with his violence, stupidity, self-loathing, and paranoia, his flight from the Bronx seems to exacerbate those problems. Pam Cook suggests that because he comes from an Italian American immigrant community, LaMotta is "caught up in the American Dream, which offered success and power at the same time as it insisted on the innate inferiority of the Italian immigrants." But LaMotta's assimilation into mainstream society does not offer an easy escape, because it involves "the loss of the integrity and the unity of that community and the break down of the traditional Italian family" (179–80). LaMotta retires from boxing and moves his family to Miami around 1956. In Florida, he becomes so overweight that his breathing is labored. His shirt no longer covers his gut, and the exposed flesh hangs over his tight-fitting pants (fig. 7). His lack of social acumen causes problems. After openly joking with the state's at-

Figure 7. Robert De Niro as Jake LaMotta caged in a Miami phone booth in *Raging Bull*. Removed from the predictability and comfort of his New York neighborhood, LaMotta struggles to fit in and adjust to life in South Florida.

torney about making shakedown payments, LaMotta kisses the attorney's wife, spilling a drink on her in the process. LaMotta solicits kisses from two fourteen-year-old girls, serves them alcohol, and is charged with "introducing them to men," an accusation he does not deny.[45] Throughout these scenes, Scorsese emphasizes the precariousness of LaMotta's situation with low-angle shots. As LaMotta totters and bumbles his way through the nightclub, the shots highlight how far the character has to fall. In the last interior scene of the sequence, an obviously fatigued LaMotta pours champagne into a tower of five glasses. The Hearts' "Lonely Nights," featuring lines like "Please, come home, I miss you so" and "I will die," plays on the soundtrack. With his life out of control, LaMotta starts to lose the things that are most important to him. His wife decides to divorce him, and in a final unsuccessful attempt to avoid prison, he destroys his championship belt, stripping it of its jewels.

Two years later, LaMotta returns to New York, still obese but now alone. His sparsely attended stage performances draw jeers, but returned to his old environment, he is able to begin the process of renewal and healing. He runs into his estranged brother and begs his forgiveness. After some hesitation, Joey promises to call Jake. LaMotta is far from redemption, but repairing some of his past wrongs seems possible now that he has returned to New York.

Ethnicity is bounded by geographic space in Scorsese's Italian American–focused movies. In one extreme long shot from *Mean Streets*, the lights of Little Italy's San Gennaro Festival occupy a small portion of the bottom-right quadrant of the frame while the illuminated Empire State Building looms above at the top. Surrounding and separating Little Italy and Midtown is a sizable and daunting void of blackness. Because of its isolation, the neighborhood naturally ingrains itself in its inhabitants' worldviews and actions, becoming an essential part of their identity—so essential, in fact, that attempts to excise it are both self-serving and self-destructive.[46]

Scorsese's fascination with and admiration for Catholicism also help to define and limit these characters, just as it had JR and Charlie. Catholicism is basic to Scorsese's account of Italian neighborhood culture in New York. It provides a spiritual and ethical background that motivates the deep sense of guilt experienced by characters like Charlie and Jake—characters who, in betraying their better selves, seem aware that they have been disloyal to their religious values and beliefs. Throughout *Raging Bull,* we see symbolic references to Catholicism. Frank P. Tomasulo suggests that Jake's mouthpiece resembles a Communion wafer ("Bully" 183), and Morris Dickstein sees the film as "a boxer's story [turned] into a Stations of the Cross movie" (661). The scene of Jake's despair in prison is a powerful scene of spiritual suffering, guilt, and the desire for God's forgiveness; it makes possible a sense of at least partial redemption at the end of the movie.[47]

* * *

Scorsese's critical evaluations of Italian ethnicity are a necessary step in the evolution of ethnic depictions in Hollywood movies, but they create a unique set of problems. By focusing so intently on Italian American neighborhoods that are isolated from assimilated America, the filmmaker unintentionally perpetuates the idea that racism, homophobia, and sexism are Old World, and perhaps even specifically Italian American, problems. Those of us who grew up outside of these communities or do not or cannot claim Italian heritage can use our ethnic or class standings or both as a way of distancing ourselves from the characters and their exclusionary thinking. Such risks are particularly important to consider since Italian Americans have been cast as one of the most intolerant U.S. populations. In an effort to combat such thinking, Scorsese has targeted these issues in both his films focused on Italian Americans and those that look across ethnic boundaries and aspire to build alliances between marginalized and previously marginalized groups. In this way, films like *The Neighborhood* (2001) and *Gangs of New York* attempt to achieve what Shohat and Stam see as the goal of multiculturalism: "seeing world history and contemporary social life from the perspective of the radical equality of peoples in status, potential, and rights [by] decoloniz[ing] representation not only in terms of cultural artifacts—literary canons, museum exhibits, film series—but also in terms of power relations between communities" (5). Unfortunately, the films' attempts are not always successful.

Crossing Ethnic Lines:
The Neighborhood and *Gangs of New York*

In the wake of the September 11, 2001, attacks, a stellar group of musicians gathered in New York City for a benefit concert. For the occasion, several prominent New York–area filmmakers were asked to contribute a short film about the city. Scorsese's film *The Neighborhood,* introduced by Italian American actors Leonardo DiCaprio and Robert De Niro, was the first shown and served as a celebration of both Little Italy and the ethnic diversity that Scorsese identifies as the city's strength. Amid daily news reports of anti-Arab sentiments, *The Neighborhood* became a plea for ethnic tolerance, in addition to a promotional film for his soon-to-be-released *Gangs of New York.*

The Neighborhood begins with home movies of an Italian street festival, shot by Scorsese's uncle in 1940. After giving a brief history of his family's immigration, Scorsese offers, "This is how it goes. My grandparents were Sicilian. My parents became Italian American. I think of myself as an American Italian, and I suppose my children . . . well, my children are American." The film then dissolves from the black-and-white home movies of the past to color shots of Scorsese's infant daughter in the old neighborhood in 2001. Scorsese take viewers on a tour of Little Italy, painting the neighborhood as a defining influence in his life and work.

About midway through the short, the movie's focus shifts. "Today, on the surface," Scorsese intones, "it seems obvious that the neighborhood has changed. I mean it's Asian American, mainly Chinese now." Shots of Asian Americans walking the streets of Little Italy appear on-screen. "But, it's not that simple," Scorsese continues. "This is Di Palo's Cheese Shop. It's on the corner of Mott and Grand, and it's been there for over seventy-five years." Accompanying this narration is a shot that begins as a medium shot of two Asian Americans—a younger man and an older woman—walking down the street that then zooms outs and pans right to reveal a long shot of Di Palo's. As the Asian Americans walk past the shop, a white man exits and walks toward the left side of the frame. The symmetry of the movements mimics the intersection of the two cultures. Inside the shop, Scorsese and Mr. Di Palo discuss the neighborhood. Di Palo says, "People say, 'This is not Little Italy anymore.' And I tell 'em, 'You're wrong. You're wrong. The spirit of Little Italy, the immigrants that came here, my great-grandfather and grandparents, they struggled. And you look outside, and you look down the street, and you see this whole group of people,' I said, 'that's the same exact thing as my parents and great-grandparents. This neighborhood hasn't changed.'" Scorsese agrees, "It's the same story." As the two converse, Scorsese cuts to home movies of Little Italy's Italian immigrants, visually juxtaposing the two stories.

Scorsese next stops outside a neighborhood church to discuss the church's importance in the community. As a child, he says, he wondered why a church would be called St. Patrick's in a neighborhood that was all Italians. "Then," Scorsese says, "I began to realize that, of course, we weren't the first ones here." At this, Scorsese moves from the present day back to the 1860s, when anti-Irish prejudice flourished, and not coincidentally the time period during which *Gangs of New York* is set. Accompanying this narration are shots of Little Italy's St. Patrick's Cathedral in 2001 and re-creations of historical events from *Gangs*. Scorsese recounts that when a group of bigots marched to attack the Irish, they turned back when they saw St. Patrick's guarded by not only Irish men but also women and children. He concludes, "That was the beginning of the end, the change, the changeover, acceptance of what America is supposed to be. Letting in the immigrants, letting in other cultures, other religions, other races, and everybody living together . . . in freedom." Near the end of *The Neighborhood,* a dissolve is again used to bridge historical eras, generations, and ethnicities. A group of Italian children marching in the Scorseses' home movies transitions into an image of what appear to be African American and Latino/a schoolchildren clothed in St. Patrick's sweatshirts marching in a similar progression in 2001.

Gangs of New York picks up on some of these same themes and underscores the idea that ethnically based prejudice is a characteristic of American culture that needs to be changed. By focusing on the intolerance that a now accepted ethnic group suffered, Scorsese implicitly points to the erratic nature of American ethnic chauvinism. The prejudice always exists, but its target varies from era to era. Ethnics who may be intolerant of today's immigrant groups are the descendants of individuals who were themselves forced to the margins of American society.

Scorsese's representation of the treatment of Irish immigrants is best encapsulated by one of the film's long takes. The scene begins with a two-shot of Amsterdam and Bill the Butcher (Daniel Day-Lewis). As they walk away from the camera, it pans to the left and tracks along the dock to follow a line of newly arrived Irish men. They are being offered their U.S. citizenship in exchange for their enlistment in the Union army. The camera tracks down the line of would-be citizens and captures one man signing the necessary forms. Others are being outfitted with uniforms, and uniformed men are being issued muskets. The camera continues its track, revealing several new

Irish American soldiers waiting to board a boat that will take them to the battlefield. As the line of soldiers advances, three women run to one of the men and embrace him. We overhear comments that make it clear that the men are unaware of the ship's destination. The camera continues its track, and an Irish accent can be heard asking, "Do they feed us now, do you think?" As the camera cranes up, it reveals several dozen uniformed men scattered along the ship's deck. A casket floats in front of the camera, and the camera pans back to follow it. As the coffin hovers over the dock, we see rows of other caskets.

This shot, like the rest of the film, is "very monochromatic," a choice that Ferretti says was motivated by a desire to strip any sense of hope from the characters' lives (Magid 51). Slightly more than a minute long, this long take demonstrates Scorsese and cinematographer Michael Ballhaus's strategy of using "a highly mobile camera and a variety of in-camera effects to visually underscore the instability and excitement of the period" (Bosley 44). In addition to its formal mastery, the shot sums up an entire narrative that is missing from most histories of the United States. Here, we see what the "land of opportunity" offered many nineteenth-century immigrants, and although it may be melodramatic and oversimplified historically, the general impression it offers about the treatment of American immigrant populations by American citizens and institutions may not be far off the mark: they were used as cannon fodder.

Scorsese, however, uses other aspects of the film's form to convey how deeply pervasive cultural mixing is in *Gangs*. Like the Italian Americans in *Mean Streets* and *Knocking*, Bill the Butcher is unable to isolate his Irish community from ethnic outsiders. As Duncan notes, this confluence of cultures exists at the level of the film's soundtrack. He writes, "The music for the pre-fight sequence sounds like Irish pipe and drums but is actually the African bamboo flute and drums of Otha Turner. . . . During the Chinese Pagoda sequence Bill asks for real American music, and the band plays 'Gerry Owen,' an Irish song" (148). Although the film's plot recounts the Irish immigrants' struggle for acceptance, the film's soundtrack shows that they have already ingrained themselves into the American fabric.

Nonetheless, while the film works to build modern-day multiethnic alliances by cultivating an appreciation for the Irish's struggles in America, it also romanticizes that history and the Irish's ability to overcome prejudice.[48] *Gangs of New York*, as Jacobson suggests, "rests on an interpretation of race, ethnicity, and history replete with assertions of 'natural' alliance, 'natural' conflict, solidarity, prior right, competition, or betrayal" (*Roots* 319). With the tagline "America was born in the streets," the film defines American identity as one of ethnic struggle. In order to become Americans, these Irish characters must fight. By defining this story as *the* American narrative, Scorsese unwittingly normalizes the prejudice leveled against immigrant groups in the twenty-first century. In essence, *Gangs* suggests that we should expect or even demand the same degree of struggle from today's immigrant groups, and we should impose the same standards of Americanness that were imposed on immigrants before them. *Gangs* does not mind the ethnic strife; it romanticizes it in an effort to laud the bravery and courage that made the Irish into Irish Americans.

Scorsese rejects such readings in his public comments. "I hope that [*Gangs*] will show people that the things they've had since they were born, the world around them, did not just fall into place, that this idea of a country, this idea of equality of race, color, creed, this sense of independence, this separation of church and state, was a very real struggle" (quoted in Baker 54). Many reviewers have praised the film for this. A. O. Scott applauds the director for not offering "the usual triumphalist story of moral progress and enlightenment, but rather a blood-soaked revenger's tale, in which the modern world arrives in the form of a line of soldiers firing into a crowd" (quoted in Palmer 318), and J. Matthew Gallman argues that the film "reveals complex ethnic, religious, and racial tensions" that are "important corrective[s] to common portrayals of a generally homogeneous North" (1126).[49] But for others, the film's blind spots, particularly as they relate to race relations, have potentially dangerous implications. Critics charge that the film ignores the historical fact that the Draft Riots were "race riots as much as attacks against the government" and that "the factions were not white Irish versus white Protestants, but white Irish men, women, and children (and some white Protestants) against blacks" (Justice 214).[50] Looking to Hollywood productions for "accurate" historical reproductions limits the potential of film as an art form and rests on the idea that *a* historical reality is easily defined and knowable.[51] However, movies like *Gangs of New York* help to shape our collective memory of the past, which has important implications for how we understand the present and formulate policies for the future. As Scorsese recognizes, "What happens in *Gangs of New York,* with immigration, is happening now in France, in Italy, in England" (quoted in Baker 56).

Ultimately, though, *The Neighborhood* and *Gangs* focus on non-Italian ethnic groups in an effort to build tolerance and understanding. These films ask viewers to see those that currently endure prejudice and discrimination not as abstract others but rather as hardworking individuals concerned for the well-being of their families (and, at times, the modern-day equivalents of their own ancestors). By recognizing and understanding one's "self-difference," viewers are encouraged to grapple with the treatment of marginalized groups on a personal level. Perhaps assimilated viewers will be less willing to tolerate more subtle and accepted forms of prejudice, because films like these allow them to feel personally affected and historically connected to the treatment of marginalized groups.

Nevertheless, in an effort to build a multiethnic alliance, *Gangs* and *The Neighborhood* risk simplifying ethnic differences to a homogenous standard. The Irish are the same as the Italians, and the Italians are the same as the Chinese. Although there may be some parallels between these groups, ignoring the specificity of each group's experience(s) perpetuates the sins that Jacobson suggests drive the White Ethnic Revival's neoconservatism.[52] If all these groups are the same, and if the Irish and the Italians have overcome prejudice and succeeded in America, then after a brief period of exclusion and discrimination, so too will the Chinese or the Latino/as or the Middle Easterners. The films imply that the current system does not need to be changed, because sooner or later these groups will pull themselves up by their own bootstraps.

The Departed

During the promotion of *Gangs of New York,* Scorsese commented on the similarities between Irish and Italian cultures. "I find Irish and Italians to be so similar," he said. "Maybe that's why they can't get along" (quoted in Blake 157). In their reviews of *Gangs,* critics also drew connections between the two white ethnic groups. David Henkin wrote, "Amsterdam Vallon's church-restoring Irish immigrants stand as heroic prototypes for Italians of a later period" (621). Scorsese clearly felt a sense of community with the Irish depicted in *Gangs.* The Five Points became the neighborhood where many of his formative experiences occurred, and Catholicism created a common bond between the two communities.[53] Perhaps it is not surprising, then, that Scorsese would return to the Irish in *The Departed.*[54]

In the opening lines of the film, Frank Costello (Jack Nicholson) intones, "I don't want to be a product of my environment. I want my environment to be a product of me." Throughout his career, Scorsese has critically evaluated the baggage his childhood environment bestowed upon him, struggling to author an identity that was distinct from the ethnic neighborhood. Intertwined with this environment was his spiritual background, which exerted a tremendous influence on his gender politics and personal behaviors. Like many of *The Departed*'s characters, Scorsese has resisted the temptation to be a product of his environment, but as the film shows, one's environment always frames one's identity.

Scorsese has been interested in this issue throughout his career, and he has returned to it in both his movies and his interviews. In 1990, he said, "People are usually the product of where they come from, whether you come from a small farm in Iowa and you had your best friend next door and you went swimming in the old swimming hole. In other words—whether you had an idyllic American childhood or you were a child in Russia or you were a child on the Lower East Side—the bond you made, the codes that were there, all have a certain influence on you later on in life" (quoted in DeCurtis 460). Whereas characters like Charlie in *Mean Streets* were skeptical or ignorant of their ability to author their own identities, *The Departed*'s Costello, Costigan, and Sullivan are overly confident, even arrogant, about their ability to rise above their surroundings.[55]

Soon after Costello's opening lines, we enter Park Luncheonette, where Costello is collecting a "tribute" payment from the store's owner. A young Colin Sullivan watches the gangster closely as he intimidates the shop owner and flirts with the owner's teenage daughter. Costello recognizes Sullivan and orders the shop owner to put together a package of food and comic books for Colin. Scorsese cuts to a close-up of Colin's hand; Costello grabs it, fills it with less than a dollar's worth of change, and tells Colin if he ever wants to earn extra money, he should come by Costello's hangout. "There is something so complete, so absolute, and so unstylish," writes Jean-Pierre Gorin, "about the buying of Colin Sullivan's soul" (30). The sequence reminds us of the Mob's seduction of Henry Hill in *GoodFellas*. The environment where these characters grow up defines them. From the moment Sullivan goes in with Costello, his life's plan is determined.

Later in his life, Colin will fantasize about a political career and talk about leaving Boston, but he cannot follow through on either dream.[56] Scorsese uses the film's form to reveal Sullivan's other fantasies. When Sullivan starts his job as a state trooper, Scorsese irises out from the character (a technique Scorsese would use again in the premier episode of HBO's *Boardwalk Empire*), revealing a larger world. The shot mimics Colin's more global thinking, but the job does not offer him the freedom he thinks it does. For Sullivan, there is no escaping his environment. His relationship with Costello constrains his available actions, even after he kills Costello near the end of the film.

Likewise, Billy Costigan thinks he has escaped his environment after entering and graduating from the state police academy. The son of an airport-baggage-handler father and an upper-middle-class mother, Costigan spent his weekends with his dad in the South Boston housing projects and his weekdays with his mom on the well-to-do North Shore. By the time he graduates from the academy, both his parents are dead, and he has cut ties with both families. When he walks into Captain Queenan's (Martin Sheen) office, he believes he has begun to author his own identity, but Sergeant Dignam (Mark Wahlberg) quickly intrudes upon this fantasy, framing Bill as the relative of known criminals rather than a real state trooper. As they converse, Costigan's face registers sadness, frustration, and anger. When he is told he will not be a Massachusetts state trooper in five years, Costigan looks resigned and defeated. But when he realizes he can be an undercover officer, Costigan (like Sullivan) believes that his ability to sustain multiple selves will allow him to author his own identity eventually.

The film's famous Chinatown sequence highlights the similarities between Costigan and Sullivan. As Costigan chases Sullivan, one gets the sense that he is chasing more than Costello's mole. In a particularly arresting shot, Costigan looks through several small mirrors hanging in a restaurant window. As he does, the image changes from a reflection of his face to an image of Sullivan's back as he ducks out the back door of the establishment. The effect is one of doubling; we see Costigan chasing himself in addition to his nemesis. And both images, of course, are the product of the environment in which the characters find themselves (fig. 8).[57]

Frank Costello not only believes he can escape his environment's influence; he thinks he can bend it to his will and mold its identity. As a mobster, Costello wields a significant amount of power in his neighborhood. However, the pressures of always being pursued by the police have begun to undermine his effectiveness as a gangland leader. Knowing that there is a mole in his midst inspires increasingly erratic behavior and ultimately renders him so vulnerable that the police gun him down, with Sullivan delivering the coup

Figure 8. Leonardo DiCaprio as Billy Costigan looks into a fragmented mirror in *The Departed*. Costigan sees his reflected eyes, Colin Sullivan's (Matt Damon) back and jacket, and even a cartoonlike image of a man that is visible just to the right of center screen.

de grâce. However, even when Costello is at the height of his power, his environment clearly frames his character's identity.

Most assume that Costello is Irish American. Based on "Whitey" Bulger, one of Boston's most villainous Irish American gangsters, the Costello character is constantly defining himself in opposition to other "others"—"guineas from the North End, down Providence," "the black chappies," and even "the Church." Additionally, he offers lines like "Twenty years after an Irishman couldn't get a fuckin' job, we had the presidency."[58] But Costello's namesake was one of the most notorious men in the history of the Italian American Mafia. The leader of the Luciano crime family, Frank Costello became particularly infamous in the early 1950s when he testified before the Kefauver Committee.[59] For LoBrutto, the use of this name in *The Departed* "works against the Irishness of the character" (384). Yet for many viewers, Nicholson's character is defined not by his Italian American name but rather the Irish American neighborhood he inhabits and the Irish American men that surround him.

The Departed has been rightly criticized as melodramatic and obvious. Nicholson's performance, which includes his impersonation of a rat and a scene where he discusses John Lennon while waving a severed hand through the air, is over the top.[60] The film's last shot of a rat crawling along a railing is equally overblown, lacking a level of creative ambivalence that we have come to expect from Scorsese.[61] Nonetheless, the film continues to investigate many of the issues and themes that have characterized the director's career. Ultimately, *The Departed* is about individuals who struggle to reconcile their desire for an individual identity with their need to be a part of a larger (ethnic) community.

Nostalgic Visions of an Ethnic Past?
Italianamerican

Whereas Scorsese's fictional cinema tends to offer a critical acceptance of Italian ethnicity, his documentaries lean toward a more nostalgic treatment. Though somewhat apparent in *The Neighborhood*, Scorsese's nostalgia is most prevalent in *Italianamerican* (1974), a fifty-minute installment in the PBS *Storm of Strangers* series and a work that the director has labeled "the best film he ever made" (Dougan 44). Jacobson has disagreed, calling it "among the most complete fossilized records of [the] impulse to recover ethnic heritage" (*Roots* 53). For Jacobson, the film's nostalgia softens the claims of the civil rights movement by making white Americans feel less white and more distant from their racist past.[62] Jacobson is right to argue that the film embraces Italian American ethnicity, but the implications of this representation are not as simple as he suggests. Appreciating Italian American ethnicity affords an attendant degree of respect to Scorsese's ancestors, whose voices, like the voices of most Italian Americans and their communities in the first half of the twentieth century, had been marginalized.

In addition, Jacobson ignores the relationship between *Italianamerican* and Scorsese's other films. What Jacobson sees as the nostalgic celebration of the Scorseses' realization of the bootstraps myth, for instance, becomes something different when viewed in this context. If Scorsese is celebrating his parents' survival in the United States, he is also lamenting the fact that a tiny apartment literally across the street from where they grew up is as far as they got.[63] In many ways, Scorsese's parents did not achieve the bootstraps myth; they remained trapped in the neighborhood in dead-end jobs, just trying to get by. This perspective extends to Scorsese's grandparents, who "limited their ambitions to the preservation and continuity of their families" (Casillo, *Gangster Priest* 43).

Jacobson's argument misses the complexity of the film, because it overemphasizes a large historical discourse and suggests that all cultural productions conform similarly to it. From this perspective, *Italianamerican* becomes just like any other product of the White Ethnic Revival. However, the film emphasizes the importance and the diversity of individual historical actors and embraces the diversity of U.S. culture, society, and history. It undermines the very conservatism that Jacobson says it supports.[64]

Additionally, *Italianamerican,* like many of Scorsese's other movies, is critical of Italian Americans. Scorsese's father (Charlie), for instance, expresses prejudicial views of the Irish, and Scorsese's mother (Catherine) takes exception to her husband's opinions. Rather than ignoring the history of prejudice within Italian American communities, Scorsese depicts it rather plainly, using his parents and their racial politics as representative of Little Italy's Italian American working-class culture.[65] Further, when Catherine Scorsese indicates to the camera crew (but not to Charlie himself) that she disagrees with her husband's views, we catch a glimpse of the problematic gender politics that characterize many Italian American families (and, as will be shown, become the target of Nancy Savoca's cinema).[66] So, on the surface, *Italianamerican* might offer a more recuperative perception of Italian ethnicity, but many of the same thought patterns that are condemned in other Scorsese works are condemned here as well. Through works like *Italianamerican,* the contradictions of ethnic identities can be seen as they are enacted on a daily basis. The works of the White Ethnic Revival (and White Ethnic Revival artists) contain similar contradictions and need to be evaluated not just in terms of the historical and institutional pressures that influence them but also in terms of the individual voices expressed within them. In this way, we can understand the goals they work to achieve, the assumptions they make, and the relative use they might have to create a more ethnically and racially sensitive world where alliances between previously marginalized and currently marginalized groups can be forged.

* * *

Mark Jolly has written of Scorsese, "Nobody else in his business extracts so much beauty from so much ugliness" (249). Indeed, Scorsese creates an uncomfortable cinema, in which individual characters and the audience are asked to confront the less appealing aspects of their identities and the limits of their individualism.[67] It is a cinema not limited to the ethnic Italian neighborhoods of Manhattan but one that applies to anyone who conforms to the standards of behavior dictated by a given culture, whether that culture be assimilated or ethnic, corporate or academic, regional or national. Scorsese's is a perspective that for far too long was marginalized within the Hollywood studio system and one that was possible only once an appreciation for ethnic difference was developed. Despite Jacobson's claims to the contrary, filmmakers like Scorsese critically evaluate the norms of their ethnic background, and through their work we are offered an opportunity to come to a better understanding of racial and ethnic prejudice, gender inequality, and sexual intolerance in the United States. Scorsese is certainly influenced by the historical context that surrounds his work, but he is also an individual historical actor with a unique voice.

Scorsese has said of the experience of watching a movie, "What happens is that these people are up there on the screen behaving. And they're not really behaving for themselves, they're behaving for a whole culture of that time" (quoted in Greene 232).[68] The characters in his films become a kind of window into the working-class Italian American cultures of some New York neighborhoods. Through them we come to a better understanding of those cultures while also realizing the costs of escape.[69] Both the choice to stay and the choice to leave are fraught with peril. As Paul Duncan suggests, "There is never any hint that [Scorsese's] characters can change that society—the society is stronger than any single person" (16).

In writing about Tony Soprano, a character who appeared more than twenty-five years after the release of *Mean Streets,* Gardaphé writes, "Without a solid sense of self, he constantly wavers from the various attacks on his ego." Tony is so obsessed with his ethnic past, Gardaphé says, that "his sense of the future is undeveloped" (*Wiseguys* 154, 156). The same charges might be leveled at many of Scorsese's characters. Their tragic flaw is that they have allowed their culture to author their identities. Through his cinema, Scorsese resists the same fate, critically evaluating the ethnic culture that shaped him while attempting to come to an understanding of his identity as an Italian American who escaped the neighborhood.

3 Nancy Savoca

Ethnicity, Class, and Gender

When you ask Nancy Savoca if she considers herself to be Italian American, she laughs and says, "Yes and no. And yes and no. And yes and no." Unlike Capra and Scorsese, Savoca's ethnic roots are a little more garbled. "I think that there is a very specific thing that people think about when they think of the Italian American experience," she says. "I have some of that experience, but I also have a really different experience. My parents came here from Argentina. . . . My father is Italian, born in Sicily, but was raised in Argentina." Savoca's parents immigrated to the United States just before she was born and settled into a working-class existence in the Bronx, New York, where financial and social pressures made their day-to-day existence tumultuous and tenuous. "Every couple of years," she remembers, "[my parents] would say, 'I can't take it here anymore. We gotta leave'" (interview with author, March 17, 2008). When Savoca was five, her family actually did return to Argentina, but soon after moved back to the United States.

The uncertainty that defined Savoca's upbringing inflects her films and differs greatly from Scorsese's. Scorsese also comes from a working-class background, but in his films, a stubborn rootedness plagues his characters, making escape difficult. In Savoca's movies, we see instances where the isolated nature of the neighborhood defines characters and limits their potential. *True Love,* for instance, follows Donna and Michael, a young couple trapped in the mind-set of their neighborhood who marry despite having serious reservations about their commitment to one another and the overall health of their relationship. Other Savoca movies like *Dogfight* (1991) and *Dirt* (and to a lesser extent *Household Saints* [1993], *If These Walls Could Talk* [1996], and *24 Hour Woman* [1999]) investigate characters who are forced to negotiate an ever-changing world. It is not a desire or an inability to escape the neighborhood that defines them but rather the conflicts that ensue and the compromises that must be made when their limited financial resources collide with the dreams and aspirations they have for themselves and their loved ones. Additionally, while Scorsese's characters often contend with the threat of violence, Savoca's confront the threat of dislocation, financial insecurity, and the numbing effects these situations can have on their emotional well-being. In that way, Savoca's films seem more like Capra's, where individual characters negotiate the traumas associated with relocations.

Savoca witnessed and experienced similar situations in her own life, and they have had a lasting impact on her politics and her worldview. After moving to Argentina and back to the United States as a child, Savoca was once again facing the prospect of a transnational relocation in her preteen years. She remembers:

> When I was eleven or twelve, it was happening again where we sold everything. . . . So, I'm really depressed, because I've got my friends. I was eleven. I'm saying good-bye to everybody. . . . One day, my father looked at me while I was packing [and said], "What's the matter with you?" And I said, "I'm sad." "Why are you sad?" "Because we're leaving, and I'm losing all my friends and my life and everything I know." And he turns to me and says, "Pretend they all died." And that's it, because it's just a terrible time and then that's it. Move on! At the time, of course, that totally devastated me. But now, I look back, and it's hilarious. It's that immigrant thing, survival! Don't spend too much time getting all mushy, move on. (interview, March 17, 2008)

Savoca's father saw the world as a place that was sometimes cruel and often-times dashed people's hopes and dreams. From his perspective, the more emotional baggage one carries, the harder it is to endure and make the decisions that are necessary to ensure the family's financial survival.

If class is important in determining what is believed to be possible, gender and ethnicity work to define what is expected. "There's supposed to be submission," she says. "There's supposed to be the guy who calls the shots and the woman who is supposed to follow, but it doesn't really happen that way. I watched my parents often, because their personalities were at odds with that. . . . They were like ill-fitting clothes sometimes—the things they had to act out." This too has become a defining characteristic of her movies. She says, "Everything I do has people's roles, usually gender roles, at the heart of it . . . people trying to act out these roles that are prescribed, and it's just not working" (interview, March 17, 2008).

Savoca's decision to concentrate on female Italian American characters in films like *True Love* and *Household Saints* provides a necessary and valuable complement to Italian American directors like Scorsese and Francis Ford Coppola, who tend to explore the experiences of women superficially.[1] Savoca targets what Edvige Giunta has labeled the "double marginalization" of Italian American women.[2] Banished from assimilated white American culture because of their ethnic identities and marginalized within their ethnic group because of their gender, these women struggle to find a place within their neighborhoods and families. This exposes some Italian American families as "instrument[s] for female oppression" (Jacobson, *Roots* 275). Women are entrapped by a narrow set of life choices and opportunities, and this blinds them to the possibilities that might exist beyond the neighborhood. Nevertheless, Savoca's female characters should not be reduced to a state of victimization. They are not victims. Instead, they are tough, independently minded women who work to balance their desires to author their own identities with their prescribed roles.

Art, Gender, and Class in the Savoca Household and at NYU

Savoca's cinema recognizes that class, gender, and ethnic identities are not easily separated. Her movies focus on the collision of multiple identities rather than isolating one at the expense of the others. Given the thematic content of movies like *True Love,* many assume that Savoca grew up in an ethnically homogeneous, closed Italian American community, but that is not the case. She first lived in a Jewish and Latin neighborhood, then in a racially mixed neighborhood with mostly African Americans and Latino/as. When she was sixteen, the family moved to Morris Park, a heavily Italian American section of the Bronx. "I remember writing in my diary at that time, 'There's a lot of white people here,'" she says. "I was just so used to people being all different, and I went to this Italian American neighborhood, and I was just shocked that there wasn't this variety" (interview, March 17, 2008).

There was certainly variety in the Savoca household. Savoca's extended family is spread across three continents.[3] Her mother, unlike her father, was of Spanish descent and came from a family who had been in Argentina for several generations. This mix of ethnic and cultural backgrounds created an incredibly diverse environment. Savoca spoke Spanish at home and English at school. She understood the Italian that some of her relatives spoke, but she could not speak the language herself (interview, March 17, 2008).

Gender was also an issue in Savoca's upbringing. When she was eleven years old, an English teacher assigned Piri Thomas's *Down These Mean Streets.* Since Thomas's autobiography was so controversial, Savoca needed parental consent before she could read it. Savoca's mother balked at the idea when the future director's older brother told her that the book contained explicit language, sex, and drug use. The persistent eleven-year-old pleaded, and, finally, the elder Savoca said she would grant her permission if the priest granted his. The director recalls, "I was so pissed off that it was the priest. I was eleven years old, so I couldn't tell you that it was sexist or anything. But I was pissed off that it was the brother and the priest who were going to tell me whether I could read this or not. So I just faked her signature, and I read it" (interview, March 17, 2008). *Down These Mean Streets* was a revelation for Savoca, because the story was recognizable.

The Savoca household was similar to many other working-class Italian American families in that reading was "totally not endorsed."[4] Nonetheless, throughout her childhood and teenage years, the arts helped Savoca to understand her identities and offered her different views of life. Her mother wrote and performed poetry in the home. Her father and cousins used a shared love of music to bridge generation gaps, and everyone could recite tangos. Film also played a prominent role.

When Savoca was a teenager, her older brother began introducing her to an eclectic set of movies. "Besides reading the book *Down These Mean Streets*," she says, "the other thing that made me want to make movies was John Cassavettes." *Husbands* (1970), in particular, shocked Savoca, especially when she learned that the characters were actors. Neither Thomas, a black male of Puerto Rican and Cuban descent, nor Cassavettes, a white male of Greek parentage, shared Savoca's gender or ethnicity. But their work featured "a sense of emotional realism" that resonated with the future director (interview, March 17, 2008).

Scorsese's *Mean Streets,* though not having the same formative impact as Cassavettes's films or Thomas's memoir, was also influential. When her brother told her that *Mean Streets* was on television, Savoca thought it was a filmed version of Thomas's book. *Mean Streets* opened the door to a world Savoca knew existed but one of which she had no direct experience. She knew that the young men in her life "had a life outside of what [she] knew life to be." Often after family gatherings, "all the guys would leave to 'play cards,'" she recalls. "I never knew where they went. . . . To me, *Mean Streets* was I got to go see what happened." Scorsese's intense focus on Italian American male characters offered Savoca a wider perspective of her ethnic background and the gender norms that defined it. As Savoca ventured outside of the neighborhood to pursue an undergraduate film degree at NYU, an interest in the dynamics of her upbringing combined with the intimacy and "emotional realism" of artists like Thomas, Cassavettes, and Scorsese would ground her work. At NYU, Savoca came to appreciate how much of an influence her working-class background had on her identity, especially when she began working on the sets of student films. "[We were] always shooting on location . . . in [my friends'] houses," she recalls. "These houses were amazing. . . . Those were the shocker moments for me" (interview, March 17, 2008).

Tensions also surfaced at home as Savoca tried to convince her parents that becoming a filmmaker was not "dangerous." "The fights were spectacular in my adolescence when I started heading down this road," she remembers. At one point, she had to move out of her parents' house to continue her studies, but eventually her parents came to accept her choices. Savoca's first student film was a fifteen-minute black-and-white short about a woman getting a divorce. When she brought it home to show it to her mother, the elder Savoca leaned over to her daughter and said, "That's very neorealistic." Similarly, Savoca's father became quite interested in what she was doing and even asked her to write down what she was studying. When the aspiring director asked why, he responded, "Because I'm telling everybody at work you're doing this, and I don't know what that's called, so I got to show them the paper." As her career took off, her parents were often at her premiers.

True Love

Savoca's first feature film, *True Love,* won the Grand Jury Prize at the Sundance Film Festival. After securing financing for the movie, the director went to see Norman Jewison's *Moonstruck* (1987). The film's characters seemed far removed from the reality Savoca knew, and she began to see *True Love* as an attempt to counter more stereotypical representations of Italian Americans. *True Love* drew on Savoca's ethnic Italian background and was "emotionally autobiographical" (interview, March 17, 2008). The film tells the story of Donna (Annabella Sciorra), a young Italian American woman who is engaged to marry Michael (Ron Eldard), an immature Italian American boy. Because she cannot imagine an alternative to married life within the neighborhood, Donna settles for Michael. As the film progresses, tension develops between the couple as a result of Michael's irresponsibility. When the couple is finally joined, they fight at the reception; Michael wants to leave Donna and spend his wedding night hanging out with his male friends. At the end of the film, the characters stare blankly at the camera in medium close-up as their wedding pictures are taken. They are together, but the closeness of the shot reveals their confusion and the emotional distance between them (fig. 9).

True Love looks candidly at "inter-gender power struggles" (Sautman 239), treating them in an ethnically specific manner. Although she may not realize

Figure 9. Donna (Annabella Sciorra) and Michael (Ron Elderd), the mismatched wedding couple, in Nancy Savoca's *True Love.*

it, one of the reasons Donna weds Michael is because marriage is one (and perhaps the only) way for her, or any other Italian American woman in her neighborhood, to garner respect and secure power. Robert Orsi has shown that female power within late-nineteenth- and early-twentieth-century Italian Harlem was centered in the *domus,* which he defines as the Italian home and family. Orsi writes, "The domus was the center of the life of the community, and women were the center of the domus; the burdens and complexities of life in the domus-centered society fell most heavily on them" (129, 131). Whereas Orsi's study focuses specifically on Italian Harlem, Mary Jo Bona's analysis of Italian American women authors identifies a similar dynamic in literature. Bona writes, "Upward mobility and separation from the family are deemphasized in these novels while an emphasis on seeking work within the community and maintaining family relations is essential to each author's definition of success" (19). Many of the same cultural codes, norms, and goals dominate in Savoca's fictional film about the Bronx. By marrying Michael, Donna creates her own family and secures a more important social role within the community. Her decision is based less on undying love than a desire to advance beyond a state of childhood. As Edvige Giunta writes,

"Donna chooses marriage not because she has found 'true love,' but because she lacks any sense of real or even imaginary alternatives to the wedding. She cannot *imagine* herself outside this fiction. She is the created rather than the creator. The American frontier has closed in on these characters: it does not go beyond New York State" (271).

Like Scorsese's boys, Donna "struggles between self-definition and cultural definition" (Giunta, "Quest" 264). The environment that surrounds her and her inability to break with tradition limit her options. At one point, she ponders calling off the wedding but rejects the possibility. She reasons that she would have to move upstate if she did. Attending college, moving to another New York City borough, or simply staying single in the neighborhood is not even recognized as a possibility. Donna needs to be in the neighborhood to have any sense of self. And in order to stay in the neighborhood, she needs to conform to its cultural codes.[5] Her actions are driven by *la bella figura* as much as JR's in *Who's That Knocking*.

Yet the cultural codes she must live by create a social hierarchy in which certain aspects of her life will go unfulfilled. The gender inequalities that characterize the neighborhood subordinate heterosexual relationships to same-sex friendships, just as they did in *Who's That Knocking* and *Mean Streets*. Donna will always be more honest with her female friends than with Michael, and Michael will always be more honest with his male friends than with Donna.[6] As a result, *True Love* oftentimes presents a cynical perspective on ethnic life, suggesting that for the most part, the only way to remain in the neighborhood is to conform to its cultural norms regardless of one's comfort level with them.

Given the film's cynicism toward ethnic culture, it is easy to see *True Love* as a scathing critique of working-class ethnic life and the sexist thought patterns that sometimes dominate it. But *True Love* also holds genuine affection for the neighborhood and the relationships that are established there. The same-sex friendships that both characters have, which seem rather commonplace in this environment, are important and valued aspects of their lives. These characters would struggle to make friends and maintain relationships that were as intimate outside of the community. Savoca emphasizes this point by confining most of the narrative to the geographic boundaries of the neighborhood, and on the rare occasion when characters venture outside of those boundaries (as Michael and his buddies do when they travel to Atlantic City as part of his bachelor party), they do so as a group. In a sense, the neighborhood is always with them, offering comfort and sheltering them from the outside world. Thus, while the film certainly sees faults in the characters' closed-off ethnic culture, it also shows why the characters love that environment and resist leaving it. The neighborhood cannot be rejected in toto, so balancing the competing demands of friendships, relationships, and community mores becomes the defining struggle of the film.

A scene between Donna and her father conveys this theme beautifully while capturing the kind of intimacy that Savoca appreciates in the work of Cassavettes and Scorsese. On Donna and Michael's wedding day, Donna and her father, Angelo (Vincent Pastore), are traveling to the ceremony in the back of a chauffeured car (fig. 10). As the shot begins, Donna is staring out of the car's window, and her father stares out the opposite window as he adjusts his tuxedo. Both are obviously uncomfortable, and the moment is awkward. Savoca emphasizes this by keeping the characters in a medium two-shot and by shooting the scene as a long take. There is no relief for the viewer as the scene progresses. Donna's father turns toward his daughter, grabs her hand, and says, "Donna, if you're not sure about this whole thing, this marriage—." Donna interrupts him, saying, "I'm sure." The conversation continues stilt-edly, with Donna's father assuring her that she could change her mind and Donna assuring him (not too convincingly) that she wants to go through

Figure 10. Vincent Pastore's Angelo rides with his daughter Donna to her wedding in *True Love*. Angelo puts aside his neighborhood's cultural norms to tell Donna he will support her if she decides to back out of the ceremony.

with it. They move on to discussing Michael, and then the conversation is cut short when the car arrives at the church. It is a brief moment in the film, but one that stands out for the genuine affection and regard Donna's father has for her. Whatever the norms of the neighborhood, Angelo puts his daughter first and will respect her decisions. This moment counters the sexism and the lack of respect that many of the film's male characters accord the women in their lives. It also balances a critique of the neighborhood's norms with admiration for the ways in which protecting the family and family members guides the characters' actions.

In some ways, *True Love* approaches the same cultural norms that were targeted in *Mean Streets* but from a perspective that emphasizes the female characters. As previously stated, this is an important contribution to the cinematic representations of Italian Americans by Italian American directors. However, *True Love* and other films like *Household Saints* do not just delve into the world and the personalities of the films' female characters. They are also heavily invested in analyzing the world of the films' male characters.[7] We see Michael at work. We see him at home with his family. We see him at the bar with his friends, and we see him in Atlantic City. In movies like *Mean Streets, Raging Bull,* and *The Godfather,* we rarely see the female characters. When we do, it is usually because their paths or lives have crossed with the films' male characters.[8]

Household Saints

Savoca returned to the subject of Italian America in 1993. *Household Saints,* based on Jewish American author Francine Prose's novel, spans three generations and interrogates the ways in which religion, spirituality, and the growth of a post–World War II consumer economy helped to nurture or dissolve ethnic traditions and some inequalities. In this film, Savoca offers a more optimistic view of the neighborhood. Here, the individual is able to fight for a place within the culture, and the culture changes (if slowly).

The film begins at a family gathering set in the present, where younger family members ask their elders about the old neighborhood. As the grandmother begins to tell the story of the Santangelos, the grandfather taps her on the arm and goads her to tell the story correctly. He says, "We used to say, 'And it happened by the grace of God that Joseph Santangelo won his wife in a pinochle game.'" At that point, the film flashes back to 1949. Santangelo (Vincent D'Onofrio), a New York City butcher, is playing a pinochle game, when his friend Lino Falconetti (Victor Argo) bets his daughter Catherine (Tracey Ullman). Joseph wins the hand, and eventually the oddly matched couple weds. Joseph's mother, Carmela (Judith Malina), however, criticizes Catherine constantly for falling short of the standards set for Italian American women. When Catherine's first child is stillborn, Carmela blames the terrible event on Catherine's insistence on working during her pregnancy. This drives Catherine to the brink of insanity and demonstrates how Old World superstitions can be used to justify the relegation of women to the domestic sphere.[9]

Once Carmela dies, Catherine gives birth to Teresa (Lili Taylor). Unlike her parents, Teresa embraces superstitious beliefs and conservative values. She imagines a personal relationship with God and desires to become a nun. After telling her boyfriend (Michael Imperioli) and her parents that Jesus visited her, she is placed in a home for mentally ill individuals. One night, Teresa dies in her sleep, and the snow of the previous day gives way to flowers. Some believe that this proves Teresa was a saint; others reject the idea. The film returns to the present day. The grandparents conclude their story, and the younger generation dismisses any supernatural explanation of the recounted events.

Irena Makarushka argues that *Household Saints'* critique of traditional gender norms begins when the grandfather taps his wife's arm and cajoles her to recount the story correctly. "The grandfather's usurpation of his wife's power to tell the tale," Makarushka writes, "confirms the cultural silencing of women and the politics of patriarchy" (84). Makarushka posits that this structuring encourages viewers to be mindful of the narrator's biases, and she is right to suggest that Savoca's movies often target gender norms and inequalities. However, in this particular case, Makarushka misses several key aspects of the film that work to undermine her thesis. First, the grandfather takes over the story in an exceedingly gentle manner. This is not to undermine his dominance of the moment, but it is to point out that the female characters in the scene—both his wife and the adult women (his daughter and granddaughter) who are listening to the story—accept this turn of events without protest. If Savoca is targeting the grandfather's dominance of the situation, she may also be targeting the women's acquiescence to and complicity in such dominance. Second, when the film returns to the present in the movie's last scene, the grandmother is narrating the story. This suggests that the film's narration is shared.

Throughout the narrative, we see female and male characters who do not fit neatly into their environment. Joseph, as Makarushka has shown, "[acknowledges] Catherine's freedom and [allows] himself to take on the 'feminine' role of the emotional and distraught parent" upon Teresa's death. In contrast, Catherine "resists traditional religious and ethnic signifiers and projects a coolness and rationality culturally attributed to male behaviour"

(90–91). They are, as Savoca has said of her parents, trying to perform roles that "are like ill-fitting clothing." In order to find happiness, Joseph and Catherine must reject the neighborhood's superstitious beliefs and some of its cultural norms.

Teresa shares this rebellious streak, but whereas Catherine faced pressure to accept the mystical beliefs and traditional roles of an older generation, Teresa faces pressure to accept her parents' modern views of religion and gender. Teresa embraces her grandmother's traditional notions of the world and adheres strictly to the superstitions that Joseph and Catherine reject. When she tells her parents that she wants to join the Carmelites, Joseph forbids it, and throughout the film, Catherine is openly hostile to many of Teresa's beliefs. Nonetheless, Teresa, like her mother and father before her, perseveres and ultimately carves out a place for herself and her eccentricities. Although the specific forces against which Teresa, Catherine, and Joseph struggle may be at odds, their resolve to resist societal pressures and assert their own identities is a shared experience. This structure complicates the audience's reaction to the characters. The film encourages viewers to empathize with Catherine and Joseph initially as they try to navigate their relationship(s) with Carmela, but when Catherine and Joseph use similar techniques to impose their will on Teresa, audience members recognize the contradictory impulses within these characters.

Ultimately, despite pressure to conform, Catherine, Joseph, and Teresa each authors his or her own identity, but not every character is so fortunate. Catherine's brother Nicky (Michael Rispoli) is ostracized because of his fascination with Japanese culture. At one point, a middle-aged woman sees an obviously upset Nicky walking the streets. She turns to her friend and says, "That's what happens when you think you're too good for your own kind." To cope with his inability to fit in, Nicky becomes an alcoholic and then eventually commits suicide. For all of her victories, Teresa suffers a similar fate. Unable to fit into the more secular, modern world of 1960s Little Italy, she is sent off to an insane asylum, where she dies alone. Despite "advancements," individuals in this neighborhood are still judged and marginalized based on their ability or willingness to cater to the dominant culture.

Nonetheless, this neighborhood and its cultural norms are not as rigid as the ones in *True Love, Mean Streets,* and other films focused on Italian Americans. In *Household Saints,* Catherine can reject the superstitions of the neighborhood, Joseph can buck the neighborhood's standards for beauty, and Teresa can stray from her parents' beliefs. The neighborhood's acceptance of difference helps to explain why Aaron Baker and Juliann Vitullo discuss the theories of Michel de Certeau in relation to *Household Saints.* De Certeau believed that

economic, social, and political systems did not rob human beings of their individuality completely. Instead, he proposed that individuals could and often
did resist cultural ideals in favor of choices that better suited their needs. The
neighborhood in *Household Saints* becomes a place where competing views
of the world coexist within an ethnically homogeneous environment.[10]

The growth of post–World War II consumerism and a related move toward assimilation within the Italian American community aid Catherine's
rejection of the neighborhood's norms (Baker and Vitullo 55–63; Ruberto
164–76). Savoca emphasizes this trend with several shots throughout the
course of the movie. In one long tracking shot, Savoca follows Catherine as
she moves through the Santangelo home. Doo-wop music from the 1950s
plays on the soundtrack, and we see a living space decorated in a typical
1950s design. Two-tone tan and greenish-blue walls complement a yellow-
and-blue-tiled linoleum floor in the kitchen. A light-yellow sectional sofa
sits on a pale-green area rug and dominates a living room with gray walls
and a white chair rail. Catherine herself is pregnant, with her hair cut short
and curled. A few scenes later, Savoca offers close-ups of Catherine's newest
household appliances as she prepares a meal in the Santangelo kitchen. At
one point, Savoca shoots a toaster in close-up, and reflected in the toaster's
metal exterior is an image of Catherine and her surroundings. From her
haircut to the appliances she uses, Catherine has rejected a more traditional
(and stereotypical) ethnic existence.

Typically, historical trends like the moves to consumerism and assimilation are thought to bestow new freedoms and a greater sense of equality on
women. However, Baker and Vitullo suggest that the move to a more assimilated, consumer-based culture can also lionize more traditional models of
femininity. Essentially, a haze of nostalgic lament cloaks the inequalities of
the past. Ruberto expounds upon this point, suggesting that contemporary
cinematic representations of Italian American women, whether in gangster
films like *The Godfather* (1972) or "working-class" films like *Mac* (John Turturro, 1992) or *A Bronx Tale*, have helped to cement "a kind of narrative and
visual nostalgic imagery . . . that neglects female labor (inside or outside of
the home)" (166). *Household Saints* challenges this dominant paradigm by
recognizing the importance of female domestic labor. The film suggests that
Catherine's work "both within and beyond a strict domestic sphere" drives
the Santangelo family out of an isolated ethnic existence and into assimilated,
middle-class American culture (171).[11]

Savoca's willingness to see working-class Italian American women as empowered individuals whose actions help to shape the culture counters the
stereotype of the passive mama. In both *True Love* and *Household Saints*,

female characters recognize some of the inequalities of their culture, but they resist victimization by searching for opportunities to gain and wield power in their neighborhoods and in their families. Their gender heightens the consequentiality of their choices. *True Love*'s Michael and *Household Saints*' Lino can be irresponsible and immature, but Donna and Catherine are not allowed such luxuries. One misstep and their social standing is jeopardized.

Along with their gender, the working-class standing of these characters (particularly in *True Love*) magnifies the gravity of their choices. The opportunities that these characters have to attain a better life for themselves and their families are limited. This not only heightens the drama of the films but also distinguishes them from many Hollywood movies where money is seemingly not an issue. The same dynamic is evident in *Dogfight*, a studio-produced film that Savoca made between *True Love* and *Household Saints*. *Dogfight* does not focus intently on ethnic issues, but it shares an interest in gender and class with Savoca's other movies and continues to demonstrate the degree to which her films stray from and challenge the norms of typical Hollywood fare.

Dogfight

Throughout her career, Savoca has resisted Hollywood's tendency toward easy categorization. "Some people thought that [*True Love*] was a romantic comedy," she says. "In the video stores, sometimes they put it under comedy; sometimes they put it under drama. Who knows? I don't know." Despite making a film that did not fit neatly into any one genre, Savoca was courted by Hollywood after the critical success of *True Love*. Soon, she had received a script titled *Dogfight* that appealed to her. "I remember reading it and really loving the era, the time it was in," she says. "I also loved the idea of doing the Vietnam War" (interview, March 17, 2008).

The film, which is based on events from screenwriter Bob Comfort's life, tells the story of Eddie Birdlace (River Phoenix), a returning Vietnam veteran who spends most of the narrative remembering the night before he left for Vietnam. *Dogfight* opens with a haggard Birdlace limping off a San Francisco–bound bus. Clad in a military-fatigue shirt and cap, Birdlace is a lost man. He is surrounded by others but is clearly not a part of them. He eats alone and in silence during this layover, and when he returns to the bus, the film flashes back to November 1963. A younger, less morose Birdlace is on a different bus. He is full of life and surrounded by excited military men, including his friends Berzin (Richard Panebianco), Oakie (Anthony Clark), and Benjamin (Mitchell Whitfield).

This quartet has arranged a "dogfight" for later that evening. The rules of the competition are simple: the guys rent a bar; everyone chips in fifty dollars and then brings the least-attractive date they can find. Winners are awarded cash prizes. The guys arrive in San Francisco and go off in search of their dates. After being rejected several times, Birdlace meets Rose Fenney (Lili Taylor), a shy young lady with a loving but perhaps overbearing mother. After some cajoling, Eddie convinces Rose to accompany him to a party. Rose is enjoying herself, but soon she learns about the dogfight. She confronts Birdlace and runs out of the bar. Eddie and his friends go out for a night on the town, but he regrets his actions and goes to apologize to Rose. He offers to take her to dinner, and, reluctantly, she agrees. As his friends brawl with sailors, get matching tattoos, and pay for oral sex in a movie theater, Eddie and Rose walk through parks, play Whac-a-Mole in an arcade, and make love. At the end of the night, Rose hands Eddie a piece of paper with her address on it and says he can write to her if he wants. Birdlace is noncommittal and after returning to the company of his buddies rips up the paper and throws it out of the bus window.

Three years later, a missile attack wounds Birdlace's leg and kills his friends. The flashback ends as Eddie wakes up in San Francisco. He walks around the city and returns to Rose's diner. Rose's clothing, the signs posted in her restaurant, and her past interest in social-protest songs communicate her opposition to the war. After some awkwardness, Rose hugs Birdlace. The film fades to black, and viewers are left to speculate on the fate of their relationship and how Eddie will cope with the tragic events he has experienced.

After Savoca and her producer (and husband) Richard Guay made some minor revisions to the script, they realized that their vision for the project was different from that of Warner Bros. The studio thought the film should more closely resemble *Pretty in Pink* (Howard Deutch, 1986). Savoca was shocked, but despite the complications, she was still allowed to shoot the film. A disastrous test screening at a Pasadena shopping mall led Warner Bros. to lobby for changes. "The front row [of the test audience was] filled with these teenagers," Savoca recalls, "and somehow they had gotten a whiff—I guess they were River fans—about what the movie was about and the title and all this. . . . [T]hey started going, 'Dog-fight! Dog-fight! Dog-fight!' . . . [A]t that point all the blood drained from me, and I said, 'They're going to hate this movie, because they're expecting something else.'" Savoca was right. The audience was completely with the film until the dogfight ended. "They were so mad that we had geared them up for a comedy," she remembers, "and then, it had turned on them" (interview, March 17, 2008).

Among other changes, Warner Bros. wanted Savoca to shoot an alternate ending, but Savoca balked. The conflict became so heated that the studio tried to shoot one without her involvement. Ultimately, Savoca's battle to maintain her artistic vision paid off.[12] "That movie is the movie that I made," she states. "There are no excuses for anything I've made. I've always made the movies I wanted to make." Her first experience on a major Hollywood film, however, was "a hurtful [one], because in the end the movie was buried" (interview, March 17, 2008).

Dogfight shares similarities with Savoca's other movies. If *True Love* had countered representations of Italian Americans in movies like *Moonstruck,* then *Dogfight* was her answer to Hollywood's romantic comedies. Savoca's alternative visions challenge viewers' expectations by offering characters, situations, and narratives that are not easily classifiable. This frustrates some viewers and producers, because it fails to cater to standard modes of production. However, Savoca finds it to be more honest. "Life is sometimes really funny, and then in two seconds, it turns on you," she says. "To me, that's a lot more interesting and is actually more exciting" (interview, March 17, 2008).

On a related note, *Dogfight* challenged Hollywood's traditional gender norms. As Giunta has suggested, *Dogfight* "concerns the emergence of the female voice" and "provides a distinctly female narrative perspective," despite being framed within a male character's flashback ("Narratives of Loss" 171–82). As in *Household Saints, Dogfight's* narration is shared by both male and female characters.[13] This links the two seemingly dissimilar films, as does Giunta's suggestion that "Rose's critique of her society involves an attack on her mother's cultural values" (174).[14] The connections are important, because they hint at the larger arguments of Savoca's work. By showing that characters from diverse backgrounds face similar struggles, Savoca lays the foundation for a new community that is based on common experiences of gender and class rather than just ethnic or regional identity.

The film's interest in class is perhaps most apparent when Eddie tries to take Rose to dinner. The working-class couple enters an expensive restaurant, but the maître d' refuses to seat them because Eddie is not properly attired. Eddie pleads his case, asking for a table in the back and saying that it is his last night Stateside, but the maître d' stands firm in his refusal. Eddie and Rose leave the restaurant and go to purchase a jacket and tie. With the price tag still visible on the collar of Eddie's newly purchased used jacket, the couple returns to the restaurant, and the maître d' seats them begrudgingly (fig. 11). When the waiter arrives, Rose orders a full meal, while Eddie asks for a beer. When Rose learns that Eddie does not have enough money for

Figure 11. Eddie Birdlace (River Phoenix) and Rose (Lili Taylor) request a table at an expensive restaurant in *Dogfight*. The tag on Eddie's newly purchased jacket is still visible near his right shoulder.

a second meal, she shares her dinner with him. "Those are things that are never in movies," Savoca says, "because in movies, the guy pulls out the wad. There's always money" (interview, March 17, 2008).

Savoca's complementary interests in gender, ethnicity, and class come together in one of *Dogfight*'s last scenes. Birdlace has left for Vietnam, and Rose and her mother are holding each other in their diner. Tears well up in their eyes as a televised report confirms the death of President John F. Kennedy. The subtle references throughout the film to the Fenneys' Irish Catholic background and the looks of shock and sadness on their faces indicate that Rose and her mother feel a special bond with the country's first Irish Catholic president. Shot in a simple shot–reverse-shot editing pattern, the scene references an important moment from Savoca's childhood that is laden with socioeconomic implications. As her family watched Kennedy's funeral on television, Savoca's mother turned to her and said, "Look at Jackie Kennedy; she doesn't cry. That's how Americans are. You see? We've got to learn to be like this. Because they are stoic." The Fenneys' connection to Kennedy is based on national identity and ethnic and religious background, but Savoca remembers the actual events through the lens of ethnicity and class. For Savoca's mother, Kennedy's assassination was a terrible tragedy, but it also offered an opportunity to study how wealthy, powerful Americans like Jacqueline Kennedy acted in times of crisis. Savoca says, "We learned as immigrants what is to be admired and what is to be mimicked if possible." While *Dogfight* does not offer blatantly ethnic characters, it demonstrates that Savoca's vision is always inflected by her ethnic, gender, and class backgrounds. "I'm always making Italian American–Argentine films," she says, even when the movies do not engage those issues explicitly (interview, March 17, 2008).

Dirt

Savoca's most recent film, *Dirt,* was conceived as a television series. The idea was to follow a cleaning lady into a different person's home or apartment each week, giving viewers an opportunity to peek into that person's world. Rather than keeping the focus only on the cleaning lady's customers, viewers would also get to travel home with her to see how she lived. Showtime purchased the rights to the project but then balked at the idea of a television program. Savoca recalls, "When I said, 'Well, we'd like the rights back. We want to do it as an indie film,' they said, 'Well, maybe that we can do'" (interview, March 17, 2008). In *Dirt,* Savoca's representation of the interrelationship among ethnicity, class, and gender reaches new heights. Here, the writer-director rejects socially constructed boundaries that work to form communities through a process of exclusion and, as an alternative, suggests that communities can be formed around experiences that cross ethnic, gender, and class lines.

The film tells the story of Dolores (Julietta Ortiz), an undocumented worker from El Salvador who has migrated to the United States with her husband and son for the promise of economic opportunity. For more than a decade, she has worked in New York City as a maid. She and her husband hope to use their earnings to buy a house in their homeland, where they plan to retire. Mother, father, and teenage son live together and, like many immigrant families, confront the generational tensions that oftentimes surface between immigrant parents and their children. At home, Dolores struggles with her son's attempts to Americanize himself, and at work she endures prejudice on a daily basis. Throughout the film, viewers are placed in Dolores's position as assimilated Americans speak condescendingly toward her. Small in stature, she is often jostled by passersby and disregarded by many of the film's other characters.

Dolores's life becomes even more difficult when she loses her biggest client for reasons that are beyond her control. As she struggles financially, Dolores faces further hardship when her husband is killed in a workplace accident.[15] Dolores knows that her husband wanted to be buried in El Salvador, but traveling to the country might mean that she will never be able to return to the United States. Nonetheless, she heeds her husband's wishes and travels with her son to El Salvador. After the funeral and some deliberation, Dolores and her son return to the United States illegally. Even though they face restrictive immigration policies and the prospect of continued maltreatment in New York, they believe that the United States is now their homeland and that it offers better opportunities than El Salvador.

As Savoca was preparing *Dirt,* she reflected upon her experiences as an ethnic woman who grew up in a working-class family. She says, "I have a lot of people in my family who do service jobs. . . . And I just remember all my growing up and even now, sitting around the table at the holidays, and the topic of conversation being the rich people. . . . It's a study, and sometimes it's definitely about—not condemning but—judgment, and other times it's like a fascination of this other species." Since becoming a successful filmmaker, Savoca often interacts socially with the wealthy people her family continues to study. "I'm allowed to move through class effortlessly, like a ghost through walls," she says. "So I can sit in a house and have the most expensive wine one night and then go to the Bronx the next night and be with my family. And I thought that it would be fabulous to have this cleaning woman have these [same] abilities" (interview, March 17, 2008).

Throughout *Dirt,* Dolores is treated as if she were invisible. Some of Dolores's clients limit their interaction with her to notes that direct her to clean specific spots of their home. Such invisibility is characteristic of Hollywood's representations of immigrant characters, and it echoes the treatment that working-class immigrants receive in American society. But a fear of constant surveillance also characterizes Dolores's life. Her husband loses his job, because the Immigration and Naturalization Service raids the restaurant that employs him. Other residents in her building are constantly changing their names to avoid detection. And as she walks by a policeman, Dolores is careful to dispense of her litter in a trash can instead of letting it fall onto the street. For Dolores, it is a life of constant uncertainty, because the slightest infraction or chance encounter can bring her family's hopes and dreams crashing down.

In some films, this consigns the character to a state of victimization. In *Dirt,* Dolores uses her invisibility to her advantage. This is perhaps most apparent in her interactions with the Ortegas, a family of three and Dolores's biggest customer. Throughout the narrative, Dolores discovers that Mr. Ortega is having an affair, that Mrs. Ortega is disappointed in her son, and that the Ortegas' son has all of the advantages of wealth but is unhappy. This knowledge only increases Dolores's power. When she discovers Mr. Ortega's affair, for instance, he pays her more money. In another scene, when she is cleaning the Ortegas' bathroom, Mrs. Ortega speaks of her life and her pursuit of public office. Savoca offers close-ups of Dolores scrubbing the tub and toilet while Mrs. Ortega yammers on, completely indifferent to the chores that Dolores is completing. Mrs. Ortega does not see any point in asking Dolores about her family, but despite her lower socioeconomic status, Dolores faces similar challenges as a parent and, by traditional standards, seems to have built a more loving and honest marriage. By ignoring Dolores, Mrs. Ortega misses an opportunity to find a sense of community and grow as a person.

When the Ortegas fire Dolores because Mrs. Ortega fears that employing an undocumented worker jeopardizes her political campaign, Dolores is scared and heartbroken. To survive, she turns to the building's other service workers for support. The Italian American doorman (Mike), the Irish American super (Flaherty), the African American elevator operator (Gerard), and the Dominican American cleaning lady (Mona) advise her of possible employment leads, and Mona counsels her on her relationships with her husband, son, and neighbors. Despite ethnic differences, these working-class individuals form a supportive community based in common experiences, and by the end of the movie Dolores seems to have weathered an exceedingly difficult time in her life.[16]

Throughout the film, Dolores works to establish a more secure (if still tenuous) existence for herself and her family by recognizing the assumptions and prejudices of others. "Dolores in *Dirt* is frickin' smart," Savoca says, "and you have to be to make life work for you under these circumstances." In accepting that the ideals of American society are not always fulfilled by the realities of American life, Dolores is better able to navigate the culture while gaining her fellow characters' and the film viewers' respect. In one scene, for instance, an obviously wealthy white woman begins speaking quite loudly to Dolores. Savoca shoots the woman from a slightly low angle in medium shot, which places the audience at Dolores's approximate height. The unnamed character stabs the air with her index finger, speaking a pathetic version of Spanglish loudly and slowly in an apparent attempt to overcome a language barrier that does not exist. Dolores, in medium shot, stares at her expressionlessly and refuses to react. The scene recalls moments from Savoca's own childhood. "I would go to the store with my mom, and she didn't speak English," Savoca remembers. "The ladies were saying, 'Tell ya motha', she's in America now. She's gotta learn English. Don't translate fa her. She should know.' . . . I am a little kid, and this woman is talking down to my mother. And I just remember my mother turning to me and saying, 'Tell this son of a bitch that she can go fuck herself'" (interview, March 17, 2008). In both cases, an assimilated American's willingness to treat a fellow human being as inferior speaks more to the nature of the would-be oppressor than to the individuals whom they are trying to oppress. The film encourages the audience to admire Dolores for enduring this harsh treatment so calmly.

Dirt is also notable for its recognition of the diversity that exists within ethnic groups. Whereas Hollywood films tend to oversimplify specific ethnic identities by focusing on broad racial categories like "Asian" or "Hispanic," *Dirt* identifies and develops Dolores as not just Hispanic but specifically El Salvadoran.[17] When she was researching the film, Savoca says that some of her Latin friends discouraged her from focusing on El Salvadorans, because they warned, "They don't let you into their world." In Savoca's experience, this was not the case. She was acquainted with a group of El Salvadoran immigrant women whose stories "were horrific and amazing and courageous, and yet they were full of fear." Eventually, Savoca asked if she could use their stories, and the women were happy to oblige. The common perception of the El Salvadoran community as isolated and suspicious of outsiders shares much in common with outsiders' impressions of Sicilian communities—something that was not lost on Savoca (interview, March 17, 2008).

In the stories of modern-day El Salvadoran immigrants, Savoca saw the history of her own family. Certainly, specific historical challenges and ethnic norms separate U.S. immigrant groups, but too often those specificities allow assimilated individuals with ethnic backgrounds to feel no sense of connection with today's immigrants. In truth, some of the challenges that these groups face or faced as well as the pressures that they feel or felt to assimilate are quite similar. Savoca says, "Whenever I find someone who's screaming about immigration today, [I say,] 'Look at these things from the turn of the century: "Italians are dirty." "They're full of disease." "They're lazy." "They don't want to work." "They don't want to speak English."' Germans, Jews, fill in the blank, and it's whoever the immigrant is today" (interview, March 17, 2008). With *Dirt,* Savoca once again argued for the validity and necessity of an alternative means of community formation and suggested that grouping individuals together based on a shared history of immigration might be more effective.

However, Savoca is careful not to fall into the reductiveness that is sometimes apparent in movies like *Gangs of New York.* If *Gangs'* strategy of collapsing ethnic difference offers the sense that immigrant experiences can be equated, *Dirt* balances a desire to see similarities between past and present immigrant groups with an understanding that the historical moments in which these characters live are different. U.S. immigration policies became more restrictive throughout the twentieth century, criminalizing a practice that was perfectly legal until then (at least for whites and white ethnics).[18] When Italians arrived on U.S. shores in the early part of the twentieth century, it was literally impossible for them to be judged illegal (unless, of course, they had prior criminal records that would prevent their entry). If the same immigrant Italians were to face the situations that Dolores does in *Dirt,* their decisions would not be as difficult. Traveling to and from Italy for a funeral, for instance, would be relatively easy if an early-twentieth-century Italian immigrant could afford and endure the sea voyage. *Dirt,* then, recognizes that there are some similarities between yesterday's immigrants and today's, but it also appreciates that immigrant experiences are unique.

Further, Savoca's decision to base *Dirt* in the twenty-first century, as opposed to Scorsese's decision to place *Gangs* in the past, lessens viewers' ability to distance themselves from the prejudice Dolores suffers. The characters that speak slowly, loudly, and condescendingly to her or who ignore her are not the barbaric street hoods of *Gangs.* Instead, they resemble the middle- and upper-middle-class members of *Dirt*'s contemporaneous audience.[19] Viewers are meant to see themselves not just in Dolores but also in the Americans with whom she interacts. Savoca places them in a position where they are both the descendants of groups who endured prejudice and the members of groups who perpetuate similar prejudices today.

Given *Dirt*'s social importance and the uniquely balanced perspective it offers on immigrant experiences, it is a shame that the film has never been released in any video format and has received only limited distribution on television. Although changes in the leadership at Showtime contributed to the film's fate, its refusal to fit neatly into a genre or to offer characters who are easily classified as "good" or "bad" may also have been a factor. Nonetheless, *Dirt* has found an audience at festivals throughout the world. "Those issues of identity are universal," Savoca says. "Who am I? What are the rules of my society? What's my tribe make me do?" (interview, March 17, 2008). For all of their ethnic specificity, their interest in gender, and their focus on the working class, Savoca's movies develop themes that cross the boundaries that usually divide us.

* * *

Like Scorsese, Savoca has been critical of her Italian American background—a culture that has given her a strong sense of identity while also limiting her individuality and opportunities. Films like *True Love* and *Household Saints* are attempts to work through the contradictions and tensions within a culturally specific worldview so that a better understanding of the dynamics in individual identity constructions can be reached. The view of the Italian neighborhood and family that is offered in these films does not fit neatly into Jacobson's argument that the White Ethnic Revival lauded ethnics and the bootstraps myth in an attempt to level racial and ethnic prejudice. Savoca's films are often quite critical of ethnic perspectives, showing us characters who are disempowered by their environment. The neighborhoods' encouragement of exclusionary thinking inhibits personal development and encourages patriarchy. We are not given the chance to marvel at an American success story, nor are we encouraged to see white ethnics succeeding where other minorities have failed; rather, we are offered an opportunity to critically evaluate a carefully documented and sometimes lovingly depicted culture whose sexism is seen as unjustified and illogical on both a societal and an individual level.

But Savoca's characters refuse to be easily classified. A character like Eddie Birdlace is simultaneously a shallow, sexist teenager who joins in "dogfights" with his immature friends and a young man from a working-class background who sees the injustices of the world, raises his voice in occasional protest, and grows into adulthood by critically evaluating his own behaviors. The character frustrates traditional Hollywood expectations, because he both repulses and charms. A similarly conflicted response characterizes reactions to *True Love*'s Michael and Donna and *Household Saints*' Joseph and Catherine Santangelo. Savoca's ability to simultaneously criticize these characters while finding their humanity works to promote understanding and tolerance rather than judgment.

4 Francis Ford Coppola

Ethnic Nostalgia in the Godfather *Trilogy*

In *The Godfather, Part II,* ten-year-old Vito Andolini (Oreste Baldini) flees
Corleone, Sicily, where Mafia chieftains are attempting to kill him. He arrives
at Ellis Island and undergoes what many consider to be the typical experience
of American immigrants. First, Andolini encounters an immigration official
who does not speak Italian and who, in his haste and lack of interest, renames
him Vito Corleone. Then Vito sees a doctor, is diagnosed with smallpox, and
is quarantined. The sequence concludes with Vito entering a small room,
walking up to its window, and staring out at the Statue of Liberty (fig. 12). In

Figure 12. The American Dream deferred. A recently arrived and newly
quarantined Vito Corleone (Oreste Baldini) stares out of his Ellis Island cell
in *The Godfather, Part II.*

a beautiful shot, Francis Ford Coppola captures the deferral of the American Dream. Shooting from outside the room's window, Coppola frames Vito in a medium close-up. As Vito moves to the right half of the screen, a reflected image of the Statue of Liberty occupies the left. Having arrived in America, Vito must wait for his shot at the American Dream, and the Statue of Liberty, the visualization of the dream for so many, appears only as an illusion. Vito moves away from the window and back into the room. Coppola cuts to an interior shot as the young Vito sits in a chair, and we look over his shoulder. The image of the Statue of Liberty is a dominating presence, yet it remains out of focus, out of reach, and behind a pane of glass.

Ironically, these images were photographed not in New York Harbor but in Trieste, Italy.[1] Many of the ideas that have come to characterize Italian American ethnicity are as artificial as these images, and they can lead to potentially destructive consequences. Maria Laurino, in her memoir *Were You Always an Italian?* writes, "Without a fuller understanding of history, nostalgia fills the void and we become appendages to someone else's past, daylight somnambulists seeking peace with the spirits; or we create dangerous fictions, clutching a lost time that at all costs must be preserved undisturbed" (33–34). But how does one capture historical truth when the life experiences of many Italian Americans today are far removed from the ones their ancestors knew? How does one achieve "a fuller understanding of history" while recognizing that grand historical narratives are told from a specific perspective with specific political goals? How does one arrive at any sense of historical truth when all perceptions and memories are relative, selective, and limited by the experiences of the individual?

Rather than attempting to uncover a historical truth, the aim of this chapter will be to interrogate the myths that have sprung up around Italian American ethnicity, the assumptions that ground these myths, and the goals these myths seek to achieve. The *Godfather* trilogy is an apt object of study for such an undertaking, since the films have become so prominent in American and global culture and since they are directed by an Italian American whose work has been consistently concerned with issues of family and nostalgia. Ultimately, *The Godfather* and *The Godfather, Part II* deploy familial loyalty rhetorically, creating a nostalgic portrait of the past.

For Pam Cook, nostalgia is "a state of longing for something that is known to be irretrievable, but is sought anyway" (3).[2] Cook argues that in addition to being potentially regressive, nostalgia "can be perceived as a way of coming to terms with the past," since it is "predicated on the acknowledgement that the past is gone forever" (4). In Cook's assessment, nostalgia does not condemn cultures or individuals to repeating the past, nor does it relegate them to a state of complacency or eternal regret in the present. Instead, it is helpful in allowing them to move beyond what has been. However, while nostalgia might acknowledge the loss of a past, it might also be in denial of having lost it forever. In the *Godfather* films, and other Coppola movies, nostalgia exists as a critique of the present, but Coppola's nostalgia is also stubbornly romantic. He laments a lost time, which is as much about values (family, loyalty, respect) as a historical moment, and, occasionally, one gets the sense that Coppola is such an idealist that he believes "it could be that way again."

At times, the *Godfather* films seem regressive. The films' nostalgia is seductive and encourages the embrace of a conservative worldview that relegates women and minorities to a subordinate status, sees American culture as the corrupter of a pristine and idyllic Italian culture, and works to endorse the neoconservative impulses that Jacobson sees at the heart of the White Ethnic Revival.[3] Nevertheless, the *Godfather* films are also critical of the Corleones, never allowing viewers to forget that this seemingly ideal Italian American family is sustained by bloodshed, extortion, and murder. *The Godfather, Part III* (1990) plays more like a Scorsese film, where ethnic dysfunction is dramatized through a series of images, scenes, and intratextual references that comment upon and starkly undermine the comforting myths of the previous two installments.

Coppola and *The Godfather*

Mario Puzo's novel *The Godfather* was published in 1969 and quickly became a best-seller. To date, it has sold more than twenty-one million copies, making it almost as well known as Coppola's film series. Given the ways in which the novel, its characters, and the subsequent films derived from it have permeated American culture, it is easy to forget that *The Godfather* was not the only late-1960s cultural production to investigate the Italian American Mafia. Peter Maas's nonfictional *The Valachi Papers* (published in 1968) was adapted into a Hollywood feature in 1972, the same year that *The Godfather* was released. According to Michael Schumacher, *The Valachi Papers* "whetted the public's appetite for information about the secretive mobster society" (88). In 1968, Paramount released *The Brotherhood,* directed by Martin Ritt and starring Kirk Douglas as a Mafia don who seeks to retire to Sicily after double-crossing his New York partners.[4] *The Brotherhood* bombed at the box office and temporarily threatened the cinematic adaptation of Puzo's novel.

The production history of *The Godfather* films has been well chronicled, but the reasons for Coppola's involvement are worth revisiting.[5] When Paramount green-lighted the film, Coppola was a young filmmaker with only four Hollywood features to his credit. None was tremendously successful; most were low budget. So, it was not his record of profitable blockbusters that made him attractive to Paramount. In fact, it does not seem that Coppola was attractive at all initially. Paramount offered the film to several directors who rejected the project. Even Coppola declined the proposition the first time it was made to him. Eventually, he realized that the salary the job carried was too great to turn down, especially with his nascent American Zoetrope facing bankruptcy.

Coppola was offered the job for a number of reasons. Michael Goodwin and Naomi Wise suggest that Robert Evans, Paramount's vice president of production, and Al Ruddy, the producer of *The Godfather*, "needed a director, ideally a hungry director who would work cheap, who knew how to shoot fast and inexpensively, and who wouldn't argue with Paramount's decisions and priorities" (112). Coppola seemed to fit the bill, though he later disagreed with many of Paramount's suggestions.[6] He was also an Academy Award–winning writer, and so Paramount could secure a writer and director for one salary. Equally important was Coppola's Italian heritage.[7] Evans believed that gangster films like *The Brotherhood* had failed because they were movies about Italians usually made by Jewish producers, directors, and actors.[8] An Italian American director, he thought, would lend an added sense of authenticity to the Corleone saga.

In Coppola, Evans chose an individual who had been defined significantly by his Italian heritage, and Coppola drew on that background in the *Godfather* films.[9] Coppola was born in Detroit, Michigan, but was raised largely in Queens, New York. His father was a moderately successful conductor and flutist, and the family enjoyed a middle-class life, though reports indicate that their standing was not always secure.[10] As a child, Coppola was stricken with polio and had to spend much of his preteen years isolated from family and friends. After miraculously beating the disease, he attended high school but was later sent to a (much loathed) military academy. After graduation, he went to Hofstra University and became a prominent student leader within the drama community. Coppola then entered the graduate program in film at the University of California at Los Angeles and was later hired by Roger Corman, beginning his career as a screenwriter and director in the early 1960s.

Peter Cowie writes, "Nothing has influenced Coppola's life and work so dramatically as his Italian blood." From an early age, Italian ethnicity was not something that imprisoned him, as it did Scorsese and Savoca, but something of which he could be proud. Coppola says, "We were taught that Italians had great culture: like Fermi, Verdi, and so on" (quoted in Lebo 15). With middle-class respectability gained through his father's profession as an artist, Coppola was allowed to embrace his Italian roots as a unique aspect of his personality and identity that did not threaten his sense of opportunity and social advancement in the post–World War II era.[11] Nonetheless, Coppola's public image has been saddled (or aided) by many of the stereotypes that have plagued Italian Americans.[12] He has been referred to as "like a Mafia godfather" (Lindsey 134). George Lucas has described him as "very Italian and compulsive" (quoted in Phillips, *Godfather* 52), and Cowie suggests that he is melodramatic and blames his sexual politics on "the conservatism of his Italian background" (*Coppola* 194, 7). Coppola has encouraged some of these remarks by saying that he operates "very affectionately with people" and frequently linking his Italian background with a "family attitude" (Cowie, *Coppola* 6). Nonetheless, one cannot help but recognize the degree to which critics use Coppola to validate more widely held Italian stereotypes.

While the *Godfather* films would become the ones most associated with a specifically Italian ethnicity, a more general interest in ethnic characters is present in many of the director's other films. The main character in *The Rain People* (1969) is Natalie Ravenna (Shirley Knight), an Italian American wife on the run, in a film that features a brief *Godfather*-esque wedding sequence. Coppola's *Tetro* (2009) tells the story of two Italian American brothers living in Argentina and was promoted by the director and his American Zoetrope company as "semi-autobiographical." *Finian's Rainbow* (1968) focuses on two Irish immigrants and is tied thematically to the first two *Godfather* films.[13] And *The Cotton Club* (1984) delves into the interaction among Irish, Jewish, and African American characters during the Harlem Renaissance. These last two films reveal an approach to race that is fairly typical of Hollywood. *The Cotton Club,* for instance, sets up a dichotomy between the criminal activities of "bad" or "negative" whites and the artistic expression of "good" or "positive" African Americans, but it marginalized (and marginalizes) African Americans in its production and its narrative.[14] Ultimately, it is white actor Richard Gere who stars in a film that is supposedly about the Harlem Renaissance. As in many Hollywood movies, African American characters are subordinated to white ethnic or nonethnic characters in an effort to appeal to a mass audience.

The Godfather's conservative impulses are cloaked within a more nostalgic view of the past and coexist with metaphorical overtones that challenge, but do not completely undermine, the film's politics. As a result, the film's conservatism becomes less apparent and somehow more negligible. We should recall that *The Godfather* was released at a time of uncertainty and unrest in American culture. William Malyszko writes of the period, "Americans were quite critical of their leaders. The Vietnam War and the Nixon administration, which led to the Watergate scandal, had created considerable unrest. The central metaphor of the Mafia as representative of corporate America would not be lost on many members of the audience" (8).[15] However, whereas the film invites a critical view of the dominant culture, its apparently noble and benevolent Mafia don invites a less radical response. "Perhaps, [The Godfather] indicated a change in thinking," writes Schumacher, "an indication that the public, weary of what it considered to be a free-wheeling, overly permissive society, was willing to embrace a more rigid, almost Machiavellian leadership in exchange for order in the house" (93). While sanctioning multiple viewing positions, Coppola's deployment of ethnicity smuggles traditionalist messages into the films and makes them acceptable.[16] The first two Godfather films are marked by an obsessive interest in ethnic detail, an endorsement of the sanctity of the patriarchal family, a need to defend and protect familial loyalty, and a consistent effort to tone down the rawness of the Old World characters of Puzo's novel and make them more appealing to moviegoing audiences.

Puzo's Novel versus Coppola's Film

Coppola and Puzo engaged in a long-distance collaboration on the screenplay for the first Godfather, but even Puzo concedes that the finished product was largely Coppola's.[17] Critics have noted Coppola's "more engaging" gangsters (Cowie, Godfather 16), the absence of sinister words like omertà, Moustache Pete, and 90 calibre (Lebo 32), and the transformation of Fredo from the novel's more competent and brutal character to the film's bumbling nice guy gangster (Phillips, Interviews 178). Noting the differences between the two works is a useful first step, but scholars must strive to move toward a type of analysis that interrogates the reasons for these changes and the general goals they serve.

The difference in Puzo's and Coppola's visions (in spite of their shared ethnic background and gender) further exposes the diversity that exists within ethnic groups. Gardaphé suggests that the differences between the novel and the film are attributable, at least in part, to the generational differences between the works' authors. He writes, "For the most part, Coppola follows the direction of Puzo's novel, but the choices he makes when changing the story are made from a perspective that reflects the generational differences between Puzo, the son of immigrants, and Coppola, the grandson of immigrants— a perspective that reflects attitudes towards masculinity that had changed drastically in one generation" (Wiseguys 38).[18] However, whereas Puzo's novel offers a more critical representation of the Don (Marlon Brando) and his

Old World norms, the films romanticize the Don's regressive masculinity. With details such as the killing of Vito's brother in Sicily (in the film but not the novel) and the ignorant, callous immigration official who changes Vito's last name (in the novel, Vito changes it to the name of his hometown for sentimental reasons), Coppola creates an environment in which Vito's embrace of an Old World notion of masculinity is treated symptomatically. Gardaphé writes, "Coppola simply piles up a number of reasons why Vito must demonstrate his manhood in order to right wrongs committed against him and his family" (*Wiseguys* 39). As a result, the films associate regressive masculinity with a seemingly more benign and "natural" Old World ethnic culture (*Wiseguys* 38–42).

Since Santino (James Caan) cannot control his temper, and Fredo (John Cazale) consistently fails to protect his father, control his wife, or otherwise perform an acceptable masculinity, Michael (Al Pacino) is the only Corleone son capable of inheriting "the Don's sense of manhood, and, thus, control of the family" (*Wiseguys* 38). Yet Michael fails, too. His murder of Fredo at the end of *Part II* is simultaneously a critique of traditional masculinity, a critique of the influence American capitalism can have on individual actions, and a critique of Michael's character. Nonetheless, throughout *Part II* there is an effort to distance Michael's principles from those of his father. Michael embraces the regressive masculine norms of an older generation, but he does so with little regard for other Old World values. His fratricide is less a critique of his father's (and the culture's) regressive masculinity than a critique of Michael's inability to balance Old World values. In attempting to control his family, Michael destroys it.[19] In "acting like a man," he ruins the thing that (according to his father in *Part I*) makes him a man.

Ultimately, despite rare critiques of Michael's treatment of Kay (Diane Keaton), the films work to endorse an Old World view of gender norms, lamenting the loss of a time that was less complicated, when social roles were more clearly defined and men were in charge. One can see Coppola's efforts to facilitate this nostalgic view of hierarchical gender dynamics in the ways he romanticizes characters that Puzo's novel made less appealing. Don Vito Corleone and his enforcer Luca Brasi (Lenny Montana) are transformed from mobsters and murderers in the novel to men with at least some likable qualities in the film. The Don values family above all else and resorts to violence only when he feels there is no alternative. Brasi's loyalty to and respect for the Don paint him as a selfless servant who fumbles over his words when he is in the presence of Vito because he has so much respect for the man.

These representations are in sharp contrast to the ones offered by Puzo's novel. Far from being a lovable, bumbling friend to the Don, Brasi is a gruesome murderer whose rage and violence are incredibly sadistic. In the novel, when Al Capone sends two hit men to assassinate Vito Corleone, they are met by Brasi. After binding the two men and stuffing bath towels in their mouths, Brasi murders them in a manner far more ghastly than anything depicted or discussed in Coppola's film. Puzo writes:

> Brasi took an axe from its place against the wall and started hacking at one of the Capone men. He chopped the man's feet off, then the legs at the knees, then the thighs where they joined the torso. Brasi was an extremely powerful man but it took him many swings to accomplish his purpose. By that time of course the victim had given up the ghost and the floor of the warehouse was slippery with the hacked fragments of his flesh and the gouting of his blood. When Brasi turned to his second victim he found further effort unnecessary. The second Capone gunman out of sheer terror had, impossibly, swallowed the bath towel in his mouth and suffocated. (215–16)

Filming such a scene may have garnered a commercially daunting "X" rating for *The Godfather,* but Coppola's decision to not even mention this event in dialogue creates a more palatable image of Brasi and Vito. The most heinous act we hear about in the film is when Brasi holds a gun to the head of Johnny Fontane's manager, and Vito assures the manager that "either his signature or his brains would appear on the contract."

In a later scene in the book, Michael meets a woman named Filomena, who he suspects can tell him the story of how Brasi came into his father's employ. After Filomena learns that Brasi has died, she agrees to tell Michael the story.[20] Filomena used to be a midwife in New York. One night, Luca Brasi forced her to accompany him to a house, where she found a pregnant Irish prostitute. The woman was having a baby that Brasi had fathered. But, he said, he did not want "any of that race to live."[21] After Filomena delivered the infant, Brasi threatened to kill her if she would not throw it into a furnace. Filomena begrudgingly obliged the request, and Brasi was later arrested for murdering the child's mother. Filomena went to Don Corleone, and the Don "assured Filomena that she had nothing to fear from either Luca Brasi or the police." The police could not prove their case in court, and Brasi was released. Soon after, he went to work for Don Corleone (344–47).

In addition to painting Brasi as a heinous character, these stories paint the Don as a monster. What kind of a man hears this story about Brasi and sees an opportunity to hire a new employee? What kind of man dispatches this monster to hack off the limbs of would-be assassins? Puzo's Don is a cold-blooded killer who is just as violent as his competitors, if not more so. Further, whereas Coppola makes a conscious effort to portray the Don mostly as a father figure, Puzo is more interested in representing him as a businessman.[22] Throughout the novel, Michael frequently refers to his father as "the Don"; in the film, he usually calls him "Dad" or "my father." Additionally, in the film, Vito tells Michael that he hoped he would be a senator or a governor, but in the novel, Vito clearly has plans for Michael to enter the family business.

Interestingly, Coppola filmed scenes for the *Godfather* films that would have offered a less romanticized view of Vito. In one, Vito travels to the hospital with his three sons, Tom Hagan (Robert Duvall), and Fontane (Al Martino) to visit Genco Abbandando, the Corleone consigliere prior to Hagan. Before entering Genco's room, Vito pulls Michael aside. The patriarch complains that Michael does not come to him "like a son should" and indicates that he has plans for Michael's future. By omitting this scene (it is in the novel), Coppola paints the Don as a more accepting patriarch, one who respects his son's independence and even admires him for looking for opportunities outside the family, as opposed to the more controlling father who is less willing to exempt his son from the family business.

Each of these incidents renders a more critical perspective on the crime family and aligns Puzo with what is typically thought to be a second-generation perspective. Puzo represents ethnic identity as a prison.[23] Michael seems trapped within the confines of his ethnicity. He visits Kay's family and is marked as an outsider. He cannot escape his fate as the heir to the illegal Corleone empire. His Dartmouth education and war record are valiant attempts to break away from the family business, but they prove unsuccessful. What is more, in the novel Michael comes to enjoy the life of a Mafia don. When he offers to "hit" Sollozzo and McCluskey, Puzo affords him more dialogue than Coppola does: "'Then you have to hit Sollozzo right away,' Michael said. 'We can't wait. The guy is too dangerous. He'll come up with some new idea. Remember, the key is still that he gets rid of the old man. He knows that. OK, he knows that now if he's going to get killed anyway, he'll have another crack at the Don. And with that police captain helping him who knows what the hell might happen. We can't take that chance. We have to get Sollozzo right away" (131). As Michael immerses himself in the chess match of Mob hits, readers get a sense that the highly intelligent Michael enjoys this high-stakes game. This feeling is absent in the films, where Michael, coldhearted and stone-faced, describes his plan tersely and resignedly. A man "stalked by his fate" (Coppola, *Part II* DVD commentary), the film's Michael finds little if any enjoyment in the life he lives. Coppola emphasizes this point with numerous close-ups that highlight Pacino's consistently, almost unwaveringly, solemn visage.

The result is that Coppola's filmed version of *The Godfather,* in Puzo's words, "had softened the characters" (*Papers* 56), making them "too nice" (quoted in Biskind 25).[24] Viewers *liked* Coppola's Corleones.[25] To varying degrees, viewers found Michael to be somewhat sympathetic. Jack Shadoian, for instance, writes, "If Michael is a monster, we realize and accept why he has to be one. The man must do what he does; his choices are made *for* him and not by him" (270).

The Godfather film became a story about family as much as crime, and the good of the family becomes the barometer for the acceptability of all the actions that are taken. If Coppola's Vito carries out an act of violence against an individual, viewers believe that the victim had it coming because he had threatened the sanctity and security of the family. When Jack Woltz (John Marley) finds Khartoum's head in his bed, few viewers will feel sorry for the unreasonable, brash, racist Hollywood producer. When Vito dispatches a couple of thugs to secure justice for the undertaker Amerigo Bonasera (Salvatore Corsitto), few would lament the punishment that will befall the men that sexually assaulted Bonasera's daughter (especially since it is not represented on-screen). The Don's justice is proportional. The same cannot be said of the novel's Don.

What emerges, then, in the *Godfather* films is an idealized portrait of Mob life and Mob justice, which is gradually eroded as time passes and modernity overtakes Old World values. Mafia hoods repair the American courts' and American government's mistakes and oversights. Mob families maintain clear gender roles, and individuals know their roles and their duties. If these norms are respected and maintained, one need never fear for his (and almost always it is "his") life, but if the norms are broken, justice is meted out swiftly and mercilessly. As Judith Crist famously (and melodramatically) remarked, "The whole function of the film is to show us that Hitler is a grand sort of family man, gentle with children" (quoted in Biskind 65).[26] Yet because the film renders such a nostalgic atmosphere for this Old World patriarchal system, viewers find themselves longing at times for the vigilantism and simplicity of the Don's world, despite the morally reprehensible nature of the family business.[27]

Nostalgia, the Family, and Ethnicity in the Films of Francis Ford Coppola

Nostalgia and a preoccupation with the family are thematic mainstays of Coppola's movies. Films like *Dementia 13* (1963), *The Rain People,* and *You're a Big Boy Now* (1966) focus on families whose stability is placed in jeopardy, while *The Cotton Club, Rumble Fish* (1983), *The Outsiders* (1983), and *Tetro* investigate filial relationships. Malyszko suggests that Coppola's interest in the family might be more accurately described as an interest in "familial breakdown and failure" (20), but in many of his films, the family pulls together and defeats the odds, remaining generally intact. Coppola's interest in nostalgia is most apparent in films like *Tucker: The Man and His Dream* (1988), *Peggy Sue Got Married* (1986), and *The Outsiders,* where the past is not only a more idyllic time but one that is imaged in gold tones.[28] Eventually, the formal nostalgia of these films gives way to bleak and tragic events, thus juxtaposing nostalgia and tragedy and resulting in an ambiguous statement that simultaneously romanticizes the past while creating a "realistic" sense of darkness and doom.

The *Godfather* films are similarly ambiguous. The first film was released at a time when multinational corporations were exerting more influence on government policies, when Vietnam raged and became a war that the United States could not win, and when the feminist movements threatened the traditional, inequitable gender norms of the past. Coppola's film responded to these changes by lamenting the role social institutions should play (and a role that, in the film's mythology, the Mafia once did) while romanticizing the gangster figure and his ethnic background, and, through them, traditional gender roles and racial hierarchies.

By focusing on the dynamics and mannerisms of New York Italian American culture, Coppola introduced an anthropological perspective to *The Godfather* that made the characters interesting not just because of their criminal lives but also because of their cultural backgrounds. Coppola provided a level of depth to the old stereotype that did not previously exist. The films emphasize the cultural norms that ground the gangster's worldview and guide his choices. Coppola's insistence on filming the movie on location in some of New York's Italian American neighborhoods, as well as including scenes that discuss in detail the care and preparation that go into making Italian gravy, for instance, work to document cultural norms (not specific to the gangster) through fictional characters and stories.[29] Within the film, ethnicity works to humanize Vito, complicating viewers' responses to and identification with him. We do not just see him as a greedy killer. We see him as a son, a husband, a father, a grandfather, and a friend. On this phenomenon, Schumacher writes, "To watch Vito Corleone gently stroking a cat, selecting oranges at the marketplace, or playing with his grandson in the garden, one might have a difficult time imagining the same man killing or ordering executions of rival mobsters, bribing judges and union officials, strong-arming the opposition, and, in general, attaining a position of wealth and influence through a life of crime" (115). This view of the Don was supported by some of the film's promotional materials. The preview for *The Godfather* features an image of Vito playing with his grandson, and in *The Godfather: Behind the Scenes*, a 1971 documentary about the making of the film, actress Morgana King (Mama Corleone) describes the patriarch as "that man from the other side of the world," saying "everything he does is for his family." This perspective advanced the generic development of the gangster film and worked to complicate and challenge many of the stereotypes that had characterized previous iterations of the genre, such as *Little Caesar* and *Scarface: The Shame of the Nation*.[30] There has nearly always been a tendency in the gangster genre to make the gangster somehow thrilling despite his evil (U.S. censors worried that films such as *Public Enemy* [William Wellman, 1931] tended to glorify gangsters), but whereas working-class ethnicity had previously served to mark the characters as different, outside the mainstream, ethnicity in *The Godfather* became something that made the characters more appealing. As Edward Rothstein has said, "At the heart of [*The Godfather*] is a forthright assertion of ethnic identity as a source of strength. That is where we find the human side of the mob" (26). Working-class ethnic Italianness became an important aspect of an attractive Old World culture that guaranteed stable families, secure social standings, and an enviable degree of loyalty.[31]

Many Italian American studies scholars have chastised Coppola (and Scorsese) for perpetuating the stereotype of Italian American gangsters. The esteemed Frank P. Tomasulo, for instance, argues that Italian American directors, by virtue of their ethnic background, are in a powerful position, because they have the potential to validate the dominant culture's stereotypes in their films. In essence, they "carry the cachet of insider knowledge and legitimacy" (70).[32] What Tomasulo and others who criticize Coppola undervalue is the extent to which Italian Mafia men are ennobled. Subtle gestures convey important information; ideals of masculinity and femininity are stressed and sometimes questioned, and a hierarchical set of values is established. Much of this ideological work is present in the film's first scenes. As Bonasera, the undertaker, asks the Don for justice, the Don's face twitches with hurt when he asks Bonasera why he has not maintained contact with the Corleone family. When Vito meets with the singer Fontane, he asks him if he is spending time with his family, "because a man that doesn't spend time with his family can never be a real man." And when Bonasera offers to pay Vito for justice, one sees in the Don's face, his gestures, and later his words that he is disdainful of Bonasera's Americanized values.[33] This look into the world of Italian American culture allows Coppola to challenge Hollywood's Italian stereotypes (D'Acierno, "Cinema Paradiso" 607). Far from simply exploiting the spectacle of the gangster stereotype, Coppola probes the cultural background of his gangster characters in an effort to understand and explain the sometimes corrupted cultural values that drive their actions.

Gardaphé's criticism of the film's outdated masculinity is worth remembering. He writes, "Against the tempest of change stand the Corleone dons, tragic and violent versions of Peter Pan, upholding all that was traditionally manly for men who were afraid of becoming feminized" (*Wiseguys* 42). How else might we explain the Don's slapping of Fontane's face as he yells, "You can be a man" at the crying and aging singer? But while one hopes that this masculinity is outdated, one must remember that in the film it is often made attractive and even just, an ideal worth embracing. Herein lies the problem. Coppola is so intent on saving Italian American culture from the gangster stereotype that he romanticizes his vision of the culture to the extent that some of the culture's less attractive and less progressive aspects are embraced and lauded as superior to American values.

Vera Dika's analysis of the film is telling in this regard. Following Frederic Jameson, she argues that *The Godfather* represents "'Le Mode Retro,' or the Nostalgia Film" (92).[34] A consistent thematic concern with Old World ethnicity is complemented by the film's form, which cinematographer Gordon Willis describes as a "Kodachromy, 1942 kind of feel" (quoted in Dika 93). The formal interest in nostalgia is confirmed at the thematic level as a conservative response to the cultural environment in which the film was released. Dika suggests that men are in complete control in *The Godfather,* and as women struggle to gain power, the family declines. Additionally, the film responds to life in the post–civil rights era by offering a fantasy of "an all-white militant group, one that exists to the exclusion of all other races and ethnic Americans" (96). This view is perhaps oversimplified; viewers tend to sympathize with Diane Keaton's Kay, the modern non-Italian woman who marries into the Corleone family. However, since Kay remains a minor character, outside the inner circle of males, and since she too is white, one can see how the film opens itself to the political criticism that Dika offers.

Jacobson emphasizes a similar point when talking about Puzo's second novel, *The Fortunate Pilgrim*. He suggests that "such texts implicitly compare the 'mighty race' of yesterday's ghetto dwellers with the ghetto dwellers of today" (145). In the first *Godfather* film, the characters are never shown rising up from an ethnic ghetto, but it is clear that the family is not far removed from its immigrant roots. Despite only two references to African Americans (Vito's suggestion that members of the group are "animals" and Sonny's use of the *n* word at the family dinner table), the film is deeply concerned with race and plays largely into the politics of the White Ethnic Revival that Jacobson describes.[35] Only seven years removed from the widely published and accepted Moynihan Report, which labeled the African American family "a tangled web of pathology" (quoted in Jacobson 148), the film held up an ethnic Italian family as an ideal (despite all of its pathological criminal activity). Says Robert Towne, who worked as a script doctor on *The Godfather*, "In the seventies, when we felt families were disintegrating, and our national family, led by the family in the White House, was full of backstabbing, here was this role model of a family who stuck together, who'd die for one another" (quoted in Phillips, *Interviews* 181). The nostalgic representation of the ethnic family in *The Godfather* leads to a hierarchical world where white ethnic men are cemented in their prominent social position among the power elite. Whiteness has indeed been relocated from Plymouth Rock to Ellis Island, as Jacobson suggests, and an Old World notion of gender and racial hierarchies becomes the solution to the social unrest that characterized the late 1960s and early 1970s.

The Godfather, Part II

In *The Godfather, Part II*, the nostalgic portrait of the Corleones' Old World culture becomes potentially more attractive, especially when Michael distances himself from the Old World values that defined his father's life. *Part II*'s dual story lines exacerbate the differences between the paths Vito (Robert De Niro) and Michael take during their thirties.[36] Michael's path represents nothing less than the corruption of the "more admirable" lifestyle of his father, while Vito's decisions have intergenerational consequences that set the parameters for Michael's available life choices. Throughout *Part II*, Michael continues to believe his more Americanized values, which treat every aspect of his life as business and none as personal, will protect his family, only to find that they help him to lose it. As Lourdeaux writes, "Michael has followed the American success ethic at the terrible price of losing his Italian family" (189).[37]

But by the end of the film, Michael realizes that his Americanization and the path to his self-destruction had been laid long ago. After Fredo is killed, Michael recalls a surprise birthday party for his father on December 7, 1941. Against his father's wishes and those of Sonny and Hagan, Michael has enlisted in the marines. (This rift is hinted at in *Part I* when Michael attends his sister's wedding as a guest, wearing his military uniform, rather than as a member of the wedding party, wearing a tuxedo.) The scene's formal aspects emphasize Michael's break with his family's beliefs. When Tessio (Abe Vigoda) arrives with the Don's birthday cake, everyone except Michael gathers on the left side of the frame to admire it; Michael remains seated on the other side of the table, uninterested. Later in the scene, when everyone leaves the dining room to greet the Don, Michael stays behind. As the rest of the family members shout "Surprise!" Coppola offers a long shot of Michael smoking a cigarette, alone with his thoughts at the dining room table. From this episode, Michael flashes back even further to a moment from his childhood. As the dining room scene dissolves, the haunting *Godfather* theme fades in. Its sad tones and slow rhythm emphasize the film's and family's nostalgic yet tragic history. A long shot, which affords viewers a more distant view of Coppola's tableau, pans right to left to follow Vito and a toddler-age Michael as their train departs Sicily. Vito holds Michael up to the window and helps him wave good-bye. These scenes represent moments of departure, when the past was left behind. The next shot, and the last of *The Godfather, Part II,* is one of arrival. As the scene dissolves from the train into a medium shot of Michael, we find ourselves closer to the powerful Don. He sits in a backyard, alone once more, this time having killed off his enemies and alienated his allies. The warm earth tones of the first *Godfather* are replaced by cold grays, blacks, and muted browns. As the music fades out, leaving nothing but silence for several seconds, Coppola tracks into a tight close-up of Michael.[38] The music fades in once more, and the screen fades to black. Is Michael's fall from grace due to his inability to escape his father's influence, or is it due to the pressures that American capitalism places on individuals to assimilate and provide ever more wealth for their families?[39] As with most Hollywood movies, the audience has an opportunity to choose between two possible interpretations, so the film will have broad appeal.[40]

If Coppola is to be believed, the demise of Michael Corleone was the reason for his undertaking a second *Godfather* film. Coppola felt that he had condemned Michael and his actions at the end of *The Godfather* and was surprised when audiences seemed to walk away liking Michael. *Part II* offers a "manifestly more cold-blooded and cruel" Michael (Schumacher 111). He may be a victim of the Old World ties he has spent his life trying to escape, but he is also much more treacherous than his father and his fate is vastly different.[41] In *Part I,* Vito dies as a grandfather playing with his grandson. He lives a life of crime, but he maintains his family and friendships and garners the audience's respect. Michael is unable to do the same. As Coppola has said, Michael was "turning into a monster—not even as warm and as somehow loveable as his father who was also a monster" (*Part II* DVD commentary). The different actions Michael and Vito take and the different worldviews that motivate those actions become metaphors for two cultures, Italian and American. Their juxtaposition in *Part II* represents nothing less than a battle between two ways of seeing the world. The film's mythology seems to be that Italian culture, represented by Vito, remains an ideal, while American culture, represented by Michael, becomes a destructive force that separates families, undermines friendships, and confuses priorities.

Part II recounts Vito's escape from Sicily following the murders of his father, brother, and mother; his arrival in America; his hesitant entry into crime; and his ascendance to the head of a local criminal empire. From the beginning of the film, Coppola presents Vito as a reluctant hero, one who resorts to crime only because he is victimized first by America and then by the powers that be within his neighborhood. In the first image of Vito as an adult, Coppola works to establish a rather intimate relationship between the soon-to-be gangster and viewers by offering a medium shot of him leaning against a wall, looking down. Having established this relationship, Coppola dissolves into a longer shot of the same image, introducing Vito's domestic space. We see that he is in his apartment, staring at his newborn son. Coppola then develops his surroundings with another dissolve that takes us to an Italian play. We see the vibrant, ethnically exclusive environment of Manhattan's Little Italy in 1917. The dissolves allow the images to bleed into one another, creating a representation that integrates private and public space. At the play, we are introduced to the local Mafia boss, Fanucci (Gastone Moschin). Clothed flamboyantly in all white, Fanucci intimidates many, including Vito's friend Genco (Frank Sivero). The film cuts to a daylight sequence, tracking Vito as he walks across a busy street, lined with vendors and bustling with activity. Using a long take, Coppola offers a crowded mise-en-scène that emphasizes the intimacy of this community while establishing Vito as a hard worker who makes an honorable, modest living (fig. 13). One day, Fanucci comes to the store and forces the owner to fire Vito and hire one of his relatives. The shop owner is apologetic, but Vito understands. When his neighbor Clemenza (Bruno Kirby) asks him to hide a package in his home, Vito does, and by chance he falls into a life of crime. He realizes he can better provide for his family, and so he follows this illegal career path.

Fanucci threatens Vito's family once more when the mafioso requests tribute. Vito meets with Fanucci and refuses to pay the full amount. Emphasizing the intimacy of this negotiation, Coppola keeps both characters in each shot of the scene. After the meeting, Vito stalks Fanucci through the *festa* he is attending and murders him in the stairwell of his apartment building.[42] In order to stress the necessity of the hit, Coppola has Vito return to "sit in innocent pleasure with his family on the stoop, wife and three children joining him in a tableau that seems to encapsulate the immigrant folk memory" (Cowie, *Godfather* 183). In medium long shot, Santino and Mama hold American flags, while Vito holds Michael (fig. 14). Coppola cuts to a medium close-up

Figure 13. Vito Corleone (Robert De Niro), the hardworking family man, navigates the crowded mise-en-scène and intimate environment of Francis Ford Coppola's *Godfather, Part II.*

of Vito and Michael. In Sicilian, the patriarch tells his infant son, "Michael, your father loves you very much." Coppola ironically juxtaposes these two identities—Vito the murderer and Vito the hardworking family man—but Vito's ability to perform both identities effectively also sets a standard against which Michael is compared.[43]

Figure 14. The Corleone family immediately after Vito's murder of Fanucci in *The Godfather, Part II.*

As Cowie argues, Michael "seems more than a generation removed from the gentility of Don Vito" (*Godfather* 188). Both are mobsters, both have committed or at least ordered the executions of dozens of people, and both have been disingenuous. But Michael's relocation of the family to Lake Tahoe indicates that the social fabric of Old World values has been worn away by modernity. Whereas Vito walked the streets of New York, becoming an organic part of the ethnically exclusive neighborhood and recognizing that accessibility cultivates affection, Michael and his family are isolated and increasingly insecure.[44] His lavish, ostentatious mansion shows that he is more like a corporate leader or a tycoon than his father had been.[45] The beginning of *Part II* shows the logical outcome of Michael's satanic turn at the end of *Part I*. The communal feel of *Part I* is forsaken for a colder existence filled with family tension.

The party for Anthony's (James Gounaris) first communion seems out of place in the western states—a point emphasized by the band's inability to play an Italian song when a tarantella is requested, resorting instead to "Pop Goes the Weasel."[46] Despite a facade of discipline and restraint, the family is in disarray. Fredo, clothed in a shiny black, tan, and brown plaid tuxedo, has married a promiscuous woman who in a drunken rage speaks badly about him and Italians generally in full view of the communion party.[47] Connie (Talia Shire), wearing an ostentatious diamond necklace with matching earrings and a fur coat, has married several times and is currently engaged to an apparent gold digger. Michael is cold, removed, and ruthless in dealing with his family and his enemies. Even the family name "has gone from four syllables to three" (Haskell 24). In part, this state of affairs stems from the nature of the Mafia, a capitalist institution motivated by wealth. But the Corleones' situation is as much (if not more) about the family as it is about the Mob. For Vito, the Mafia had been a means to provide for his family. For Michael, business and family are often at odds. "He may tell Fredo never to put anyone else before the family," writes Lourdeaux, "but he himself lets business constantly get in the way" (191).

With no one allowed to challenge his decisions, Michael has become so obsessed with power that he pursues it blindly, unable to balance it with any other values. Throughout the film, he murders any individual who disobeys his orders. He sacrifices a prostitute to ensure the cooperation of Senator Geary (G. D. Spradlin). When an old family associate, Frankie Pentangeli (Michael V. Gazzo), testifies before a congressional committee, Michael has Pentangeli's brother flown in from Italy. Michael's unstated threat is not that he will kill the brother if Pentangeli testifies (as many suspect); rather, if Pentangeli ignores the code of silence (*omertà*), the brother as per Sicil-

ian custom will have to murder Pentangeli's family in order to save face
(Bondanella 259). Even after Michael has won, he persists in his violence.
He sends Rocco Lampone (Tom Rosqui) on a suicide mission to kill rival
gangster Hyman Roth (Lee Strasberg) in an airport hit reminiscent of Jack
Ruby's assassination of Lee Harvey Oswald. Federal officers kill Lampone,
a loyal and longtime associate of the Corleones, as he attempts to flee the
scene. And, of course, at the end of the film, Michael orders the murder of
his older, weaker, less intelligent brother, Fredo.

For Michael, any challenge to the family business is treated the same
whether it comes from an old enemy, an old friend, a new brother-in-law, or
an older brother. Unlike Vito, murder is not a last resort. As Cowie suggests,
"The men killed by Don Vito 'deserve' to die. Michael's victims all possess a
certain sympathetic quality—Fredo, Frankie, Hyman Roth. . . . Coppola is
not appalled by Vito's point-blank shooting of Fanucci, but he recoils with
loathing from even the most discreet of Michael's murders. Vito possesses the
courage to carry out his own executions. Michael never soils his hands with
blood. He issues orders, condemns his victims with a nod to his bodyguard"
(*Coppola* 102).[48]

Coppola's desire to differentiate Michael's values from those of Vito seems
to have affected the editing of the picture. Many of the deleted scenes (included on the *Godfather* DVD box set) depict instances that would have challenged the film's romanticized vision of Vito.[49] In them, Vito steals dresses,
refashions weapons, and kills two aged henchmen of Don Ciccio (one as he
sleeps in a cellar and one as he fishes). In *Part I*, Coppola cut a scene where
the Don becomes aware of Hollywood producer Jack Woltz's sexual relationship with a young teenager. The Don is appalled, but his decapitation of
Khartoum does nothing to protect the young girl from the producer's sexual
perversion. In an earlier version of the *Part I* script, available in *The Godfather
Notebook* at the American Zoetrope Research Library, Coppola included
a scene that depicted the assault on the two men who attacked Bonasera's
daughter. Coppola wrote, "Just as we are coming to love and be fascinated
with the old man and what he stands for, we are given another side of it, and
though we see some justice in it, we are repelled. . . . I feel we should see the
Don right after the violence—he is responsible for it" (n.p.). Each of these
scenes makes the relationship between Michael's and Vito's monstrosity less
distinct as even the locales of Vito's murders are echoed by Michael. (Fredo
is executed while he fishes, and Hyman Roth is almost suffocated by one of
Michael's henchmen as he sleeps.) Drawing clear lines between father and son
may help the audience to recognize the film's condemnation of Michael, but
it also lauds Vito and the Mafia of the past as somehow more honorable.

Coppola's conflict between Vito's and Michael's values harks back to a tension at the center of many of Capra's films and the very idea of capitalism itself. When is enough enough? When does the pursuit of wealth threaten other values that should be preserved? Given the historical context, Vito is able to better negotiate these tensions and reach a sense of balance in his life. Everything Vito does seems to be for the sake of his family and community, and for Coppola, these are the ideals that characterize Italian culture. Michael believes that what he does is for the good of the family, but in the social atmosphere of mid-twentieth-century America, even criminal business is larger than family, and Old World values have begun to disappear. When Connie embarrasses herself at Anthony's communion, for instance, Michael is furious because of the way her actions challenge his power as a don in control of his family. Michael thinks his wealth and power are a way to ensure harmony and security within his family, but they are not. As a result, he destroys his family, while thinking he is saving it, or, in the words of Bondanella, "one 'family' destroys the other" (261).

Michael is in one sense the personification of post–World War II America, but Coppola gives us a pessimistic view of the nation. Michael has an Ivy League education, a distinguished war record, powerful allies, looks, and wealth—yet he fails. In Coppola's words, "He wins every battle; his brilliance and his resources enable him to defeat all his enemies. . . . [But] there's no doubt that by the end of this picture, Michael Corleone, having beaten everyone, is sitting there alone, a living corpse" (quoted in Phillips, *Interviews* 27).[50]

Despite its criticism of Michael, who becomes a tragic character, *The Godfather, Part II* strengthens the nostalgia for the Old World culture of ethnic Italians. Many factors could be seen to contribute to the decline of the film's ethnic family. But Michael's willingness to run the business like a modern-day corporation, searching for the easiest way to ensure profit and power with little concern for the human lives that will be affected by his decisions, is of primary importance. But just as in the first film, an implied endorsement of Old World cultural values has problematic implications for gender and racial relations in the United States. Here the choice is given much more clearly to viewers. Either they can endorse Michael's worldview that (intentionally or not) prioritizes business over family. They can live in a world where women struggle for equality, leave their husbands, and have abortions. They can be represented by a government that is corrupted and has little power to bring the leaders of crime syndicates to justice. Or they can endorse Vito Corleone's worldview, which features a paternalistic and seemingly altruistic form of crime—a world where individuals not protected by the government can go for help, where family and community are balanced, where everything, including murder, is performed in a more personal way, where gender roles are clearly defined and men work while women take care of the children, and where those in power all come from the same racial group.[51]

The family is always in jeopardy, regardless of the values espoused by the patriarch. Sons die. Assassination attempts are made on the ruling boss, and old friends betray the family. However, despite Vito's criminal pursuits and despite his unintentional limitation of Michael's options, the Don's leadership carves out a space for a loving family life. Whereas Michael suppresses his emotions, relegating all decisions and relationships to the same standards of logic he uses in his professional life, Vito recognizes the difference between his two families and makes room for his emotions at least in his private life.[52] However, both worlds remain inequitable, with women relegated to a subordinate status, which they largely accept in the first film and resist unsuccessfully in the second.[53] In the fifteen years that separated *Part II* from *Part III,* Coppola seems to have increasingly recognized the challenge of female independence. In the third installment of the series, he creates strong female characters who mildly challenge the established gender hierarchies of the first two films and hence question the nostalgia that had defined *Parts I* and *II.*

The Godfather, Part III

Part III's Michael is a man in search of redemption. He has failed to achieve his goal of legitimizing the Corleone family, probably because his criminal pursuits promised greater financial returns and because getting out of the Mob is not as easy as he would like to believe. He is wealthier and more influential than he was in *Part II,* but he has begun to recognize that he may have lost his soul in the process. Coppola has said, "Although [Vito] was in all this jeopardy he was at peace, because although he had done terrible things somehow he had managed to outwit the devil. He had managed to emerge though a murderer and a gangland leader and obviously a person who—you would have to say—[is] an evil man—he managed somehow to have us feel he was a good man" (*Part III* DVD commentary). And so, *Part III*'s Michael once again tries to live up to the standard set by his father.

In an effort to secure his salvation, Michael works to gain a majority share in Immobiliare, the Vatican holding company. Facing a cash shortfall, the Vatican wants to avoid a corruption scandal, and Michael believes his investment will legitimize the family business and save him.[54] He pursues three goals to achieve these ends and atone for his past actions. First, he attempts to negotiate the tricky politics of extracting the Corleone family from Mob life without getting himself or his family killed. Second, he tries to secure a leadership role within Immobiliare, which requires that Vatican officials consent to having a known mobster in their ranks. Third, he struggles to reconcile with Kay, from whom he has been estranged for several years. Michael fails in each of these pursuits.[55]

By the end of the film, rather than extracting the family from criminal activities, Michael has transferred power to his illegitimate nephew, Vincent Mancini (Andy Garcia). Seemingly legitimate businessmen whose maneuverings are just as Mob-like as those of Senator Geary, the Barzinis, the Tattaglias, and the Cuneos reject Michael's bid for a leadership role in Immobiliare.[56] When hit men hired to kill Michael end up assassinating his daughter, Mary (Sofia Coppola), one assumes that Kay and Michael's reconciliation is impossible. Michael dies an old man, alone in a courtyard, surrounded only by dogs. (In Italian, "May you die as a dog" is a curse that means to die alone, outside of your family.) And while Cowie argues that Michael has "suffered long and hard and paid for his sins" (*Godfather* 142), Michael might think that he is just beginning to pay for them.

Coppola has said that his understanding of the term *Mafia* is one that speaks "to the highest level of power operating on their own clandestine terms" regardless of their Italian background or the nature of their criminal pursuits. Under this definition, "the White House," "the Quirinale," and other legitimate organizations are grouped together with the Corleones' criminal enterprise and become "the *real* Mafia" (quoted in Cowie, *Coppola* 236). And so, *Part III* is to some extent an attempt to extend the central metaphor of *Part II*. The Mob is representative not just of a postwar American culture but also global history, where the exercise of power and the attainment of wealth have always been associated with deception, illegalities, and murder. Michael's famous line from the film, "Just when I thought I was out, they pull me back in," is ironic, because what he realizes is that there is no getting out. "The higher up I go," he says to Connie, "the more crooked it gets." Even if the family secures the veil of legitimacy he desires, they will still be deploying the same tactics they always have, just in a different venue.

A series of scenes that comment on the earlier films further develops this theme. In *Part III*, Mancini stalks Joey Zasa (Joe Mantegna) during a Little Italy *festa*, much like Vito stalked Fanucci in *Part II*. *Part III*'s opening scene echoes the sacramental family gatherings at the beginnings of *Parts I* and *II*, but while the family is returned to New York, the entire party takes place inside Michael's luxurious apartment rather than the outdoor settings of traditional Italian gatherings. In *Part II*, Vito watches in horror as Don Ciccio (Giuseppe Sillato) and his men kill his mother; in *Part III*, Michael watches in shock and then screams in horror as he holds his dying daughter.

In each of these scenes, the Corleone clan has fallen from the nobility that characterized Vito. Mancini begins an affair with his cousin and Michael's daughter, Mary, and the two trade stories or myths about their family. Mancini tries to emulate his grandfather, but he is too brash and interested in celebrity to be considered "the new Vito." His hit on Zasa, for instance, is not carried out secretly. Instead, he enlists several soldiers in a public ambush that disrupts the entire religious festival and exposes innocent men, women, and children to violence. The new dons are common thugs who have entered a life of crime enthusiastically, hoping to attain wealth, sexual gratification, and celebrity status. If they have families, they are, for the most part, absent from the film.

Dika argues that this representation works to undermine the nostalgia of the first two films, and no doubt that was Coppola's intention. But it is arguable whether the film is successful in this endeavor. Before Puzo died, he outlined a screenplay for *The Godfather, Part IV,* in which viewers would see Vito's ascendance to power (*Coppola and Puzo*). In discussing the project, Coppola describes a film that would resemble the structure of *Part II,* where Sonny would be the main character in one story line with Vincent Mancini anchoring the other. Sonny's story line would follow "the happy years [when] the Don reaches his zenith" (Coppola), whereas Vincent's story line would chronicle the fall of the family as it becomes more involved in the cocaine trade. Juxtaposing the rise of Vito to prominence, which among other things might chronicle the Don's association with Brasi, with the demise of the Corleone empire may have worked to undermine the depiction of a grandfatherly don and a benevolent family. If such a film were to be produced, Dika's contention might be strengthened, but without dismantling the myth of Vito as a benevolent murderer, the nostalgia of the first generation will never be undermined. Zasa and Mancini may show the Mob as the dishonorable, self-serving enterprise that it is, but viewers are left with the sense that it was different in Vito's time, that the traditionalism of Old World culture could still bring a sense of order and security to the world, and that the Mob is no different from more legitimate organizations like business or the church.

The trilogy's concluding film fails to dismantle the nostalgia of the earlier installments, but at times, it minimally challenges their traditional gender norms. In the first two *Godfathers,* women are marginalized and relegated to a subordinate position. Men assault them, lie to them, and disparage the ways that their emotions get in the way of business. Cindy Donatelli and Sharon Alward observe, "There are stretches of as long as almost forty minutes when the screen is completely controlled by men" (65). Women enjoy more high-key lighting, but, overall, they "are rendered invisible" (Donatelli and Alward 62). In *Part III*, women are still subordinated to men, but Kay can challenge Michael's controlling parenting and have him relent (and then express his gratitude) and Connie assumes a more powerful position within the family. In a preproduction discussion with Puzo and Pacino, Coppola said Connie had "become something of a Caporegime herself" (*The Godfather* Materials, Workbook, SJ2). Rather than deferring to Al Neri (Richard Bright), Connie asserts herself and acts as the don during Michael's hospitalization, approving Mancini's hit of Zasa. Despite Michael's anger, the hit is successful and works to consolidate power for the Corleones. At the end of the film, Connie becomes an assassin herself, presenting her godfather and surreptitious Corleone betrayer Don Altobello (Eli Wallach) with a poison-laced cannoli (fig. 15). From the Corleone box at a Sicilian opera house, she watches Altobello through her binoculars. Close-ups of Connie are juxtaposed with medium shots of Altobello—her body language simultaneously conveying a sense of accomplishment, regret, and resignation as Altobello ingests the poison unknowingly and then succumbs to its effects. The meek wife who endured her husband's assaults in *Part I* becomes a smart, calculating, and effective Mafia assassin in *Part III*. But this is a tragic fate for Connie and one to be lamented, because in order to become strong, she must become a criminal boss like the men before her. Connie rebels against the traditionalism of her father and brothers, only to play a pivotal role in attempting to protect the family.

Figure 15. Connie Corleone Rizzi (Talia Shire) executes her first Mob hit by presenting a poison-laced cannoli to her godfather, Don Altobello (Eli Wallach), in *The Godfather, Part III*.

The Ethnic Individual and the Assimilative System

Over the course of approximately twenty years, the story of *The Godfather* evolved considerably, but the films' nostalgic, idealized image of Vito Corleone was never dismantled or fully challenged. Vito is the key to Coppola's ambivalent embrace of Old World, ethnic Italian culture. By painting the Don as a loving family man whose actions were motivated by the best interests of his family rather than a self-serving desire for wealth or fame, Coppola created a mythical image that resonated with an American culture reeling from social upheaval and military defeat in Vietnam. By the release of *Part III,* America's global supremacy seemed more secure, but Coppola had begun to question the cost of that supremacy. His *Godfather* films continued to interrogate the assumption that criminal undertakings are solely the acts of individuals working on the margins of society and suggested that the Corleones' sins were not much different from those of supposedly legitimate institutions like the church, government agencies, and elected officials.

But although Coppola may scrutinize and interrogate American culture, the films tend to embrace Old World Italian culture despite the inequalities and prejudices that are an important and unattractive aspect of traditional Old World views.[57] In this way, the films diminish the negative and imprisoning potential of the culture that Savoca and Scorsese emphasize.[58] Perhaps Coppola's intention is not to endorse but merely to depict these norms as a fact. However, his mother and sister have both complained about the Coppola men's occasional insensitivity toward and ignorance about women (Gardner and Gardner 181). Says Talia Shire of the Coppola family, "My job as a child was to set the table in my male family. I wasn't allowed to talk" (quoted in Werner). The Coppolas' experiences are not that different from those of many other Italian Americans, and they need to be questioned. Otherwise, in our nostalgic pursuit of an imagined past, we may begin to believe that inequitable gender norms offered and continue to offer a sense of security worth preserving.

Jacobson writes that the images found in films that represent immigrants' experiences "do not resurrect memory, they have become it" (77). If this is the way history is created, as the memory of a past where the sanctity of the family was given primacy in a hierarchy of values, where "white assimilability is celebrated," and where a focus on the family and crime allowed ethnic others to rise out of poverty and into the middle class, then what are the implications for contemporary race and gender politics (175–76)? The implicit message is that individuals must adapt to their environment, no matter what. Whether it is Vito's entering a life of crime to provide for his family or Connie's engaging in murder to have a voice in the family, individuals tend to prosper who assimilate (at least partially) into the culture that immediately surrounds them (though not necessarily the dominant national culture). But the *Godfather* films also give us several characters who refuse to assimilate. Vito resists selling drugs in *Part I* until he is outvoted. Kay resists Michael's wishes in *Part II* and *Part III,* and Michael's son, Anthony, forsakes his father's wishes and leaves law school to become an opera singer.

Ultimately, then, the *Godfather* series, like most Hollywood movies, is much more about the individual than the system, and so the systemic critiques at which the films hint are underemphasized. The *Godfather* films encourage viewers to judge Vito, Michael, and others not just by the actions they take but also by the motives that they have. Both Michael and Vito Corleone are murderers, but what separates them is whom they murder, why they murder, and how quickly they resort to murder. Vito operates his criminal empire intimately, valuing community and personal relationships over excessive wealth. Michael believes that through dominance, he can extract the family from the criminal world. By becoming the system, he can escape it. Only characters like Anthony resist the pull of history, becoming successful noncriminals, but one wonders if Anthony's choice—law school or opera—is available to many. Still, Anthony succeeds by loving his father without bowing to his will.

But this character-centric perspective becomes problematic. The *Godfather* films may be the most nuanced depiction of Italian ethnicity to appear on American movie screens, but by privileging individual motives and actions, the films create a past that does not encourage changing the sociocultural and economic systems that promote assimilation. Indeed, even if characters want the system to change, they are usually powerless to do it. As a result, the films (perhaps unintentionally) encourage an acceptance of the status quo, a situation that in the films' mythology created the need for the Mafia in the first place, and they offer the hope that individuals, even Mob bosses, can be redeemed if they make the right choices for the right reasons. In Quentin Tarantino's films, the mythologies of *The Godfather* (and other movies) become the basis of characters' identity performances.

5 Quentin Tarantino

Ethnicity and the Postmodern

"Butch, I got something for ya," says *Pulp Fiction*'s (1994) Captain Koons as he sits down in front of a young boy whose TV viewing he has interrupted. He holds up a gold watch and proceeds to recount its history as a family heirloom. Bought by Butch's great-grandfather just before he entered World War I, the watch became a wartime good-luck charm and a postwar keepsake that was passed to the next generation of Coolidges when Butch's grandfather entered World War II. Before he was killed, Butch's grandfather asked a man he had never met before to deliver the watch to his infant son, and so the watch passed to its third generation of Coolidges. Butch's father wore the watch during the Vietnam War, but when he was taken prisoner, he worried that the Vietnamese would take it away. "So, he hid it," Koons says, "in one place he knew he could hide something . . . his ass." After living like this for years, Butch's father died of dysentery, and Koons "hid this uncomfortable hunk of metal up my ass two years. After seven years, I was sent home to my family. And now, little man, I give the watch to you." The young Butch's hand pops up from the bottom of the screen and snatches the watch. Undeterred by the unpleasant aspects of the story (at which most viewers laugh), Butch is anxious to feel some material connection to a father whose presence in his life has been defined mostly by stories.

"When I saw *Pulp Fiction,* the little boy watching the big TV, being alone in the room, the TV being his friend—to me that's Quentin," says Steve Buscemi (quoted in Charyn 11). But the young Butch and Quentin Tarantino share more in common than a friendship with television; both seem desperate to connect with an absent father. In Tarantino's case, the father is Tony Tarantino, an Italian American whose liaison with Tarantino's Irish

Cherokee mother, Connie Zastoupil, ended before he learned of Connie's pregnancy. Thus, while he carries his surname and is therefore marked as an Italian American, Quentin Tarantino has never met his father.[1] His work and his life become interesting case studies on what it means to be Italian American today. Is Tarantino, despite his lack of any interaction with his father, Italian American? Is Tarantino, who grew up in an ethnically mixed environment rather than an exclusively Italian American neighborhood, still connected to Italian American culture? Is being marked with an Italian American last name enough to secure one's Italianness? Can we base one's ethnic identity solely on genetic makeup? And through what other avenues can ethnic identity be communicated, understood, and felt today?

When *Playboy* asked Tarantino what the difference between a New York Italian and a Los Angeles Italian was, he responded, "There really is no such thing as a Los Angeles Italian. In New York, there are Italian neighborhoods. In Los Angeles there aren't. There is no ethnicity here. You just are who you are. Of course, most of that Italian stuff is learned from movies like *Mean Streets* anyway" (Rochlin 32). Tarantino's willingness to frame Italian ethnicity as an empty signifier is evident not only in his public comments but also in his movies, where Italian American ethnicity becomes a kind of costume that can be put on and taken off at will. Such an ironic representation is typical of Tarantino's cinema, but his critics have charged that this offers irresponsible, socially regressive, and shallow treatments of important social, cultural, and political issues like ethnicity and violence. These commentators worry that if such matters are loosed from their sociocultural and historical moorings, they threaten to become merely aesthetics.[2]

At root, many of the criticisms leveled at Tarantino represent larger concerns with life and art in the postmodern era. Following Todd Gitlin, film scholar Dana Polan agues that postmodernism is "a culture of surfaces," where viserality is rendered "so intense that it substitutes for all concern with deep meaning" (77). Critics charge that this is evident in Tarantino's films, which they judge as shallow and apathetic and which they say pale in comparison to the works of Scorsese.[3] Scorsese's violence, Toby Young asserts, "grows out of character and is essential to the dramatic arc of the story," while Tarantino's violence is there "for no better reason than because he thinks it's cool" (13).[4] Ultimately, this leads to one of two conclusions: either Tarantino believes cinema is powerless to change the world, or he does not care about the transformative potential of film and prefers instead to focus on style.[5]

Still others question the originality of Tarantino's movies. After noting the similarities between the narrative of *Reservoir Dogs* and that of *The Killing*

(Stanley Kubrick, 1956) and the violence of Tarantino's debut with that of John Woo's movies, Jeff Dawson asks, "When does *homage* end and plagiarism begin?" (88–89).[6] And Ian Penman saddles Tarantino with the label "*The Man Who Mistook A Video Collection For His Life*" (126).[7] Such views undermine the complexity of Tarantino's work and reduce him to a kind of one-trick pony who has forged an entire career on pastiche. Tarantino's movies are not just about movies, but even if they were, they would still have interesting things to say about art, the human condition, and ethnic cultures, and they would still carry political leanings worth investigating.

Tarantino's difference from previous Italian American directors is due in part to his upbringing, but it is also the product of his historical moment and his politics, which at least early in his career were oftentimes more conservative than they might have appeared at first. As widespread prejudice against Italian Americans has waned, their position within the social hierarchy of American society has offered them a greater diversity of historical experiences. In the film industry, they have attained a position where their Italianness has become less visible (and potentially less damaging). As a result, they have benefited from the privileges and anonymity of whiteness and enjoy more artistic flexibility. This has made some Italian Americans less sensitive to the continued social importance of ethnicity, but it has also put them in a position of power from which they can work against the institutional prejudice leveled at ethnically othered groups.

For Tarantino, previous movies become the raw material from which he crafts new messages, and these messages reveal the role that media productions have played in this artist's understanding of his ethnic self.[8] Early on, Tarantino's films were insensitive to the complexities of race in the United States. Between 1992 (*Reservoir Dogs*) and 1997 (*Jackie Brown*), Tarantino's dismissal of his own ethnicity was belied by his use of Italian American characters, his references to Italian American directors, and his obsessive concern with father figures (which likely springs from his personal background).[9] What resulted was a playfully postmodern engagement with Italian American ethnicity, in which cultural background became a performance that was easily accessed by any individual familiar with pop-culture products. Over the course of his decades-long career, his treatments of ethnicity have evolved into something more palatable.[10] The infamous *n* word, for instance, has not appeared in a Tarantino movie since 1997's *Jackie Brown,* and his prolific quotations (especially in *Jackie Brown* and *Kill Bill: Volume 1*) of films produced by ethnic others (and previously targeted at nonwhite ethnic audiences) have a decentering effect, reaching beyond the Eurocentric culture of the West.

The man who was once rather insensitive to ethnic issues has become a pop cosmopolitan. Through his films, he works to overcome past prejudices while complicating and challenging his previous notion that race or ethnicity is merely an act used for affect and of little "real" social consequence.

Identity as Performance

Unlike Scorsese, Savoca, and Coppola, Tarantino has never offered a character who is clearly Italian American, and his movies do not focus on immigrant and immigrant-like characters in the way that Capra's do. However, his films still present important views on the meaning of ethnicity and race in the postmodern era, and these views are often bound up with his willingness to see identities of significant social consequence as merely performative. To some extent, identities are always performed, but by suggesting that an individual could cross ethnic and racial barriers with an effective performance (as he did in his 1990s films), Tarantino forwarded a controversial racial and ethnic politics. Nevertheless, Tarantino's interest in performance is not relegated just to the ethnic and racial others in his films. Instead, it becomes a vital aspect of each of his characters' efforts to survive and succeed.

At the same time that his films were investigating performative issues, the director himself skillfully played the role of celebrity filmmaker and built his critical reputation. Today, few call his auteur status into question, even though his output seems meager when compared to other auteurs like Scorsese and Coppola. Tarantino's fragmented narrative style, his over-the-top violence, and his witty dialogue on all things popular culture are some of the unique characteristics that have come to define his movies. But it is also true that he, like many of the other filmmakers discussed in this volume, is a tireless self-promoter whose knowledge of critical trends has guided his choice of projects. A "big fan" of film criticism, Tarantino has said, "Pauline Kael was as much an influence on me if not more of an influence than any other filmmaker" (quoted in Dawson 176). His knowledge of the field stretches beyond the United States and has contributed to his popularity throughout the world. Japanese *yakuza* films, Melville's *policiers,* Italy's new Mafia movies, and Hong Kong's Triad gangster pictures have all affected Tarantino, and he has expertly translated his celebrity auteur status into commercial success. The director tends to keep his budgets low while using his name to sell his films. In fact, Harvey Weinstein was known to label Miramax "The House That Tarantino Built" (Carradine 132).

Onscreen, Tarantino's movies consistently investigate the possibilities, limitations, and implications of performances. This recurrent thematic concern relates to Tarantino's own ethnic background. Despite his Italian, Irish, and Cherokee roots, Tarantino often claims that he felt most closely tied to African American communities because of the neighborhoods in which he grew up. "Don't let the pigmentation fool ya," the director has said. "It's a state of mind" (quoted in Charity 152). This willingness to see the world as a stage where individuals can act whatever part they desire is mimicked in his films, which often highlight their own theatricality.

At the beginning of the *Kill Bill: Volume 1* preview, for instance, Tarantino emphasizes the film's "movie-ness" by including his own voice calling "Action." Uma Thurman's multiple identities as the assassin named the Black Mamba, the loving mother of her daughter, B. B. Kiddo, and the small-town wife and record-store employee Arlene Machiavelli not only underscore the wildly divergent performances that one individual can enact (Biderman 200–201) but also work to undermine the sense of familial normality that might otherwise accompany *Volume 2*'s final scenes (LeCain n.p.). B. B.'s loving parents are also professional killers who want to see each other dead.

In *Pulp Fiction,* form highlights the film's concern with theatricality. When Jules (Samuel L. Jackson) and Vincent (John Travolta) arrive early for a "hit," Tarantino emphasizes the performative aspect of his characters' identities. In the middle of a long take that lasts almost three minutes, Jules and Vincent walk away from their targets' apartment door and the camera, moving from a medium shot to an extreme long shot. They continue their "offstage" conversation about foot massages while the camera waits "onstage" by the apartment. Eventually, their conversation concludes, and Jules says to Vincent, "Let's get into character." They walk back past the camera—back onto the stage—with their closer proximity revealing the murderous scowls on their faces (Alleva, "*Pulp*" 31).

In *Reservoir Dogs,* Tarantino explores the ways in which a reliance on performance can isolate individuals from one another. This theme is crystallized in the seven-and-a-half-minute "commode story" sequence. Cutting across six different locations and recounting police detective Freddy Newendyke's (Tim Roth) adoption of his undercover identity, the sequence is expertly crafted. As Newendyke becomes more convincing in his undercover role, the camera becomes his ally. At first, it is suspicious of his story, recognizing it as a lie. When Newendyke enters the frame, it ignores him by refusing to follow him around his apartment. Eventually, however, the camera becomes absorbed in what Newendyke is saying. It begins to follow him with pans, then it tracks closer to him as he tells his story, and finally it visualizes events that never happened. The camera comes not just to enjoy the story but also to assist Newendyke by showing viewers the undercover cop's fictitious narrative.

Dogs' foregrounding of performance was not lost on critics. In his review, Richard Corliss wrote, "The sequence reveals how we all must be perform-ers, acting for our lives" ("Adding Kick" 96).[11] But it is not just this sequence that forwards that idea. *Reservoir Dogs* tells us very little about its characters' backstories, and so the ability to put on a good performance or tell a good story becomes the primary means by which one establishes his or her identity and bona fides.[12] What results for the characters is a level of anonymity that protects them should the police apprehend one of their colleagues, but a degree of alienation accompanies this apparent refuge. Anonymity prevents the formation of a community built on a shared knowledge of past actions or experiences. Anything the Dogs put forward or are told must be treated with suspicion and uncertainty. The recognition that it all may be a perfor-mance undermines the possibility of strong relationships. Like *la bella figura* in *Mean Streets,* the posturing leads to isolation, but in Tarantino's film, this results from professional obligation rather than cultural mores.[13]

The exception is the bond that develops between Mr. White and Mr. Or-ange. Both men reveal their true identities to one another, a decision that would be judged "irrational" by those around them. This exposes White and Orange to danger, but they find the possibility of forming a bond with another individual more attractive than the protection that isolation makes possible.[14] Because the other Dogs are unwilling to discuss their pasts or their lives outside of the job (Travers, "Critics' Commentary"), they rely on stories and interpretations of movies, television shows, music, and fictional characters to define their own identities and establish connections with one another. Through these conversations, they formulate acceptable masculine norms (Dargis 11), including their feelings on loyalty, betrayal, and aggression (Levy, "Critics' Commentary"). Like the real-life mobsters who began to imitate the language of *The Godfather's* cinematic gangsters, Tarantino's characters mimic the identities of fictional criminals and antiheroes. In Tarantino's own life, the movies appear to have played a similar role, especially since his father figures were an inconsistent presence.

Italian American Roots, Father Figures, and the Performance of Masculinity

Tarantino's repeated investigation of flawed relationships with father figures seems to descend directly from his own absent Italian American father.[15] In *Pulp Fiction,* Butch Coolidge (Bruce Willis) grows up without a father, cling-ing to his dad's watch as a material stand-in. In Tarantino's first script, *True Romance* (Tony Scott, 1993), Clarence Worley (Christian Slater) maintains a distant relationship with his dad, Cliff (Dennis Hopper). When they reunite, viewers learn that Clarence has not spoken with his father in three years and that when Clarence was younger, Cliff would sometimes disappear for years at a time. The relationship between White (Keitel, whom Tarantino has called "the father I never had" [Kennedy 30]) and Orange represents a surrogate father-son relationship, ending in filicide.[16] White, an older male, schools Orange, his young understudy, in the ways of crime and intimidation and protects him from others who would do him harm. Beatrix Kiddo's relationship with Bill (David Carradine) in the *Kill Bill* movies (2003 and 2004) also carries parental overtones. Once again, an older, more experienced male character nurtures his young protégée, teaching her to be a more effective and mature professional. But, once again, their relationship is dysfunctional. The series begins with Bill shooting Beatrix, who is pregnant with his child, in the head. In the script for (though not the film of) *Inglourious Basterds* (2009), Frederick Zoller (Daniel Brühl), "the German Sgt. York," recounts how his father left the family. Even the relationship between Gil Grissom (William Petersen) and Nick Stokes (George Eads) in the *CSI: Crime Scene Investigation* (2005) episode that Tarantino directed echoes these portrayals of flawed paternal relationships.[17] Yet again, an older male character looks after a less experienced, younger character who shares the elder's professional interests and some of his personal proclivities.

Critics have identified this interest in father figures as one of Tarantino's recurrent thematic concerns.[18] Jami Bernard even argues that it is *the* subject that defines Tarantino's movies. But Tarantino has said that if absent fathers are a key to his cinema, it is something of which he is unconscious while writing (Bernard 20). Still, he grants that growing up without a father forced him to "go looking for [his] father in other places" and that these places often ended up being the movies (Bernard 20–21). In effect, Tarantino looked to the movies to learn what it meant to "be a man," and his cinematic work interrogates various models of masculinity by examining the need for and place of violence and loyalty within these social structures.

Tarantino's search for agreeable and effective masculine norms often led him to films directed by Italian Americans. In *True Romance,* Clarence's masculine redemption closely resembles Travis Bickle's redemption in Scorsese's *Taxi Driver.*[19] Rather than simply paying homage to one of Tarantino's favorite films, *True Romance* is deeply indebted to the earlier picture and oftentimes seems to be commenting on it.[20] Clarence's attire when he goes to free Alabama (Patricia Arquette) from her pimp, Drexl (Gary Oldman), resembles Bickle's attire when he confronts Iris's (Jodie Foster) pimp, Sport (Harvey Keitel). Both men wear green jackets that look like military fatigues (fig. 16 and 17). Furthermore, Alabama's reluctant profession as a prostitute traces its roots to Scorsese's film. But it is *True Romance*'s performances of masculinity that reveal *Taxi Driver*'s influence most clearly. Tarantino has said, "Somebody said to me [*True Romance*] sorta picks up where *Taxi Driver* left off" (quoted in Dawson 106–7), suggesting that Clarence remembers scenes from *Taxi Driver* that not only allow him to envision Drexl speaking repulsively about Alabama but also lead Clarence to kill Drexl. As Tarantino says, "It's not because he's ever met a pimp in his life, it's just because of what he's, like, seen in the movies" (Dawson 106–7). In essence, Clarence has learned "how a man acts" from the movies he has seen.

Although Clarence's masculine redemption may be tied to Italian American culture through Scorsese, Cliff's masculine redemption is signified through a monologue about Sicilians. After their three-year estrangement, Cliff and his son reconcile in a scene that Tarantino has labeled "the single most autobiographical scene I've ever written" (*True Romance* DVD commentary).[21] Cliff learns that the police do not suspect Clarence and Alabama of murdering Drexl, and the young couple drives off to start a new life together. The next day, a quintet of gangsters assaults Cliff, but he refuses to talk. The gangsters torture him, and eventually Cliff responds with a controversial speech about Sicilian bloodlines that makes use of the *n* word (a topic to be discussed later). The monologue draws Vincent Coccotti's (Christopher Walken) ire, and he executes Cliff before he can learn Clarence and Alabama's whereabouts. Soon,

Figure 16. Travis Bickle (Robert De Niro) sits with a rattled Iris Steensma (Jodie Foster) after murdering her pimp in *Taxi Driver*.

Figure 17. Clarence Worley (Christian Slater), looking like *Taxi Driver*'s Travis Bickle, sits with a rattled Alabama Whitman (Patricia Arquette) after murdering her pimp in *True Romance*.

one of the gangsters spots the runaway couple's address on Cliff's refrigerator, and the gangsters continue their pursuit. Cliff seems to have failed, but he has succeeded and performed his masculinity admirably. He stares down his captors with bravery and panache and attempts to sacrifice his own life for the survival of his son and his son's new bride. In the eyes of the film, Cliff has been redeemed because of his loyalty and selflessness.

True Romance is a deeply personal script, and Tarantino has repeatedly acknowledged that Clarence was his stand-in in the film. But Tarantino has written other scripts that resonate with him personally, too. "If you really knew me," he says, "you would be surprised by how much my films talk about me" (quoted in Ciment and Niogret 88).[22] Critics and rival filmmakers often criticize the director by arguing that his movies are not about life but rather movies.[23] However, the lines between real life and the movies are no longer (and probably never were) as clearly drawn as this position suggests. For Tarantino, the movies *are* life. They played an essential role in the establishment of his identity and in allowing him to understand himself. They also became one of his teachers of masculinity.

Violence, Homage, and the Playfully Postmodern Ethnic

For Tarantino, masculinity is closely connected to the use of violence, and several writers have criticized the director for the violent imagery in his movies. Henry Giroux, for instance, suggests that a filmmaker plays a pedagogical role in American and global culture and "should be recognized as a type of cultural worker" (311). He chastises Tarantino, arguing that *Pulp Fiction* and similar movies "do not rupture or challenge automatically the dominant ideologies that often justify or celebrate violence in real life" (309). Giroux frames Tarantino as an unethical filmmaker whose use of violence is socially irresponsible.[24] Others suggest just the opposite. Barnes and Hearn point to *Reservoir Dogs,* asserting that "the ever-growing pool of Orange's blood . . . is a constant reminder of the director's responsible and realistic approach to de- picting brutality" (27). Using the adjective *realistic* to describe a fictional film is always a questionable choice. Still, Barnes and Hearn's willingness to see more than shock value and homage in Tarantino's violence is commendable.

Sometimes Tarantino uses violence to advance his thematic concerns or implicate the audience in the on-screen action. Many of the most violent scenes in his movies are not shown at all. They occur in the minds of viewers when the camera pans away from police officer Marvin Nash (Kirk Baltz) while Mr. Blonde/Vic Vega (Michael Madsen) slices off his ear, or when viewers turn away themselves as Vincent Vega necessarily but aggressively plunges an adrenaline shot into an overdosing Mia Wallace's (Uma Thurman) heart.[25] As Paul A. Woods says of Tarantino's violence, "It's what's implied that is more than some people can bear" (*King* 45), and Valerie Fulton goes even further, arguing that Tarantino's implied violence "asks the viewer to confront her complicity with those who produce images of violence" (178). In effect, by "completing" the violence, the viewer becomes the producer of the violent imagery. In *Inglourious Basterds,* Tarantino picks up on this theme. When a Nazi soldier refuses to cooperate, Lt. Aldo Raine (Brad Pitt) and his platoon are ecstatic. "Actually, Werner, we're all tickled to death to hear you say that," Raine says. "Quite frankly, watchin' Donny beat Nazis to death is the closest we ever get to goin' to the movies." For Raine (and Tarantino), the representation of violence is one of the thrills of moviegoing.

Movies taught Tarantino about masculinity and the role violence plays in that social construct, but they also developed his understanding of ethnic and racial identities. This aspect of his work is perhaps most apparent in the homages his films make. Despite charges of unoriginality or shallowness, the knowledge of pop culture exhibited by Tarantino's characters serves a real nar- rative function: it helps audience members to feel connected to them. "This is the kind of stuff most of us actually do spend much of our time talking about," writes Amanda Lipman, "and it puts us on a level of understanding with the characters" (51). So Tarantino's movies engage issues like violence and ethnicity in a "language" with which his audience is familiar and comfortable.

This obvious reliance on pop culture, especially in *Pulp Fiction,* has led some to focus almost exclusively on the postmodern aspect of Tarantino's work.[26] Graham Fuller has even gone so far as to brand Tarantino as a "*post-post-modern*" auteur, suggesting that many of his references "themselves spring from earlier incarnations or have already been mediated or predigested" (Peary 49–50). *Pulp Fiction* is said to have roots in everything from *Huckleberry Finn* (Page 110) to "postwar Italian fashion" (Barnes and Hearn 143).[27] Even the film's promoters were quick to recognize the film's influences. "I have this really eggheaded theory that it's like the ultimate postmodern movie," said Miramax publicist Cynthia Swartz, "because it takes fifty years of film and pop culture history and synthesizes it into something new" (quoted in Bernard 240).

The film and the time at which it was released (when I and millions of other college students were venturing onto the World Wide Web for the first time) encouraged an obsessive concern with cinematic details: What was in the briefcase? Why had many of the clocks in the film stopped? What would the narrative(s) look like if it (they) were pieced together chronologically? Which movies were being referenced when?[28] Most critics marveled at the film. "You don't merely enter a theater to see *Pulp Fiction*," wrote Janet Maslin. "You go down a rabbit hole" (C1). After *Pulp* was nominated for seven Academy Awards, Miramax arranged an advertising blitz that included hiring film scholar Thomas Schatz "to write an essay linking *Pulp* to its roots in forties film noir" (Bernard 239).[29] But even today, it is rare that we consider what all these references mean on anything more than a grand theoretical level as it relates to postmodernism. As a result, the ethnic implications of Tarantino's homages have been ignored. Just as there is more at stake than a simple laundry list of similarities and differences in Scorsese's quoting of Italian cinema, so too is there more at stake in Tarantino's quoting of previous Italian American films.

The Italian roots of *Pulp Fiction* run deep. Woods suggests that Mario Bava's *Black Sabbath* (1963) inspired Tarantino's initial ideas for *Pulp* (*King* 101).[30] But the films of Coppola, Scorsese, and other Italian American filmmakers also influenced the movie. By way of narrative situations, formal techniques, and iconography, Scorsese, Coppola, and others are not only present within *Pulp Fiction* but also used to introduce an ethnic Italian American aspect to Tarantino's work even though the world of *Pulp* seems far removed from the ethnically specific worlds of *Mean Streets* and *The Godfather*.

Pulp Fiction references Coppola frequently. In the Jack Rabbit Slim's sequence, Dawson identifies a poster for *The Young Racers* (1963), a Roger Corman–directed picture on which Coppola worked as a soundman (160). More significantly, *Pulp* is steeped in references to the *Godfather* films. Gavin Smith suggests that Winston Wolf (Harvey Keitel) resembles Vito Corleone "down to the pencil moustache and hair" (114).[31] And Edwin Page argues that when Marcellus (Ving Rhames) meets Butch, Vincent, and Jules in his club, he also resembles the Don (117). Noting similar scenes in *Reservoir Dogs* and *True Romance,* Page argues that Tarantino is trying to link his characters "with the stereotypical, Italian gangsters depicted in Coppola's film" in order to "cause audience members to recognise even more clearly how different [his] characters are from those usually seen in the genre" (117). Tarantino is certainly citing Coppola, but rather than distancing himself, Tarantino's homage is an effort to establish a community of sorts with the films and filmmakers he has loved throughout his life. By referencing their movies, he links his narratives with theirs and gives their characters a life after their original cinematic appearances. Essentially, Tarantino expands the characters' life spans and simultaneously coauthors their cinematic existence.

The scene in which Koons gives the gold watch to Butch references Italian American Michael Cimino's film *The Deer Hunter* (1978). Walken's role as Koons, a military officer and Vietnam vet who endured traumatic events and imprisonment during his tour, clearly echoes his role as Nicky in the earlier film, but it also resurrects a character who had died in a Russian-roulette scene some sixteen years before. Tarantino enacts a kind of collective wish fulfillment by bringing back to life a sympathetic character who was victimized by his youth and his government while using humor to ameliorate the disagreements caused by one of the most divisive historical events of the second half of the twentieth century. Cimino may have been trying to achieve the same goals, minus the humor. Through homage, Tarantino becomes a part of a community that includes the films, fictional characters, and filmmakers that he admires, while establishing a community with his audience with whom he shares a collective cultural experience.

Similarly, Travolta's presence, especially in the Jack Rabbit Slim's dance contest, resurrects *Saturday Night Fever*'s (John Badham, 1977) Tony Manero and *Grease*'s (Randal Kleiser, 1978) Danny Zuko (fig. 18). After entering the 1950s-style diner, the camera follows Travolta and Thurman to their table with a steadicam long take that invokes Scorsese's similar shot of Henry and Karen Hill at the Copacabana in *GoodFellas*. As Chumo writes of Tarantino's scene, "As this man walks through the restaurant with celebrity look-a-likes all around him and B-movie posters on the walls, he is both Vincent Vega, heroin-shooting hit man marveling at the spectacle so alien to him, and John Travolta, celebrity icon seeing how icons of an earlier era are recycled for their nostalgic value" (77). Travolta's star status is not concealed here. The actor is not lost in the character. Instead, Tarantino works to make both the star and the character present, adding another layer to the film, and investing in the body of Travolta multiple identities.[32]

Figure 18. John Travolta/Vincent Vega/Tony Manero/Danny Zuko dances in Quentin Tarantino's *Pulp Fiction.*

When Travolta and Thurman take to the dance floor, Travolta's previous roles are even more present. Tarantino insists that he thought of the scene before he thought of casting Travolta (Ciment and Niogret 85), and Woods traces the scene's roots to Godard's 1964 film *Bande à Parte* (*King* 113), which includes a scene where the narrative essentially pauses so that the film's characters can perform a playful dance.[33] However, neither of these points weakens the screen persona of Travolta or the effects that his presence has on an audience. As Mia and Vincent recycle dance crazes from the twentieth century, audience members are amused not just by the silly skillfulness of the dancing (an influence of the Godard film), or their own memories of performing these dances, but also by the resurrection of two lovable characters from late-1970s cinema in the form of a now aged, less agile John Travolta. "For whatever reason, people get so excited when I dance," Travolta has said. "I'm a heroin-addicted hitman with a gut. It never ceases to amaze me, but at least I didn't have to wear white polyester" (quoted in Dawson 188).[34]

Whatever Vega's ethnic background, his identity now becomes melded with that of Manero and Zuko (and to a lesser extent *Welcome Back Kotter*'s [1975–79] Vinnie Barbarino).[35] Essentially, he becomes Italian American in this scene (if he were not already) by way of the characters of Travolta's past and Travolta's own identity as a real-life Italian American.[36] The director's previously outlined concern with performance enhances the effect. Viewers can see Manero, Zuko, Vega, and Travolta all at once.

While Tarantino's cinematic references to Coppola, Cimino, and Travolta have garnered attention, his work is more often compared to that of Martin Scorsese.[37] Actors who have worked with both directors often link their directorial styles, and critics also draw comparisons.[38] The *Village Voice,* for instance, labeled *Reservoir Dogs* "*GoodFellas* minus girls"; others saw the same film as "a new *Mean Streets*" (Dawson 70).[39] Complementing their similar working styles, stylistic consistencies, and shared thematic preoccupations are a series of direct references to Scorsese's pictures. Tarantino's references to *Taxi Driver* and *GoodFellas* have been previously outlined. But he also digs deeper into Scorsese's oeuvre when the characters in *Pulp Fiction* discuss how to properly administer a lifesaving shot during a near drug overdose. A similar conversation takes place in Scorsese's obscure 1978 documentary, *American Boy: A Profile of Steven Prince* (Dawson 181).

Given these references, it is no surprise that Tarantino was dubbed "the new Scorsese" as early as 1994 (Bernard xiii). Tarantino seemed to encourage such assessments prior to *Reservoir Dogs,* but after the release of his debut, he seemed to feel an anxiety of influence.[40] "Like him, I like mixing fast-cutting scenes and more deliberate ones, and I'm very particular with the frame," Tarantino said in 1992. "But he's almost a stone around young filmmakers' necks. So many new films are aping Scorsese. I don't want to be a poor man's Scorsese" (quoted in Peary 29). After the release of *Pulp Fiction,* Tarantino continued to recognize the similarity between his cinema and Scorsese's but resisted the idea that he was simply recycling Scorsese's work:

> I make a point of not talking about Scorsese any more because everyone else does when they talk about me. I think it's unfair, but I understand it completely. I mean, here's the deal: Scorsese deals in the gangster genre; so do I. Scorsese makes violent films; so do I. Scorsese moves the camera around a lot; so do I. Scorsese uses Harvey Keitel, I use Harvey Keitel. Scorsese is a big film buff, I'm a big film buff. I mean, so what? One guy even said, you use the f-word a lot: did you get that from Scorsese? Occasionally, they'll make a good critical analogy but mostly it's all pat and easy. What matters is that the end result is so different. (quoted in O'Hagen 65)

Tarantino's insistence on the distinctiveness of his cinema is justified. He does not just recycle Scorsese. Both have their own thematic concerns, but even when their concerns overlap, the perspectives they offer frequently diverge. Among other things, Tarantino does not share Scorsese's interest in Catholicism, guilt, and sin (O'Hagen 66), and television's and Hong Kong cinema's influence on Tarantino distinguishes his work from that of Scorsese and other filmmakers of that era (Peña quoted in Bernard 212). Even on violence, an issue to which both filmmakers return, the perspectives offered are quite different. Of Tarantino's ironic treatment of brutality, Scorsese says, "I *couldn't* do what Quentin does. He does it *so* beautifully. I couldn't do it. They're not the same kind of people in his films and my movies" (quoted in

Kaplan 40). Scorsese's films tend to feature characters who cannot escape their histories and ethnic, geographic, or spiritual ties. Tarantino's characters rarely have backstories; when they appear onscreen, they have already escaped their upbringings in a way Scorsese's characters rarely, if ever, do.

Tarantino's tendency to quote western pop culture continues in *Kill Bill: Volume 1,* where he references not only Scorsese and Coppola but also two other Italian American filmmakers: his favorite director, Brian De Palma, and himself, Quentin Tarantino (Page 187).[41] The most prominent quotations of De Palma occur in the scenes between Beatrix Kiddo and Elle Driver (Daryl Hannah). By invoking the split-screen aesthetic that De Palma used so effectively in *Sisters* (1973), Tarantino draws the two adversarial characters into a more intimate rivalry.[42] Used in both *Volume 1* and *Volume 2,* the technique enhances the impression that Elle and Beatrix not only look alike but also have similar histories with Bill and similar desires as they relate to each other. Given Elle's uncertain fate (she is badly injured but still alive when we last see her) and Beatrix's miraculous recovery from being shot in the head, one wonders if the split-screen technique foreshadows a future cinematic showdown between the two blonde warriors.[43]

Tarantino's quotations of his own work abound in *Kill Bill,* particularly in *Volume 1.* Uma Thurman outlines an imaginary square with her finger as she discusses her pursuit of revenge with Vernita Green (Vivica A. Fox). Thurman draws a similar shape in *Pulp Fiction* when she tells Vincent not to be a square.[44] When Thurman's Beatrix awakens from her coma, she performs the action in a manner similar to her awakening from a near overdose in *Pulp Fiction.* Even the character Thurman's Mia Wallace played on the failed *Fox Force Five* television pilot (Raven McCoy) seems "very similar to the Bride in the Vernita Green sequence" (Charyn 133–42). Tarantino's use of Thurman as an echo of his previous use of the actor in a prior film is replicated in his casting of Michael Parks and James Parks. In *Volume 1,* Michael Parks plays the character of Earl McGraw, a Texas Ranger sent to investigate the Two Pines massacre. Parks plays the same role in the Tarantino-scripted *From Dusk till Dawn* (Robert Rodriguez, 1996). Similarly, Parks's son James plays Earl's son Edgar in *From Dusk till Dawn* (Page 191), and both actors reappear in the same roles in Tarantino's *Death Proof* and Robert Rodriguez's *Planet Terror,* the two installments of *Grindhouse* (2007).

In a slightly different intertextual strategy, Tarantino continues to use actors whose presence (like Travolta's in *Pulp Fiction*) invokes previous media productions. David Carradine as Bill reminds viewers of Carradine's Caine from the TV series *Kung Fu* (1972–75) and also of *Pulp Fiction,* when Jules tells Vincent that he plans to walk the earth "like Caine from *Kung Fu*" (Holm

87). The director's use of mise-en-scène complements the self-referentiality of his casting. Most obvious, perhaps, are the costumes of O-Ren Ishii's gang of swordsmen who dress in mostly the same attire as the Dogs from *Reservoir Dogs* and Jules and Vincent from *Pulp Fiction* (Charyn 146).

By referencing Scorsese and invoking films like *GoodFellas* (which are so tied to an Italian American milieu), by drawing on Travolta's star image and lived experience to make Vincent Vega Italian American, and even by quoting his own films, which draw on prior Italian American characters, themes, and environments, Tarantino introduces an Italian American aspect to his own cinema. But how much of an issue and what kind of Italian Americanness is it? Tarantino's representation of Italian American ethnicity through the lens of pop culture mimics one of the main avenues through which white ethnicities are learned and understood today. Ferraro writes, "It is through art and, increasingly, in the wake of the fourth generation, only through art that we come to know and to deal with what it means to feel Italian still in America" (*Feeling* 2). Ferraro's "reconstructive rather than deconstructive" cultural studies offers a more inclusive view of Italian American ethnicity, where one need not be able to claim a genetic ethnic heritage in order to "feel" some sense of community with a given culture (3, 7–8). He writes, "Italian American self-understanding and the portrayal of Italians in American culture at large, then, moved closer together, to the point where the feelings Italian Americans have for themselves, the feeling non-Italians have for Italian Americans, and the feeling they both have for the role of Italianness in America intertwine and interpenetrate: almost—but not quite!—one" (4). What Ferraro describes, and what Tarantino enacts, is one way of being Italian in the postmodern era. But this perspective or strategy privileges the consumption of pop-culture products over lived experience. Tarantino's understanding of ethnicity is solely a commodified one. As a result, it seems quite shallow to some, because it is dislodged from "real-life" experience.

In an essay that predates the release of *Reservoir Dogs* by one year, Vivian Sobchack discusses what she labels "postmodern modes of ethnicity." In an earlier time, she asserts, ethnic communities were more "coherent" and "relatively stable" (332). But by the early 1990s, "we are also part of a society which experiences the particularity of celebrity more intimately than it does the coherence of community. In this context, nearly all those visible markers that once separated the cultures of 'ethnic' descent from the 'American' culture of consent, that signaled the boundaries of otherness and gave it ethnic identity, integrity, and authenticity, are detached from their original historical roots and have become 'floating signifiers' available for purchase by anyone. Ethnicity, too, seems based on consent" (333). Sobchack may have overestimated the extent to which "the boundaries of otherness" had broken down, but her assertion that the nature of ethnicity had changed is correct. Many believed (or continue to believe) that they could access and construct their own ethnic identities "through pastiche or parody, through a scavenging or playful ironizing of those costumes, speech, and manners that once were held separate and discrete and that conferred upon a portion of the culture's members their particular identity, history, and sense of community" (Sobchack 333). Such was the environment in which Tarantino began his career and developed his early ideas about race and ethnicity. Disconnected from his own Italian American ancestors and heritage, Tarantino grasps at his Italian ethnicity through the Italianness and real-life experiences of other filmmakers like Coppola, Scorsese, and Travolta.

The Performance of Race and the Establishment of Whiteness

By the release of *Jackie Brown,* Tarantino's views of ethnicity and race had generated considerable discussion, and nothing was more controversial than his use of the *n* word. Throughout his career, Tarantino had used the word liberally. It appeared in *True Romance* when Cliff Worley recounted how the Moors' invasion of Sicily supposedly changed the appearance of Sicilians forever. Tarantino had also used it in *Reservoir Dogs.* Then, in *Pulp Fiction,* he cast himself as Jimmie Dimmick and proceeded to use the word four times in his first minute on-screen.[45] In *Jackie Brown,* the word appeared again, and a viewer decided to confront Tarantino. Following the premier screening at Britain's National Film Theater, an unidentified black male rose, professing his enjoyment of the film, but he said, "You just can't get away with all those offensive 'nigger' references." Tarantino paused and then responded, "Well, I do," grinning as the audience applauded and laughed (quoted in Hattenstone 160). Perhaps Tarantino had grown tired of being asked about this issue, or maybe he worried that his work would be reduced to it, but whatever the case, it is clear that he had fundamentally misunderstood or resisted the point of the man's question.[46] The audience member was concerned with what was socially responsible rather than what was socially possible.

Tarantino had been asked to respond to critics who targeted his use of the word before, and his responses often worsened the situation by revealing his muddled understanding of racial issues. Speaking of *Reservoir Dogs,* for instance, he said, "The thing is, do I think these guys are true racists? No. I just think they're a bunch of guys getting together and talking a lot of shit. There's a difference there. Do I think, you know, when Mr. White says a couple of things in the movie, do I think Mr. White thinks that blacks are like lesser human beings than him? No, I don't. The main thing these guys are coming from is that they don't look at blacks as professionals in their job, alright. They rob liquor stores. Now if there was like a black guy, say, a gunman that they trusted, they'd be different" (quoted in Dawson 73). If racism is making decisions about people based on their race, then looking at blacks, *all* blacks as this quotation implies, as nonprofessionals is racist. Tarantino's logic was fallacious. He was basing his claims that his characters were not racists on a flawed understanding of racism.[47]

Jim Smith has offered a more lucid defense of Tarantino's artistic choice. Smith suggests that Tarantino feels comfortable using the word because he "sees himself, and his work, as essentially post-racist." Smith writes, "Growing up where he did, around the people he did, he saw the word used in a variety of contexts and clearly came to feel, or always felt, that it had transcended its original American usage as a derogatory term used by whites against blacks in exactly the same way that the far less controversial 'boy' (when used to describe an adult) has." In a later statement, Smith seems to contradict himself when he asserts that the word's use "reflect[s] on the characters who use it, not the writer who wrote the words for the characters to say" (103). Even though Smith's writing leaves readers wondering if the word should be attributed to Tarantino or his characters, his argument is far more compelling than the usual "well, Sam Jackson thinks it's okay, so it must be all right" line of reasoning that dominates much of the discussion of Tarantino's use of the word.[48] Such a perspective relies on the idea that Jackson, because of his profession and ethnicity, can pass judgment on the word's use for an entire culture.

The problem with Smith's position is that the United States is not a postracial society, and neither Tarantino's films nor his authorship can be removed from that context.[49] As Sharon Willis writes, "What [*Pulp Fiction*] forgets to remember is that the social forces of words cannot be privatized, that it cannot cite the word 'nigger' outside a context formed by its enunciative conditions, which include the author's social location as well as the word's history" (212).

Beginning with *Jackie Brown*, Tarantino's use of the *n* word shifted.[50] In the film, only black characters use it. In recent years, this trend has continued.[51] In fact, a white character has not uttered the *n* word in a Tarantino film since *Pulp Fiction*. Put simply, the racial identity of the characters who use the word (or the authors who write it) significantly affects the word's context and therefore its meaning. Historically, whites have used (and some continue to use) the word to enforce racial hierarchies. That history surrounds whites' use of the word, even if those who use it do so with the best of intentions or artistic motivations. However, when blacks use the term, it has the potential to serve as an act of reclamation and empowerment. The word's previous use as a slur that is or was deployed to enforce hierarchies *may* transform into a sign around which those with a shared history of prejudice and discrimination can form a community. And so, while Tarantino's use of the *n* word was insensitive early in his career, its altered use or absence in his later films marks a turning point in his thinking.

Still, the racial politics of Tarantino's movies goes beyond his use of this single (admittedly important) word. Overall, his movies offer a quite complicated conception of race and ethnicity. For instance, some of his films may suggest that language, accent, and clothing can overcome racial and ethnic difference, but they also recognize that the ethnic and racial performances that characters enact can distress others and therefore that ethnic individuals are judged based on their appearances and mannerisms. As a result, Tarantino's films explicitly represent social anxieties about race (Willis 211). Nevertheless, this view highlights an individual's ability to don ethnic masks in personal conflicts while ignoring the persistence of systemic prejudice against nonwhite minorities. So Tarantino's films, essentially, reverse the power dynamics usually associated with ethnic hierarchies in the United States; ethnic minorities often appear to hold greater social power, because they can perform identities that intimidate others. Jules's performance of an aggressive masculinity in *Pulp Fiction,* for example, seems to be aided by the social anxieties surrounding black men. White characters like Brett (Frank Whaley) shirk away from Jules not just because he is armed but also because they fear the angry black male stereotype.[52]

Jackie Brown focuses on African American characters and the systemic obstacles they face more than any other Tarantino movie. In adapting Elmore Leonard's *Rum Punch,* the writer-director changed the film's title character from white to black, and the change helps the movie. As Edward Gallafent has said, Tarantino is able "to suggest, much more forcefully than if the role were filled by a white woman of the same age and history, both the difficulty of starting over and the gravity of the threat of failure" (94). Pam Grier, who played the film's title role, concurs: "The casting had nothing to do with colour blindness. A black woman has more political obstacles. She can walk into a store and the guards will wonder if she's a shoplifter. A white woman wouldn't get that attention. So it's social and political consciousness. . . . [Jackie] has more obstacles. With the ATF, the LAPD. She's not a senior flight attendant living in a beautiful townhouse on the beach, she's living on $16,000 and benefits. She should be on another economic level" (quoted in Charity 157).

The implications of race and racial identities permeate the film. In a line Tarantino added to the original source material, Ordell Robbie (Samuel L. Jackson) questions Max Cherry (Robert Forster) about why he has a picture of himself and Winston (Tommy "Tiny" Lister), a large African American man, hanging on his wall. "It was your idea to take that picture too, wasn't it?" Ordell asks. Even if some viewers are more sympathetic to Cherry, the film encourages them to confront the racial connotations and stereotypes associated with blackness. Winston may be Max's associate, but he is also a black man who is, in Devon Jackson's words, "big, cool, macho, not to be fucked with, able to wreak havoc on folk because it's in [his] 'nigger' genes" (quoted in Barnes and Hearn 125–26). The film may allow viewers to dismiss Ordell as a racist (or the oddly labeled "reverse racist"), or as someone who sees racial implications in situations where race is supposedly not an issue.[53] Nevertheless, *Jackie Brown* as a whole is more sensitive to and intelligent on racial issues than Tarantino's earlier work.

During the film's promotional tour, Tarantino continued to offer totalizing views of black and white audiences and even labeled *Jackie Brown* "a black film made for a black audience."[54] But he also drew attention to the history of prejudice in Hollywood by reminding viewers of *MTV Live* that no black actress had ever won a Best Actress Academy Award (to that point).[55] During the same appearance, he referenced several 1970s blaxploitation films and suggested that the character of Jackie Brown represented the evolution of Grier's Foxy Brown. This educated viewers and encouraged them to seek out these films. By exposing middle- to upper-middle-class white audiences (who unlike many of their working-class counterparts could afford basic cable) to movies once targeted at primarily African American viewers, Tarantino's film and promotional efforts carried progressive potential.[56] They could help to break down some of the racial barriers of the past.

Throughout his career, Tarantino has often spoken about how he went to an all-black school, how all his friends were black, how his mom had black boyfriends, and how all her friends were black.[57] Nonetheless, in *Jackie Brown*, he seemed to realize that class background was an important dimension of that bond. Speaking of the film's main character, Tarantino said on *MTV Live*, "[Jackie's] stuck in what a lot of people in this country are stuck in, where they're working to starve basically." The director's movies had always featured working-class characters or at least characters from working-class backgrounds, but with *Jackie* he showed that even individuals from the same class were divided and treated differently based on racial differences. As Grier observes, Jackie *does* face more obstacles than she would if she were white.

It is worth noting that Tarantino's so-called blackness is disconnected from any of the prejudice (institutional and personal) that typifies the experience of blacks, particularly black men, in the United States. Tarantino's white skin (not to mention his celebrity status) allows his supposed blackness to be optional.[58] Throughout his life, the director has been able to emphasize or de-emphasize, embrace or shed, aspects of his ethnic background when it has suited his interests. Even though he is one-quarter Cherokee Indian, his father's Italian name has granted him the air and privileges of whiteness, allowing him to avoid the preconceptions that might have accompanied his Native American heritage. Had his skin tone been darker, things may have been different.

For Tarantino, unlike nonwhite filmmakers, his whiteness is normative, and his movies can be all about aesthetics. As Ella Taylor writes, Tarantino "can afford to be the spokesman for art without politics. He's a straight, white male working in a genre that can do no wrong at the box office" (47). Taylor overstates the profitability of crime films. Like all movies, they too can fail commercially. Nevertheless, her recognition that Tarantino's racial background, gender, and sexuality allow him to more easily distance himself from political content is well considered. Despite his claims, Tarantino's films are very political. His cinematic style and the politics it carries have led Hattenstone to observe, "Despite appearances, there is something very conservative about Quentin Tarantino" (161). But as with most Hollywood films and filmmakers, Tarantino's politics are not so easily classified.

The *Kill Bill* Situation: How to Feel Ethnic without Being Ethnic

In his *Kill Bill* movies, Tarantino expanded his quotations of Asian and European cinemas.[59] Like his efforts in *Jackie Brown* to expose white audiences to blaxploitation films, this technique exposed mainstream American audiences to productions made by and previously targeted at nonwhite ethnic groups. As a result, the *Kill Bill* films work against cultural isolation and allow for cross-cultural influence. They also complicate Tarantino's racial politics by using homage to counter some of Hollywood's racially determined practices. For years, what was defined as "good" tended to be created by artists who were "white" and male. Other perspectives were judged "inferior," but these "inferior" movies are often the ones Tarantino quotes.[60]

In clothing O-Ren Ishii's Crazy 88, Tarantino added black masks to the now familiar costume of black suits, white shirts, and black ties (fig. 19). According

Figure 19. Gordon Liu as Johnny Mo in *Kill Bill: Volume 1* sports the now familiar Tarantino uniform (black suit, white shirt, black tie) with an added touch—Bruce Lee's Kato mask.

to Page, the masks refer to "Kato, a character played by Bruce Lee in the TV series *The Green Hornet* (1966–1967), the music for which is actually used in [*Kill Bill: Volume 1*]'s soundtrack" (198).[61] Tarantino's reference to a Bruce Lee character from an American television series introduces a Chinese American aspect to his work, but the director does not stop there.[62] He also adds Hong Kong to the mix with the yellow-and-black jumpsuit that Kiddo wears in *Volume 1*—a clear reference to *Game of Death* (Robert Clouse, 1978), one of Lee's Hong Kong productions. By including a Hong Kong reference in one of *Kill Bill*'s Japanese sequences (it takes place in Tokyo), Tarantino risks offering the impression that he is ignoring the cultural diversity that exists under the umbrella term *Asian*. In *Volume 2*, he ameliorates this feeling. When Kiddo studies under Pai Mei (Gordon Liu), the Chinese master draws clear distinctions between the linguistic and martial arts traditions of his culture and those of the Japanese, especially when his pupil seems to equate the two.

Tarantino's sensitivity to ethnic and cultural issues was also apparent in his casting of the film. The character of Pai Mei had appeared in numerous Hong Kong films, and several different actors had played the role. Initially, Tarantino was training to play the Chinese master in *Volume 2* (Carradine 44), but he later decided to cast Liu. If Tarantino had kept the role and the dialogue remained the same, the film's racial politics would have been complicated. Tarantino would have appeared in some form of yellowface, holding court on the conflicts between "his" culture (Chinese) and that of the Japanese. Liu, on the other hand, is a Chinese actor and an icon of Hong Kong action movies. Included among his credits is *The 36th Chamber of Shaolin* (Chai-Liang Liu, 1978), a film in which Liu's character, San Te, fights Pai Mei. (He had also played the samurai sword–wielding Johnny Mo of O-Ren Ishii's Crazy 88 in *Volume 1.*)

Similarly, when Tarantino cast Lucy Liu, the daughter of Chinese American immigrants, as Ishii, he demonstrated a degree of sensitivity that is not typical of Hollywood. According to the director, Ishii was "not going to be American. She was going to be Japanese—full-on Japanese from Japan," but when Lucy Liu took the part, Tarantino decided to change the character to "half-Japanese, half-Chinese, Asian American" (*The Making of Kill Bill*). Tarantino's willingness to alter the character toyed with Hollywood's tendency to equate all "Asian" ethnic groups. In a far more characteristic move, *Memoirs of a Geisha* (Rob Marshall, 2005), a studio film released several years after *Volume 1,* cast Malaysian actor Michelle Yeoh, Chinese actor Li Gong, and Hong Kong actor Kenneth Tsang in Japanese roles. In their casting, Hollywood films often group all "Latins" together as well. Puerto Rican American Jennifer Lopez and Colombian American John Leguizamo, for instance, are often cast as Italians.[63] This willingness to collapse ethnic difference is not always detrimental, since it has the potential to stress the similarities among individuals from different cultures. However, in some cases, particularly when it relates to racial minorities, these casting choices can help to perpetuate and even create the cultural ignorance that flattens the diversity within racial groups and sees all Asian and Latin American cultures as the same. An individual can be from the same *race* and still have a different *ethnic* background.

Tarantino's respect for the cultural diversity of Asia is complemented by his love of Chinese, Hong Kong, and Japanese films.[64] Not only does he make repeated references to their cinematic traditions, but he has also been a strong advocate for the U.S. distribution of films from these countries. In 1995, he formed Rolling Thunder Pictures to do just that. Not long before Tarantino's ascendance to stardom, Hollywood films mocked the poor dubbing and "cheap" aesthetics of Asian movies. Then Hollywood action-film aesthetics began mimicking those of Hong Kong movies. Hollywood studios began remaking Japanese horror films like *Ringu* (Hideo Nakata, 1998). And numerous Hollywood movies, from *The Last Samurai* (Edward Zwick, 2003) to *Lost in Translation* (Sofia Coppola, 2003), began taking a strong interest in Japanese and other Asian cultures.[65] Tarantino's work, along with the success of films like *Crouching Tiger, Hidden Dragon* (Ang Lee, 2000) and *The Matrix* (Wachowski Brothers, 1999), helped to open the door for new kinds of films and filmmakers. As both a filmmaker and a celebrity cinephile—that is, on both a textual and an extratextual level—Tarantino has helped to expose audiences to a more diverse set of cinematic perspectives.

In *Volume 2,* with the notable exception of the Pai Mei sequence, Tarantino's references shift from Eastern to Western. Allusions to Italian filmmaker Sergio Leone's spaghetti westerns come in the form of the film's "more widescreen-languorous and contemplative" nature (Clark quoted in Page 219) and its soundtrack, which features music from Leone's 1966 film, *The Good, the Bad, and the Ugly* (Page 218). In bringing Eastern and Western cinematic traditions so close together, the *Kill Bill* films forward an argument of "harmonious co-existence and balance" (Page 201).[66] Far from being dissonant, the styles are "complementary" (201). And perhaps this is the value of Tarantino's cinema. Through his movies, he has become a global sophisticate of sorts and envisioned a more tolerant class of filmgoers. His movies carry the potential to break down some of the barriers that have sprung up as a result of ethnic, racial, and class prejudice by introducing viewers from racially, ethnically, and class-dominant groups to cultural products once deemed inferior or at least interesting only to a limited audience.

Nevertheless, a familiarity with pop-culture products cannot be equated with actual experiences of prejudice. If we allow homage to be the only determinant of ethnic identity, our understanding of these socially significant categories would become very shallow indeed.[67] Still, the sheer form of Tarantino's cinema says quite a lot about race and ethnicity and the ways in which those social identities are learned, lived, and understood in the postmodern era. For many today, ethnicity (particularly white ethnicity) may not be as connected to a specific historical experience as it once was, but then being ethnic (Italian American or otherwise) regardless of historical era cannot be reduced to an essentialized understanding of identity. This is not to suggest that we live in a posthistorical world. Rather, it is to recognize that there are always multiple ways to understand and perform one's ethnicity.

The Limits of Performance and *Inglourious Basterds*

Inglourious Basterds marked another shift in Tarantino's cinema. Whereas *True Romance, Reservoir Dogs,* and *Pulp Fiction* had (to varying degrees) suggested that individuals could transcend ethnic and racial barriers by enacting effective performances, *Inglourious Basterds* contends that one's actual ethnic background greatly aids or restricts his or her ability to perform different identities. The leader of the Basterds, Lt. Aldo Raine (Brad Pitt), who is part Apache but not Jewish, restricts membership in his unit to willing "Jewish— American—soldiers."[68] Raine implies that Jews have a more personal connection to the Holocaust than non-Jews and that some might have a more visceral and violent hatred of the Nazis. Thus, ethnic background in tandem with historical events carries a social and emotional value that is difficult to re-create with a mere performance. *Basterds* also hints that Raine has confronted situations where violent racism was directed at him personally. In the script, Tarantino writes, "Lt. Aldo has one defining physical characteristic, a ROPE BURN around his neck. As if once upon a time, he survived a LYNCH-ING. The scar will never once be mentioned" (18). Given the ethnically (and sometimes sexually) charged nature of lynching, one can only assume that the scar resulted from a run-in instigated by Raine's Apache heritage.[69]

Later in the film, three members of the Basterds (including Raine) impersonate Italian filmmakers in order to infiltrate a Nazi film premiere. As they speak Italian with terrible accents, they wear what the script labels "goofy spaghetti bender smiles" (134). Nazi colonel Hans Landa (Christoph Waltz) exposes the Basterds' plot and captures Raine and Utivich (B. J. Novak). In the film, as Landa converses with the two captured Basterds, he mentions "your *paesanos,* Sergeant Donowicz and Private Omar," and calls them "your two Italian saboteurs." The script went even further, with Landa asking the Apache American Raine, "Italian? Really? What could you have possibly been thinking?" Raine responds, "Well, I speak alittle Italian—" To which Landa replies, "I speak a little Tagalog, but I wouldn't begin to presume I could pass for Filipino. Don't get me wrong, I understand you were in a pickle, what with you losing your Germans. And I have nothing but admiration for improvisation. Still . . . Chico Marx is more convincing. If the three of you had shown up to the premiere dressed in woman's attire, it would have been more convincing" (142). Once again, the film demonstrates that some barriers cannot be crossed by a performance.

During an interview with Brad Pitt and film critic Elvis Mitchell, however, Tarantino talked about how effective linguistic performances during World War II might allow an individual to cross enemy lines. "World War II was the last time a whole bunch of white people fought a whole bunch of other white people," Tarantino says. "So, you have a situation that if you can pull off the lingo, if you can pull off the language, you could survive in an enemy territory. You could infiltrate a different army" ("Roundtable Discussion").[70] The Basterds' recognition of this fact drives their fear that former Nazi soldiers might pass as average citizens after the war. When a captured Nazi private by the name of Butz (Söenke Möhring) wins his freedom from the Basterds by divulging the positions of German forces, Raine asks what he will do with his Nazi uniform when he returns home. The private says, "Not only shall I remove it, but I intend to burn it." Raine responds, "You take off that uniform, ain't nobody going to know you's a Nazi. And that don't sit well with us." Raine unsheathes his knife, saying, "So, I'm gonna give you a little something you can't take off." Two shots later, we see Butz with a swastika-shaped scar on his forehead. This disfigurement has become Raine's trademark. By mutilating Nazis, he negates the possibility that they will ever be able to perform an identity disconnected from their Nazi past.

Sgt. Hugo Stiglitz (Til Schweiger) and Cpl. Wilhelm Wicki (Gedeon Berkhard) stage the film's only successful performances. Both are members of the Basterds who sometimes dress as Nazis and then ambush their unsuspecting targets. Stiglitz is a former Nazi soldier, and Wicki is an Austrian who immigrated to the United States before he could be sent to a concentration camp. As a result, Stiglitz's performance as a German is not a performance at all, and his performance as a Nazi resurrects one of his past identities. Wicki's performances are indeed performances, but given the similarities in language and perhaps even culture between Germany and Austria, Wicki's ability to cross these boundaries convincingly is easier than other nationality-bending performances might be. In fact, Stiglitz and Wicki are found out only when they team with British lieutenant Archie Hicox (Michael Fassbender), whose masquerade as a Nazi is exposed.

In the final analysis, *Inglourious Basterds* seems more willing to frame ethnic background and ethnic experiences as both socially significant and as inaccessible for individuals who are not members of the group. Raine's disfigurement of his Nazi foes goes even further, denoting contempt for those who enact performances for self-serving ends. All of this represents yet another turning point in the films of Quentin Tarantino, but it is also clear that his work has been moving in this general direction for quite some time.

Conclusion

Ancestral Legacies and History's Lessons

There is a connection between the ways we think about ethnicity and the ways in which the movies represent ethnic identities. It is not as simple as the movies show us Italian gangsters, and therefore audiences assume that all Italians *are* gangsters. Among other factors, real-life experiences of Italian ethnicity and real-life interactions with Italian Americans affect individual readings of mediated images. Nonetheless, regardless of background or experiences, the movies can and do affect our perceptions of ourselves, others, and the world.

I began this study with my reactions as an eleven-year-old to Brian De Palma's film *The Untouchables*. In the years since, I have been exposed to many representations of Italian American ethnicity, and some have been more enlightening than others. In 1997, for instance, Stanley Tucci and Campbell Scott's *Big Night* (1996) was playing at the Foundry, a two-dollar theater in Georgetown. The Foundry was a popular destination for college students who loved the movies and were spending way too much on tuition. The screens were small, and the floors were flat, which sometimes made it difficult to see over the people in front of you, but the management kept the screens filled with mostly independent movies, and the theater, which was within walking distance of campus, represented an affordable alternative to most of Georgetown's restaurants. I loved going to the Foundry (which has now closed and been replaced by a megaplex that does *not* offer two-dollar tickets), and it was with some delight that I passed my money through the box-office window and made my way into the theater. I do not remember hearing much about *Big Night* beforehand, but two of my friends, Emily (who was from Chicago) and Cristina (who was from Spain), had, and they thought it would be a good way to kick off our spring break. Neither Cristina nor Emily was Italian.

Big Night blew me away, and it is still one of my favorite movies. The film's representation of Italian Americanness was so different from most of what I had seen before. I was thoroughly enjoying the film when I started to suspect that my reactions were slightly different from those around me. Everyone was smiling and laughing. Everyone was reacting to the same images, characters, and narrative situations. But I could not help but feel that I did so for different reasons. After the film ended, we exited the theater and started talking about how much we enjoyed the movie. "But," I told my non-Italian friends, "you guys were laughing because you thought it was funny. I was laughing because I've been there." Indeed, *Big Night*'s extended dinner sequence, featuring multiple courses and bestowed upon a grateful dining party at a long rectangular table shrouded in a white cloth, reminded me of one family dinner in particular. A few years before, my godmother had arranged a gathering in honor of her two children (who had just graduated) at Bona Fides in New York's East Village. I looked at *Big Night* and I smiled, because I saw me and my family on-screen. My non-Italian peers were amused by the same images but had not had the same kind of experiences.

Years later, after a particularly challenging week of graduate school, my friends decided to lift my spirits. "We're gathering at my place on Friday night to watch a movie," my friend Jeff told me. "You pick what we're watching." I might have picked *Big Night,* but it had been a tough week, so I picked *Good-Fellas.* Some of my friends had not seen the picture, and *my* feelings about the film had changed quite a bit since the first time I watched it. My dad and I had rented it when I was still in high school, and we were shocked not by Scorsese's artistry (I did not know who Scorsese was), not by the Copacabana long take (I had no understanding of film construction), but by the language. We commented on it while the video ran, and when the movie ended, my dad turned to me and in a matter-of-fact voice said, "That was a bad fucking movie." I rarely heard my Dad drop the "*f* bomb." We had a good laugh.

But now, *GoodFellas* was the film to which I turned to feel better after a bad week, and I was looking forward not just to seeing one of my favorites again but also to seeing how my friends, especially the non-Italians who had never seen *GoodFellas,* would respond. We were about halfway through the movie when Henry walked up to Bruce (Mark Evan Jacobs) and pistol-whipped him for assaulting Karen. There were audible gasps among my friends. One even mumbled, "Oh, my God." I sat there, understanding that this was some pretty brutal violence, but also thinking that Bruce was getting what he deserved. I am not proud of that. I would not condone such behavior in everyday life, and

I do not mean to suggest that *all* Italian Americans have the same reaction that I do; they do not. However, in the context of *GoodFellas,* I find the fate that befalls Bruce to represent some kind of justice, and many of my friends watch the same film and are appalled and repulsed by this scene. It remains a moment when once again a movie and an audience's reactions to it allowed me to see the difference of my views. At the time, I attributed some of that difference to my ethnic background. Other scenes in the film, like the one where the guys make the "sauce" in prison, left me with a similar feeling.

In *An Offer We Can't Refuse,* George De Stefano writes of *The Godfather's* Corleones, "I recognized these people, their appearance, mannerisms, behavior, and attitudes. And I identified with them. . . . Vito and Carmela Corleone were my grandparents" (105–6). Even though De Stefano comes from a family that is not Mob connected, he was able to see himself in *The Godfather's* gangsters, and they helped him to better understand his own ethnic background. Salvatore Iaquinto, an Italian American delegate who serves in the Virginia General Assembly, seems to have a similar relationship with *The Godfather.* During his 2008 campaign, Iaquinto used the *Godfather* films to define or at least underscore his Italian American identity. To promote one of his fundraisers, Iaquinto printed fliers that drew on the iconography of *The Godfather, Part III's* movie poster. Replacing Al Pacino was Iaquinto, lit in golden tones, his hands clasped in prayer, eyes staring straight into the camera. Many Italian Americans criticized the public official for his mobilization of an Italian American stereotype; others defended him.[1] But both his use of the imagery and the debate that swirled around it represented a fight over the public face of Italian Americans, a fight that centered on the use of a media production to understand and define what it meant to be Italian American.

A similar controversy accompanied the HBO cable series *The Sopranos* (1999–2007). During its eight-and-a-half-year run, some Italian Americans railed against what they saw as the stereotypical representation of their ethnic group on the David Chase series. Congressional representatives of Italian American descent introduced resolutions condemning the program.[2] Organizers of New York's annual Columbus Day parade famously banned actors who worked on the show from marching, and groups like the American Italian Defense Association (AIDA) were so angered by *The Sopranos* that they sued HBO to have it taken off the air.[3] Yet during the same time, critics hailed the show as one of the finest on television, and the Academy of Television Arts and Sciences recognized the program with more than one hundred Emmy nominations and twenty-one Emmy Awards. There was more to *The Sopranos* than the gangster, but that does not mean that the gangster stereotype should be ignored, especially since all representations are political. By attacking the show as stereotypical or by defending it, critics necessarily advanced their political views, goals, and agendas, particularly as they related to issues of ethnicity.

In 2001, as the series was nearing the end of its third season, New Jersey congresswoman Marge Roukema rose on the floor of the U.S. House of Representatives to offer a resolution condemning the program.[4] Roukema asserted that the stereotypical depiction of Italian Americans in the media, and especially on *The Sopranos,* represented nothing less than "ethnic profiling." "If this kind of ethnic profiling were being directed at African-Americans and Hispanics they would have been marching in the streets," Roukema said (Hernandez B2). Roukema's assertion worked to collapse ethnic difference and prejudice, so that being an Italian American became the same as being an African American or a Hispanic. In fact, Roukema's rhetorical use of the phrase *ethnic profiling* was meant to equate the Italian American stereotypes on a critically acclaimed fictional television show with controversial law enforcement practices that use ethnic and racial identities "as one set of characteristics among others to decide whom to stop, question, search, or otherwise investigate for as-yet unknown criminal offenses" (Harris 67).

Not surprisingly, Roukema's resolution was offered at a time when the racial profiling practices of the New Jersey State Police were under scrutiny. In November 2000, the state attorney general released more than ninety-one thousand pages of documents that chronicled the existence and use of racial profiling by New Jersey State Police officers dating back to 1985. Although state law enforcement officials publicly denied its use, racial profiling became a primary, if ineffective, weapon in the "war on drugs," as minority motorists accounted for 80 percent of the vehicles stopped in some parts of the state.[5] This debate was clearly in Roukema's mind when she offered her resolution, but in a letter to the *Bergen County Record,* she denied that she was "playing politics" with the *Sopranos* issue. Near the end of her letter, though, Roukema once again equated *The Sopranos* and racial profiling practices using largely the same language she had used in her congressional resolution (including the term *ethnic profiling*) (May 16, 2001).[6]

Historically, Italian Americans were subjected to brutal prejudice in America, but it is irresponsible to suggest that their experiences today even approach those of other racial and ethnic minorities. It is true that *The Sopranos* makes use of a stereotype long associated with Italian Americans, but the stereotype is more complex than is sometimes recognized. Today, prejudice against Italian Americans is largely mitigated, as evidenced by Italian Americans' positions in the highest offices of government, business, education, and virtually every other field. As a result, the stereotypes of *The*

Sopranos did not and do not have the same social and cultural power that they once did. At one point in history, a show like *The Sopranos* might have contributed to the continued marginalization of Italian Americans, but that is no longer the case.[7] Says Michael Imperioli, an actor and writer who played Christopher Moltisanti on the program, "*The Sopranos* is not going to keep some kid who's Italian American from getting into a good college because the dean thinks his father is a mobster because he happens to be Italian. I mean we're past that, you know" ("Michael Imperioli's Mob Scene").

Italian Americans have come a long way since the days of Frank Capra when stereotypes plagued *our* public image, when congressional representatives introduced legislation to deport *us* to solve the Great Depression, and when *we* were targeted for discriminatory practices and interned during World War II. Today, those kinds of treatment are reserved for other ethnic groups, and it seems that some Italian Americans struggle with the degree to which their group has assimilated and attained a position of social power.[8] As a whole (and there are exceptions particularly in working-class areas), Italian Americans do not face the discrimination and pressure to assimilate that they once did. In fact, I can only recall one incident in my life when my ethnic background made me a target of genuinely derogatory speech. In the summer of 2001, an older white man who worked at the front desk of a Wyoming hotel was talking to me about another Italian American and said, "I don't know about you, but I think they're pretty boring." As the book before you indicates, I did not agree. But I do remember being stung by the statement, so much so that a decade later, I can still recall the insult, even though it carried no real social power. The man could not prevent me from getting a room or a job. And although it may be true that I have been lucky, I suspect that plenty of Italian Americans enjoy an existence closer to my own than the one that my grandfather lived as the son of immigrants throughout the middle years of the twentieth century. He endured ethnic slurs, prejudice, and discrimination repeatedly throughout his life. I have not.

Even the media representations of Italian Americans have changed. In addition to the gangsters on *The Sopranos*, characters of Italian American descent have been attorneys (Jimmy Berluti on *The Practice*), presidential campaign directors (Bruno Gianelli on *The West Wing*), surgeons (Dr. Robert Romano on *ER*), white-collar office workers and shop owners (*Jungle Fever*), and small business owners (*Return to Me*), and that is just a sampling from the past fifteen years. Contrast that with De Stefano's experience as an Italian American who came of age in the late 1960s: "From television shows like *The Untouchables*, I learned that the government personified by Eliot Ness and his posse of FBI agents, had its hands full trying to bring to justice bad guys with Italian last names, the only Italians I recall seeing on TV except for the occasional comic type, like the voluble barber speaking broken English. It wasn't until the seventies that Italians were seen on the other side of the law, in cop dramas like *Baretta* and *Columbo*" (98). De Stefano overstates the case slightly. One of Ness's untouchable agents was Enrico Rossi (an Italian American character played by Greek American actor Nicholas Georgiade); another was Agent Lee Hobson (played by Italian American actor Paul Picerni). Still, the television landscape with which I grew up was much more diverse. It seems to me that by focusing so intently on *The Sopranos,* Italian American groups and individuals have missed an opportunity to applaud the diversity of Italian characters offered by today's media.[9]

Nevertheless, Italian American ethnicity remains an important identifying marker even if it has become more accepted. For Italian American filmmakers like Sofia Coppola, Italian ethnicity seems to be of less thematic interest, perhaps because of the relative absence of anti-Italian prejudice or the seeming inconsequentiality of Italian ethnicity socially (though not personally). When *Lost in Translation* was released in the fall of 2003, most reviews hailed the arrival of a new talent. Coppola had previously directed *The Virgin Suicides* (1999), but her second feature-length film garnered more critical acclaim and, unlike *Suicides,* was the product of an original screenplay. Critics marveled at the performances by Bill Murray and Scarlett Johansson, the stunning cinematography (which is a characteristic of all of Sofia Coppola's work), and the languid, absorbing pace. Within months, Coppola was the first American woman to be nominated for an Academy Award for direction. Although she lost the directing award to Peter Jackson, she won the Oscar for "Best Original Screenplay," becoming the fourth Academy Award winner from the Coppola family. It was a moment of vindication for Coppola, whose performance as Mary Corleone in *The Godfather, Part III* had drawn the ire of critics and fans.

But not everyone was enamored with *Lost in Translation.* Four weeks prior to the Academy Awards ceremony, Asian Media Watch launched http://www.lost-in-racism.org, a Web site designed to dissuade Academy voters from honoring Coppola or her film.[10] "*Lost in Translation,*" the Web site charged, "provides a biased and offensive portrayal of the Japanese people and perpetuates negative stereotypes that are harmful to the Asian American community." Several respected critics agreed. "When the characters are not mocking Japanese pronunciation, the movie treats the city dwellers as either spookily serene, as in the flower-arranging class that Charlotte visits, or comically excitable, like Bob's greeting party," commented Ryan Gilbey in *Sight and Sound* (52). In *Time,* Richard Corliss charged that Coppola's film "makes too much easy fun of the Japanese: that they are a short people who speak in very long sentences and mix up their ls and rs" ("A Victory") (fig. 20). Film scholar Peter Brunette concurred: "Since all the jokes are at the expense of the Japanese—'these people are, really, just so weird!!'—the humor grates after a while" (n.p.). And in *Cineaste,* Maria San Filippo observed, "The film is largely credited by Japanese crewmembers, yet no sympathetic or even fleshed-out Japanese character is portrayed on screen" (28).[11]

When asked about the ethnic aspects of the film, Coppola acknowledged that some of the representations were stereotypical but rationalized them by arguing that the characters were based on real people. "If you're going to observe and put in details, you can't just be nice. You have to put in things that are real, and it isn't always politically correct," she said. "We make fun of Japanese businessmen, but we also have some cool, interesting Japanese artists" (Charity "Big in Japan").[12] Although it is tempting to become preoccupied with identifying stereotypes, it might be more beneficial to interrogate their narrative function.[13] *Lost in Translation* is about the dislocation that Bob Harris and Charlotte feel in their own lives. Coppola, it seems, misses an opportunity to use the difference of the Japanese to enhance the characters' feelings of dislocation. Instead, viewers are invited to *join* Bob and Charlotte in laughing at the Japanese. "In the hands of a more experienced director," writes Brunette, "this confrontation with a very foreign culture could have been a chance for some deep thinking about American naivete and innocence, but Coppola seems to be as much at sea in this foreign land

Figure 20. Bob Harris (Bill Murray) towers over the stereotypically short Japanese men who surround him in Sofia Coppola's *Lost in Translation.*

as her characters" (n.p.). Far more experienced filmmakers have offered far less sensitive representations of Asian peoples. Michael Cimino's *Year of the Dragon* (1985), for instance, presents a more sadistic and sexualized portrayal of Asian Americans.[14] Nonetheless, Brunette's assessment of the racial dynamics of *Lost in Translation* is convincing.

Where some see a lack of depth, Pam Cook sees a budding auteur. For Cook, Coppola is an interesting filmmaker with a keen aesthetic eye. And although some criticize her for her repeated interest in the problems of privileged people, it is important to remember that Coppola's focus on female characters provides a valuable perspective that remains somewhat unusual in Hollywood narratives. Nevertheless, critics like Nathan Lee castigate Coppola for her representation of class privilege. "*Marie Antoinette* [2006] is not the place to go for a critique of privilege," Lee writes. "It wouldn't know 'the masses' if they rose up and smashed the furniture" (25). For Sofia Coppola, the great-granddaughter of Italian immigrants, gender and class seem to be of more interest than ethnicity. Perhaps this is because she herself is more likely to be marked as different because of her gender or socioeconomic status.

There were at least two types of Italian immigrants, and the Coppola family belonged to the more educated, wealthier sort. But although Coppola's interest in class issues may be tied to her personal history, it is also indicative of a larger sociological trend within Italian America as a whole. As Italian Americans have become more assimilated, they have been afforded greater economic opportunities, and their cultural background has become less of an issue, at least for the public at large. In and of itself, this shift seems innocuous enough, but oftentimes a certain class of immigrants and immigrant descendants can become so absorbed into a world of quasi-aristocratic privilege that they are blinded to the ways ethnic identities, especially for nonwhite groups, continue to matter.

Sofia Coppola's focus on class and relative lack of interest in ethnicity (to date) exposes one of the biggest challenges facing Italian Americans and Italian American communities. How will they use the social power that their (relatively) new status as assimilated white Americans grants them? Because of the leadership positions Italian Americans have attained, they now play a more powerful role in sculpting the dominant culture's norms. Which of history's lessons will they embrace? Will they perpetuate the ills of the past and leverage their own power by discriminating against current immigrant groups? Or will they work to create a more accepting culture, in which today's immigrants are not forced to sacrifice their cultural ties in order to create a more assimilated American identity?

Unfortunately, in recent years, several prominent Italian Americans have gained national media attention by arguing against illegal immigration. Former Colorado congressman Tom Tancredo, the grandson of Italian immigrants, "[speaks] out against the ills of the illegal immigrant invasion" (n.p.).[15] Former Hazleton, Pennsylvania, mayor Lou Barletta (now a U.S. congressman), the great-grandson of Italian immigrants, has become a national political figure by proposing regulations that enforce immigration on a local, rather than a national, level. And in a case that garnered more than its fair share of media attention, Joey Vento, the grandson of Italian immigrants and the owner of Philadelphia's famous Geno's Steaks, was slapped with a discrimination suit (which he later won) when he hung a sign on his business that read, "This is America. When ordering—please speak English."

Like most previously marginalized groups, Italian Americans endured terrible prejudice. It is somewhat understandable that a bitter taste would be left in the mouths of some Italian Americans who want to honor their ancestors. But perpetuating the discriminatory practices of the past does not honor our ancestors at all. It merely imposes the same hardships they faced on others and makes the perpetuation of prejudice one of the trappings of the American Dream. Far from being disconnected from larger political debates like these, the controversy over media productions like *The Sopranos, The Godfather,* and *Lost in Translation* indicates that discussions about the media continue to be a forum for political discourse in which the meaning and shape of Italian ethnic identity are negotiated. Each of the directors investigated in this book has contributed films that continue to fuel these debates and shape the way we view our culture. Inevitably, this process of negotiation is tied to the relative acceptance of Italian Americans in American society, their standing within the film industry, and their personal backgrounds.

Unfortunately, focusing on individual directors has become a somewhat rare enterprise in academic film studies. Esteemed scholars proclaim auteur studies "a convenient fiction" in some of our introductory-level textbooks, dismissing what is thought to be a rather old-fashioned approach to film studies (Lewis, *American Film* 209).[16] The study of directors, critics charge, undermines the labor of others who work on a production, fails to question the ways Hollywood uses "auteurs" as a marketing ploy, and oftentimes ignores historical and industrial contexts. What we are left with is an approach that serves the economic interests of a commercial system by feeding the hysteria around star directors. These are serious and valid concerns, and we can and should account for them in our studies of filmmakers. But as scholarship on the industry and its audience(s) has come to dominate, the attention (at least within academic circles) offered to individual artists working within the system has been increasingly tapered.

It is clear that we can no longer treat individual directors as immune to industrial, cultural, and historical pressures. Still, the fact remains that in Hollywood, the director *does* matter. Her or his voice has not been usurped entirely by the system, and her or his individual politics and backgrounds (ethnic or otherwise) influence the perspectives that her or his movies offer. The idea that individuals can and do make a difference may sound overly romantic, especially in a climate that tends to emphasize the cynical (though oftentimes legitimate) belief that economically driven systems exercise an increasingly powerful hold over our actions, beliefs, and desires.[17] But the belief that these systems have won works to cultivate a kind of fatalism and despair that discourage resistance and hinder our ability to enact change.

Cultural studies and film studies should point to the problems with the system, but they should also be working toward effective solutions. We cannot ignore the economic realities of Hollywood productions, and we should be critical of the ways that movies and their makers become and are commodities. However, we cannot forget that film is also a very powerful art form and that it has the potential to change the way its audience views and understands other groups of people, political issues, themselves, and even the world. The five Hollywood directors investigated in this book have been afforded an influential voice within American culture and have shaped our collective perception of what it means to be ethnic in the United States. Through their movies and their public images, Frank Capra, Martin Scorsese, Nancy Savoca, Francis Ford Coppola, and Quentin Tarantino have worked to construct the imagined community of Italian America and have shaped the ways individual Italian Americans understand their own ethnic identities. By charting the ways in which their movies mobilize Italian ethnicity, we can better understand the relative acceptance of Italian Americans in American society and the Hollywood film industry at different historical moments. We can also see how individual class, gender, and regional backgrounds work to mold and shape a collective ethnic identity and how the various rhetorical strategies used in their films encourage us to conceptualize ethnicity.

Their works' importance goes beyond their individual backgrounds and even the wildly diverse Italian American community. As Paul Giles has shown, scholarship on ethnic groups needs to move beyond the autobiographical, because such a perspective "tends to refer conceptual questions inward to the upbringing of the writer or subsequent issues of personal beliefs, rather than outward to the more complex business of how such variations become disseminated and inflected with the larger amorphous structures of culture and society" (121). My hope for this volume is that it rests somewhere in between a strictly autobiographical approach and one that ignores the filmmakers in favor of an emphasis only on the system or only on the audience or only on the text. Popular films exist in a kind of dialogue with their audience, and it is important to understand not just the conditions under which they are made or the individuals and groups who view them but also the individuals who help to bring them to the screen. The works of these filmmakers have become a pervasive aspect of the cultural discourse not just on ethnicity but also on assimilation, acculturation, immigration, and tolerance.

For Capra, the movies became a forum where he could subtly challenge the dominant image of Italian Americans and immigrants. Through his films, he worked to recoup marginalized white and white ethnic groups by framing them as the living embodiment of dominant American ideologies such as the Protestant success ethic. By the time Martin Scorsese began his filmmaking career, the relative acceptance of Italian Americans had increased, and this afforded Scorsese greater artistic freedoms when it came to representing his ethnic group. For Scorsese, ethnic Italianness meant isolation from mainstream society and carried the potential of limited opportunities and problematic racial and gender politics. His films offer a critical view of the culture in an effort to make it more tolerant, more progressive, and less imprisoning. Nancy Savoca's arrival in the late 1980s advanced the thematic concerns investigated by Scorsese. Savoca's movies are interested in the isolated nature of Italian American neighborhoods, but she also examines the financial insecurity and emotionally numbing effects that dislocation from the neighborhood can bring. By focusing mainly on female protagonists, Savoca works to expose the "double marginalization" of Italian American working-class women. Savoca's representations also challenge the more nostalgic image of Italian American ethnicity that is offered in Francis Ford Coppola's *Godfather* trilogy. Conceived by an Italian American filmmaker with a more privileged background, the *Godfather* films advance beyond stereotypes to offer a complicated vision of Italian American gangsters, but the films' characterization of Vito Corleone embraces an Old World perspective that tries to negotiate the complex relations between family and business. Unfortunately, many of the gender and racial hierarchies of Old World Italian culture escape the film's full criticism. Nevertheless, the *Godfather* films and others that focus on Italian Americans became one of the main avenues through which Italian Americans like Quentin Tarantino learned about ethnic Italianness. Whereas Tarantino's early films treat ethnic identity as merely performative, his most recent movies question that notion and at the same time expose mainstream Hollywood audiences to genres and national cinemas outside the United States.

The study of Italian American directors is of consequence not just for Italian Americans but for all ethnic groups. Each group confronts its own stereotypes and history, but the process by which the dominant culture attempts to assimilate a small, less socially powerful group is unfortunately a characteristic of American modernity. Italian Americans are one example of a much larger historical trend, and the strategies that the filmmakers outlined in this study mobilize might also be apparent in the works of Irish American, Jewish American, Greek American, Asian American, African American, or Latino/a directors. Investigating directors from ethnic backgrounds such as these and reading them in relation to other directors from the same ethnic group or even directors from different ethnic groups enable us to see that the Hollywood cinema, usually seen as a cultural institution that works to assimilate ethnics, has also been a forum where assimilation is resisted.

Furthermore, the racial and ethnic politics of all media productions should be of concern, especially in the post–civil rights era. As some previously marginalized ethnics shed their ethnic identities in favor of class-blind "Americanness," there is a tendency to believe that all ethnic groups suffer the same prejudice. Other ethnics embrace their roots to the point that they see their group as superior to others, since they have overcome past prejudice. Both perspectives can lead to ethnic chauvinism and cause members of a once marginalized group to look at currently marginalized groups as inferior. This viewpoint discounts the fact that some groups are the subject of more prejudice than others and that the institutional racism of the past continues to affect the socioeconomic opportunities of marginalized groups today.

In April 2007, *The Sopranos* returned for its last nine episodes. In the first, entitled "Soprano Home Movies," Bobby Baccalieri (Steven Schrippa) sits on the shores of a lake in upstate New York, near the Canadian border.[18] With his wife, Janice (Aida Turturro), and Tony and Carmela Soprano (James Gandolfini and Edie Falco) present, he recounts how his grandfather emigrated from Sicily to Montreal and then crossed into the United States illegally. Carmela asks why his grandfather did not come through Ellis Island, and Baccalieri responds, "Got mixed up in some shenanigans on the other side—antigovernment or something, had a police record." They all pause, and then Baccalieri concludes, "They oughta build a wall now, though. I'm telling ya." Each character nods, and Carmela says, "Amen."

Baccalieri's desire to essentially pull the ladder up behind him is indicative of a larger trend within American culture that is neither foreign nor specific to the descendants of Italian immigrants. Perhaps if the descendants of immigrants saw those that suffer through discrimination and prejudice today not as abstract, inferior others but rather as the modern-day equivalent of their own ancestors, they would be more tolerant, understanding, and accepting. Rather than ignoring the experiences of yesterday's immigrants, such thinking would recognize injustice and work to ensure that inequitable practices are not perpetuated now or in the future. By studying the artistic expression of directors from a once marginalized ethnicity, teachers and scholars can work to achieve this goal by initiating discussions that personalize history for Italian Americans and non-Italian Americans alike.

In the summer of 2006, while he was touring the United States, Bruce Springsteen (who is half Italian American) debuted what he labeled "an immigrant song."[19] "American Land" recounts the allure that drew so many immigrants to the United States. The first several verses paint America as a land of plenty—diamonds line the sidewalks, women wear satin, gold rushes out of rivers, and "there's treasure for the taking for any hard working man." But as the song nears its conclusion, Springsteen offers a darker perspective on the immigrant experience. His last verse reads:

> They died building the railroads
> Worked to bones and skin
> They died in the fields and factories
> Names scattered in the wind
> They died to get here a hundred
> Years ago, they're dying now
> The hands that built the country
> We're always trying to keep down

Springsteen is suggesting that limiting the potential of immigrants through prejudice and discrimination robs the country of its full potential. Both the immigrants and the country are being robbed of opportunity. This was as true when thousands of Italian immigrants arrived in America as it is today. The study of ethnic filmmakers can uncover the injustices of the past, personalize the prejudices that immigrants endured, and work to create a more accepting culture where the United States might reach its full potential.

Notes

Introduction

1. Anthony Tamburri advocates the use of a slash to separate the words *Italian* and *American* when used as an adjectival phrase. However, for clarity and marketing purposes, many publishers opt for more traditional punctuation practices. For a more detailed discussion of the hyphen as it relates to ethnic Americans, see Aaron; and Tamburri, "To Hyphenate or Not to Hyphenate."

2. For a discussion of national, regional, and local perspectives as they relate to late-nineteenth- and early-twentieth-century Italian immigrants, see T. Guglielmo, *White on Arrival* 15.

3. I borrow the notion of "imagined communities" from Benedict Anderson.

4. Accounts vary as to the number of Italians lynched in New Orleans. Salvatore LaGumina puts the number at eleven. Selwyn Raab writes that there were sixteen victims. The best history of the lynching is Richard Gambino's *Vendetta*, which (like LaGumina's account) puts the number at eleven. Gambino's book was adapted into an HBO movie of the same title in 1999. Although the New Orleans lynching is the most infamous, Italians were lynched throughout the United States. For a general history of Italian lynchings, see Heather Hartley's documentary *Linciati: Lynchings of Italians in America* (2004). For a general sampling of the caricatures and prejudice directed at Italians during this period, see LaGumina.

5. See "Drive for Law."

6. For a thorough account of what Italian Americans label *una storia segreta* (a secret history), see Di Stasi.

7. Gardaphé's work is also deeply concerned with television writer, director, and producer David Chase's (born David DeCesare) HBO series *The Sopranos* (1999–2007). See Gardaphé, *Wiseguys* and "Class Act."

8. Casillo's definition disqualifies films like *Scarface: The Shame of the Nation* (Howard Hawks and Richard Rossen, 1932) because of the ethnic (or nonethnic) background of

its directors, but also excludes filmmakers who do not focus on what are perceived by Casillo to be "Italian American subjects." This approach neglects the many ways one can be "Italian" and instead perpetuates the idea of *an* Italian American experience.

9. There are, however, Italian American writer-directors who have crafted films that exist on the margins of what might be considered Hollywood's usual narratives about Italian Americans. Stanley Tucci's *Big Night* (cowritten with Joseph Tropiano and codirected with Campbell Scott, 1996) and John Turturro's *Mac* (cowritten with Brandon Cole, 1992), for example, both offer a more complicated perception of the American success story. Nevertheless, Hollywood studios distributed these films, which also feature mainstream Hollywood stars.

10. Whenever terms like *black, white,* or *Asian* are used in this study, they should be understood as culturally constructed categories based largely on skin color that erase the cultural diversity that exists within a given racial group. Paul Gilroy argues that the continued use of racial categories perpetuates the racist thinking of the past. Gilroy's position is a valid one, but racial categories continue to be of social consequence today. I cannot in good conscience write a study that ignores race in the hope that my not using (or even ignoring) racial categories will contribute to the abolition of racist thinking. However, whenever it is appropriate throughout the study, I prefer to use the term *ethnic,* because I believe its basis in cultural as opposed to racial thinking is more productive and accurate.

Chapter 1. Frank Capra: Ethnic Denial and Its Impossibility

1. In *Italians in America* (Greystone and A&E, 1998), Phillip Cannistraro recalls a meeting in which Capra denied that his ethnicity had any effect on the films he made. Similarly, in 1958, Capra composed a letter that discussed the musical talents of his father and four brothers. As if to mock the notion that his family felt tied to Italy, Capra wrote that what they most regretted about leaving was that they had to give up their monopoly on the local choir (Frank Capra Collection, Box 1).

2. The term *lost film* refers to a work of which there are no known existing prints.

3. Many of these pieces are available in Poague, *Frank Capra: Interviews.*

4. In *Regarding Frank Capra,* Eric Smoodin notes his discovery of at least two fan letters (in the Frank Capra Collection at the Wesleyan Cinema Archives) from Italian Americans who mention the director's heritage. Smoodin concludes, "To at least some audiences in the United States, apparently those with a familial link to Capra's heritage, the director was viewed as signifying the possibilities of the melting pot and the potential for increased understanding among national, racial, and ethnic groups" (205). Members of the Wesleyan Cinema Archives' staff have informed me that the collection also includes several more fan letters from individuals with Italian last names. Many are written in Italian, and because Capra answered most of his fan mail personally and kept copies of his replies, the collection also includes his responses. Usually, if Capra received a letter that was written in Italian, he replied in Italian. Additionally, the Wesleyan Cinema Archives includes a story entitled "Letters of the Duchess of Berry to Her Son" that Capra wrote in 1916 for the *Tech*—an annual Throop Polytechnic Institute (now California Institute of Technology) student publication. In it, the Duchess writes to her son about his father—a man of

Neapolitan heritage who dies when the boy is young. The letter has obvious similarities with Capra's life. His father had died the year before in a machinery accident.

5. In *The Classical Hollywood Cinema,* David Bordwell, Kristin Thompson, and Janet Staiger outline the tenets of classical Hollywood's mode of production (3).

6. The editors of the *Nation* surveyed the "editorial columns of foreign newspapers and periodicals" and concluded that they "show a remarkable unanimity of opinion: that something is radically wrong with US justice" ("World Opinion" 72).

7. It must not be forgotten that while Capra's involvement with *The Strong Man* may be more interesting to viewers and scholars today, the film was initially conceived as a star vehicle for Harry Langdon.

8. The name Zandow would have reminded contemporary audiences of Eugene Sandow, a famous strongman who promoted a patented exercise program.

9. An intertitle describing the town reads, "Justice and Decency had fled before the new law ~ ~ money." Similar to the agrarian philosophy that Capra subscribes to in *American Madness* (1932), this quotation demonstrates a critique of twentieth-century modernity, generally viewed as the American way of life in the 1920s.

10. Many scholars argue that critics have been too quick to dismiss Langdon. See F. Thompson; Rapf; Schelly; and Rheuban.

11. *The Strong Man* offers a number of scenes that will become more famous in other Capra films. The transformation of Cloverdale, for instance, foreshadows the transformation of Bedford Falls in *It's a Wonderful Life. The Strong Man* also includes a slide down a banister, which will be reused in *Mr. Deeds Goes to Town;* a reference to the Walls of Jericho, which will be recycled in *It Happened One Night;* and a character's mistaking the steps of a ladder for the stairs of a staircase, which will reappear in *A Hole in the Head.*

12. One of the title cards states this rather bluntly, "Mary Brown, the Parson's daughter, saw the world through the eyes of optimism ~ ~ perhaps because she was blind."

13. See Ray; and Slotkin.

14. Ray writes, "Embodied in the adventurer, explorer, gunfighter, wanderer, and loner, the outlaw hero stood for that part of the American imagination valuing self-determination and freedom from entanglements. By contrast, the official hero, normally portrayed as a teacher, lawyer, politician, farmer, or family man, represented the American belief in collective action, and the objective legal process that superseded private notions of right and wrong" (59). Bergot may start out a kind of outlaw hero, but he ends the film as an official hero.

15. Given the description of the film, it seems as if *Three Men and a Baby* (Leonard Nimoy, 1987) would serve as a modern retelling of this tale.

16. Although the ethnic fathers and Mary are never identified as immigrants, we can safely assume that they are not far removed from immigration based on where they reside and the historical context that surrounded the film's release.

17. Sollors sees a similar synthesis between consent and descent in the novels of James Weldon Johnson and Abraham Cahan (173).

18. Morris, Birdie, and Eddie Lesser are depicted as both children and adults in the film. The credits listed refer to the actors who played the characters as adults.

19. For Muscio, the tracking shots and largely horizontal shot compositions "downplay verticality" in a way that is unusual for films set in urban areas and with "a key narrative

interest in upper mobility" (313). Rogin is more interested in Capra's use of sound. Whereas *The Jazz Singer* relegated the patriarch's dialogue to intertitles, *The Younger Generation* offers spoken lines to characters from both generations.

20. Even when Birdie visits Eddie in prison, the action takes place outside. Capra uses exterior shots showing the couple standing on opposite sides of a chain-link fence. In contrast, the formal techniques used to shoot Morris's apartment frame the opulent space as the more daunting prison.

21. The first store bears the name "Julius Goldfish & Son." The next storefront features a sign that reads "Goldfish & Son Antiques," and the final shots show an ornate building with a sign that reads "Antiques" and a smaller barely decipherable sign that reads "Morris Goldfish, Importer." This montage has a secondary effect. According to Muscio, "In itself the shop window is highly symbolic of the city, but also of exteriority. This montage keeps us outside the store, where we can see the effects of work, but not work itself" (318).

22. While Morris is courting the Kahns' daughter, his parents enter the Fifth Avenue apartment building carrying packages from the old neighborhood. The doorman stops them, thinking they are laborers, and tells them they must use the service elevator. Instead of defending his parents, Morris labels them servants and tells the Kahns how difficult it is to get good employees these days.

23. See Capra, *Name* 93.

24. In *The American Dream*, Jim Cullen argues that there are a number of different American Dreams (including upward mobility, equality, and home ownership). But, he says, the contemporary use of the term *American Dream* seems "to mean that in the United States anything is possible if you want it badly enough" (5).

25. Riskin was the son of immigrants, and some have argued that he was the creative force behind Capra's most famous pictures. See McBride; and I. Scott. However, prior to and after his work with Riskin, Capra's work offers a remarkable degree of thematic and formal consistency.

26. As Jonathan Munby has shown, the use of accents in 1930s Hollywood films, particularly in the early gangster films, expanded the visual aesthetics that previously marked characters as ethnic. Unlike *Scarface*'s Tony Camonte (whose accent fades as he ascends to the heights of his profession), Capra's characters always speak in assimilated voices.

27. According to Elizabeth Kubek, Riskin changed the main character in *Lady for a Day* from Madam La Gimp, "an immigrant dancer," to Apple Annie, "an American peddler" (42). Riskin's screenplay also included an Italian garbageman named "Armetta." Kubek writes, "The published screenplay opens with an Italian garbageman finding a statue of Cupid in a barrel of rubbish. The garbageman, Armetta, defies the statue in stereotypical broken English: 'In theesa town, that arrow she'sa no good. Whadda you want is a machine gun.' When Cupid's arrow (its flight line drawn by the camera) singles out Apple Annie, Armetta sneers: 'Whatsa matter you? Apple Annie in love? You crazy!' Armetta is also given the final lines of the screenplay: 'That's the trouble witha thisa town. Everybody she's tough. Nobody she's got any heart.' Riskin envisioned that, accompanying the fadeout, we would hear Armetta singing 'L'amour, toujours l'amour'" (52). Unfortunately, Kubek treats Capra's decision to omit the stereotypical Armetta rather dismissively. "Understandably," she writes, "Capra disposed of this heavy-handed stereotype" (52). However,

Capra's 1930s films include a number of stereotypical Italians. They appear briefly in such films as *American Madness* and *It Happened One Night* (1934), and they are rather portly figures with mustaches who speak with accents and gesture with their hands. Nonetheless, they also demonstrate intelligence and loyalty to the films' most sympathetic individuals. Perhaps Capra's decision to omit Armetta was predicated on an anxiety that the ethnic Italian played too significant a role in the film.

28. For a more lengthy discussion of *Forbidden*'s importance in Capra's filmography, see Cavallero, "*Forbidden.*"

29. This thematic move in his film may have paralleled a similar move in his personal life. McBride writes, "It was only as Capra grew up and experienced discrimination that he lost his early sense of kinship toward blacks" (35).

30. Groups like the Boy Rangers in his home state counter the power elite of Washington by representing an ideal social community. Yet they too are overpowered by entrenched interests, and their efforts to sway public opinion are futile.

31. Nick Browne has argued that effective public speaking allows Jeff Smith to grow into adulthood. However, the necessity of learning a new vocabulary shares much in common with the way some immigrant groups were forced to learn English when they came to the United States. See Mangione and Morreale 160–62.

32. Carney writes, "Deeds and Bennett (and later Saunders and Smith, and after them Willoughby and Mitchell) are forced to leave behind the styles of gesturing, speaking, and consciousness with which they began their films and to invent new styles in their place" (282).

33. Despite Capra's conservative politics, it is worth noting that the conflict between democratic ideals and fascist principles was negotiated repeatedly in 1930s cultural productions. For a description of the Popular Front, see Denning.

34. When Smith first begins his filibuster, Taylor tells Paine, "If he even starts to convince those other senators, you might as well blow your brains out, you know that, don't ya?"

35. See Richards.

36. In addition to Capra, La Guardia and Sinatra were among at least ten Italians or Italian Americans who complied with requests to appear on this program.

37. It seems that most, if not all, of the programs ended the exact same way.

38. Author Lisa Scottoline uses the history of Italian American internment during World War II as the backdrop for her best-selling novel *Killer Smile* (2004).

39. According to McBride, when Capra had enlisted in the army for World War I, he had learned that he had not yet been naturalized as an American citizen. However, he was allowed to enlist with his application pending. Ann was under the mistaken impression that marrying an American citizen had naturalized her (450).

40. In December 1917 while an undergraduate at Throop, Capra wrote "A Treatise on Moving Pictures." A copy of the paper is available in Wesleyan's Frank Capra Collection. In it, he labels film "the best spreader of any sort of propaganda" (8).

41. Although Capra's name did not appear on prints of "Why We Fight," his involvement with the series was well publicized.

42. Kathleen M. German provides a notable exception to this trend. In "Frank Capra's 'Why We Fight' Series and the American Audience," German treats *The Battle of China*

as a kind of anomaly in the series. She writes, "Though they are an American ally, the Chinese are visually rendered as the enemy" (245).

43. See Bohn; and Ewing.

44. See MacDougall 61; and Koppes and Black 58–77.

45. Gardaphé finds the roots of the gangster archetype in the mythical character of Hermes, but he focuses his analysis on Italian American–authored gangsters from the mid-1960s to the twenty-first century (*Wiseguys*).

46. Munby suggests that during the 1930s, the Hollywood gangster, regardless of who "authored" the character, helped to bridge ethnic divides. This framing suggests that viewers were more sympathetic toward the gangster than contemptuous (although Munby does acknowledge that the stereotype simultaneously cultivated a greater fear of the "other" [5]). The treatment of actual Italian Americans in the press and beyond and the representation of Italian gangsters as stupid and immature would seem to challenge Munby's optimism.

47. At other points in the series, other individuals and groups of individuals are labeled "Hitler's stooge."

48. A similar portrayal of Mussolini can be found in Charlie Chaplin's film *The Great Dictator* (1940). Chaplin's Hynkel (an obvious stand-in for Hitler) is treated as a clown, but Jack Oakie's Napoloni (an obvious stand-in for Mussolini) is depicted as his foolish stooge.

49. Within the era's comic books, "the lesser enemy of fascist Italy was deemed a suitable foe for Wonder Woman" (MacDougall 65).

50. According to historian Stephen Fox, Mussolini did become a source of comedy when Fox screened some of the "Why We Fight" films for his undergraduate students. Oftentimes, they would laugh when Mussolini was shown gesturing or speaking (e-mail to the author, October 20, 2002).

51. *Prelude to War*, like all of the other "Why We Fight" films, is a compilation documentary. Shots from fictional Hollywood films were often used to complement the "bastardized" enemy newsreels, staged reenactments, and Allied battlefield footage.

52. In *Scarface: The Shame of the Nation*, the following brief exchange occurs between an Italian and a non-Italian. The non-Italian offers, "Put teeth in the Deportation Act. These gangsters don't belong in this country. Half of them aren't even citizens." The Italian, complete with his accent, responds, "That's true. They bring nothing but disgrace to my people." This conversation was added at the behest of the Production Code Administration, and all of the other Italians in the film are either gangsters or individuals who associate with gangsters.

53. It is interesting that Italy and the other Axis powers are castigated by the film for walking out of an organization that the United States refused to join.

54. See Steele 228; and Rollins, "Birth" 68.

55. Anti-Asian racism permeated the United States throughout the war years. Immigration authorities treated Chinese immigrants so harshly that the Chinese often referred to immigration officials as "gestapo" (Dower 140).

56. Greg Garrett notes, "Of the best-known documentary films made during wartime, only three actually include racial diversity: Frank Capra's *War Comes to America*, John Ford and Gregg Toland's *December 7*, and John Huston's masterpiece, *Let There Be Light*"

(73). Garrett's claim is somewhat oversimplified. After all, the widely distributed film *The Negro Soldier* (1944), assembled by Capra's team, deals extensively with issues of race and race relations.

57. The Japanese, however, fail to make the list of ethnic groups who immigrated to the United States. Thus, *War Comes to America* quashes the possibility that Japanese people could be Americans.

58. The image of the Japanese as "bucktoothed" was often compared to Bugs Bunny and prompted Warner Bros. to release a short film entitled *Bugs Bunny Nips the Nips* in 1944 (Dower 84). In an even more racist moment, *Know Your Enemy: Japan* notes, "[The Japanese soldier] and his brother soldier are as much alike as photographic prints off the same negative."

59. For a more in-depth analysis of Valentino's star image and its cultural significance, see Studlar 150–98.

60. Actress Angela Lansbury, who worked with Capra on the 1948 film *State of the Union,* has echoed these sentiments. In *Frank Capra's American Dream* (Bowser, 1997), Lansbury, an immigrant herself, says, "I think being an immigrant, in other words, coming to this country from Europe, makes you supersensitive to what this country looks, sounds, represents, is all about." Katharine Hepburn has expressed a similar if less critical sentiment. McBride quotes her as saying, "I think immigrants know more about what this country means than those of us who were born here and criticize it. Those of us who were born here, we tend to take it for granted. Capra's outlook was that of a fellow from Sicily coming into this country: that was his politics: 'Pleased to be here'" (261).

61. See Ignatiev; Jacobson, *Whiteness;* Roediger, *Wages of Whiteness* and *Working towards Whiteness;* Rogin; and T. Guglielmo.

62. Russo suggests that the film's source material leads to a movie that mixes Jewish and Italian American elements "at times, to a careful eye, not seamlessly" (298).

63. See Bondanella.

64. See T. Guglielmo; and Lipsitz.

Chapter 2. Martin Scorsese: Confined and Defined by Ethnicity

1. References to Scorsese's Italianness often mobilize stereotypes. Mark Carducci writes, "Like every Italian worth his pasta, Scorsese uses numerous hand gestures as he speaks" (48), and when commenting upon Scorsese's desire to stay out of the limelight, Mary Pat Kelly offers, "Some would say that is very Sicilian" (*First* 26).

2. Generally, Scorsese's authorship is established in one of three ways. Connelly writes, "Scorsese's artistic signature comes across in his choice of characters and actors; in the stories he chooses to tell and the emotion he invests in telling them; and in the look and bold camera movements of his films" (157). An array of different, though largely similar, descriptions of the typical Scorsese protagonist have been offered. Thomas Wiener has defined them as "fighters of a sort" who "reflect in no small way their creator [Scorsese]" (119). Duncan suggests that they are "driven by the pressures and needs of his [*sic*] environment and his [*sic*] inner nature" (11). Lawrence S. Friedman describes them as "guy[s] trying to make it" and suggests "that is mainly what the cinema of Martin Scorsese is all about" (38). And Gavin Smith holds that "Scorsese's films are almost always constructed

around narcissistic protagonists who typically deny or defy reality in order to inhabit increasingly lonely, paranoid fantasies of supremacy and control, sustained by forces of both repression and anarchic violence" ("Art" 237). Those who look to thematic consistencies within Scorsese's films tend to focus on select themes that are analyzed repeatedly. Dougan writes, "The broad-brush theme that unites all of Martin Scorsese's early films is the combination of sin and redemption" (53). Bliss, Kelly, and Keyser see this as deeply tied to Scorsese's Catholic upbringing. Scorsese himself has suggested that an interest in "obsessive behaviour" (among others) defines his work (quoted in Dougan 101). Almost all critics agree that Scorsese's cinema is a personal one, springing from his childhood upbringing and often recounting stories from his life. See Kelly, *First Decade;* and L. S. Friedman.

3. As a result, some of Casillo's readings derive from the conclusions he aspires to reach rather than coming organically from the texts he investigates. In writing about *Mean Streets,* Casillo argues that spiritual pride is "for Scorsese as for Italian Catholics the worst of sins" (189). Such assertions risk reducing the diversity that exists within an ethnic group to a homogenous standard.

4. "The establishment" can take a number of forms. In *The Aviator* and *King of Comedy,* it is Hollywood. In *The Departed,* it is the Massachusetts State Police and organized crime. In *Raging Bull,* it is professional boxing.

5. As Casillo has written, many of Scorsese's characters belong to all-male peer groups whose members exhibited neither true individualism nor self-mastery but a conformist adherence to the nonindividualist values of both their communities and the peer group itself, to the point where their displays of "'individuality' consisted of no more than a solicitation of group approval" (387). Casillo's perspective is quite totalizing, offering little sense of the ambiguity and ambivalence that we see in Scorsese's narratives. Nevertheless, the general theme he describes is present in the director's work.

6. Scorsese was surrounded by family members in an isolated, closed, prideful community where two kinds of people wielded power—the priests and the wiseguys. As a child, he witnessed a number of violent acts and was confused as to how the incidents he saw could be reconciled with the lessons he was taught in the church. See D. Thompson and Christie 3, 9.

7. For a discussion on the privileges of whiteness in twentieth-century America, see Lipsitz.

8. Casillo rightly defends Scorsese against critics who charge that he has betrayed or capitalized on his ethnic background by glorifying the mobster stereotype, arguing that his films "treat the Mafia in a distinctly ironic mode, as a virtual parody of Catholicism, in which the basic elements of Catholic teaching are inverted in a demonic register" (388).

9. Quart and Rabinow go on to suggest that *Mean Streets* "profoundly subverts most of Hollywood's Italian American fantasies" (43), and this was intentional. Coscreenwriter Mardik Martin has said, "*The Godfather* was a big book at the time, but to us it was bullshit. It didn't seem to be about the gangsters we knew, the petty ones you see around. We wanted to tell the story of real gangsters" (quoted in Dougan 35).

10. See Dougan 7, 38, 93; and D. Thompson and Christie 48.

11. Lesley Stern's *Scorsese Connection,* for instance, argues that Scorsese's films often represent a reworking of prior movies, but of the almost 150 titles surveyed, only 4 come

from Italy. Beyond minimizing Scorsese's eclectic influences and perpetuating hegemonic ideals by focusing almost exclusively on Hollywood movies, this oversight effectively minimizes the role that ethnicity plays in Scorsese's work.

12. A number of homages to French New Wave filmmakers are apparent in Scorsese's films. LoBrutto identifies *Jules and Jim* (François Truffaut, 1962) as a pervasive influence. The shot of Travis Bickle staring at a dissolving Alka-Seltzer tablet in *Taxi Driver* is a clear reference to a close-up of a cup of coffee in Jean-Luc Godard's *Two or Three Things I Know about Her* (1967). Bickle also writes in his diary about stomach cancer, a reference to Robert Bresson's *Diary of a Country Priest* (1951).

13. In his review of *Gangs of New York*, A. O. Scott notes the similarities between it and Visconti's *Senso* (1954) and *The Leopard* (1965) (35).

14. British cinema, especially the work of Michael Powell and Emeric Pressburger, has also been an influence. In fact, Scorsese has said he desires to complete documentaries on French and British cinema that would be similar to *Mio viaggio in Italia* and *A Personal Journey with Martin Scorsese through American Movies* (codirected by Scorsese and Michael Henry Wilson, 1995).

15. Moments like these are countered by moments when Scorsese clearly sees himself as an American. While he was married to Isabella Rossellini in the late 1970s and early 1980s, Scorsese spent some time living in Rome. Scorsese recalls, "I liked the style of living, taking it easy, moving at a certain pace. But one thing I realised when I lived in Rome with Isabella was that I'm American" (quoted in Behar 187).

16. Ferretti has been Scorsese's production designer on *The Age of Innocence* (1993), *Casino, Kundun, Bringing Out the Dead* (1999), *Gangs of New York, The Aviator,* and *Shutter Island* (2010).

17. Allen Mandelbaum (Kelly, *First* 78) and Scorsese himself have recognized the influence of the earlier Fellini film, but the degree to which it has informed Scorsese's understanding of Italian culture and ethnicity has been neglected.

18. Bondanella points out the similarities between these two films and investigates what it tells us about the creation of art and the influence of art on artists (79–82). However, he is less concerned with the similarities between Fellini's and Scorsese's treatment of Italian American ethnicity and culture.

19. In his essay on *I vitelloni,* Frank Burke underestimates the importance of such protocols. Burke writes, "The main characters refuse to respond creatively to irrational change and end up surrendering catatonically to the rational, tightly controlled world of town and family" (119). While Burke faults the *vitelloni* for not being individuals, he underestimates the extent to which their "tightly controlled world" is strongly defined and policed by ethnic culture.

20. Both Lucia Santa and Don Vito Corleone, by Puzo's own admission, were based on the author's mother.

21. There are exceptions to this general rule. *Boxcar Bertha* and *Alice Doesn't Live Here Anymore* (1974) take females as the main characters.

22. Interestingly, Scorsese's cinema rarely offers representations of the characters' actual fathers. *Italianamerican* and *Cape Fear* (1991) provide notable exceptions, with *Boxcar Bertha, GoodFellas, Kundun,* and *Gangs of New York* offering very brief appearances by the main characters' fathers.

23. Scorsese, himself, has said he did not get *Knocking* "right, except for the emotional aspects of it" (quoted in DeCurtis 451).

24. Martin became a two-time Emmy winner and is the sister of Scorsese's NYU classmate and screenwriting partner Mardik Martin (Sangster 8).

25. Scorsese has described *Knocking* as "a dramatic version of *Murray*" (quoted in Kelly, *First* 16). Grist has argued that *Murray!* is much more condemning of assimilated materialism and that in *Knocking*, "the girl's educated sophistication" is lauded compared to JR's worldview (41).

26. As Bliss writes, "J. R. refuses to be reasonable since, in his distorted view, to accept the girl as flawed would be tantamount to admitting that she was his equal, a situation that would entail his loss of power over her, something he could not tolerate" (*Martin Scorsese* 44–45).

27. Rebecca West writes, "[J. R.'s] attraction to the 'girl's' otherness is, I believe, motivated as much by his desire to escape the limits of his ethnically determined world as by her blond purity" (332).

28. A number of critics have commented on Scorsese's formal choices in *Knocking*. See Bliss, *Martin Scorsese* 37; West 332; LoBrutto 77; Dougan 29; and Casillo, *Gangster Priest* 144.

29. See Grist 42; and L. S. Friedman 26.

30. In comparing this aspect of *Knocking* with *Murray!* even Grist acknowledges, "J. R.'s treatment of the girl invites [the Madonna-whore complex's] condemnation" (42). And according to L. S. Friedman, "Scorsese now calls the sexual conflict of this film *medieval*, marveling that he made a movie about sexual repression in the age of sexual revolution" (25).

31. Scorsese shot a scene for *Mean Streets* in which Charlie walks through the San Gennaro Festival. According to Sangster, "Scorsese neglected to obtain permission to film [during the festival]. When the festival organisers sent him the bill for $5,000, Scorsese borrowed the money from Francis Coppola" (38).

32. See Bliss, *Word*.

33. See Luconi; and Sciorra.

34. Selwyn Raab argues that the Mafia plays an important role in discouraging non-Italians from entering Italian American neighborhoods, arguing that this is one way the Mob protects its interests (x).

35. Maurizio Viano and Stephanie Hull have judged Scorsese's representation of race to be superior to that of other Italian American filmmakers like Francis Ford Coppola and Brian De Palma.

36. These characters are also anti-Semitic. They assume women who seem to be promiscuous are Jewish and that Jewish women are promiscuous. When Johnny Boy enters a bar with two Jewish females, Charlie refers to them as *matta christos,* which translates to "Christ killers" (LoBrutto 145). In another scene near the bloody conclusion of the film, Charlie labels an adversary "a Jew bastard" even though he does not know his background.

37. Just as Charlie and Johnny Boy become a pseudocouple, so too do Michael and Tony. Tony seems jealous of Michael's interest in other women. When Michael is showing

off pictures of his new girlfriend, it is Tony who asserts that he saw her kissing another man. And when Johnny Boy and Charlie want to throw Benton and Sammy out of Michael's car, Michael resists because he fears they will be interrogated about the shooting at Tony's bar.

38. A similar tension is apparent in *Who's That Knocking* where JR and his male friends often "share" the same women. Whereas Grist and Keyser suggest that such scenes represent the repressed homosexuality of Scorsese's male characters, Casillo argues that such interpretations are "too easy, too predictable, and too boring" (*Gangster Priest* 162–63).

39. In *GoodFellas*, Henry Hill and Jimmy Conway are part Irish American.

40. In *The Madonna of 115th Street*, Robert Orsi suggests that the *domus* is the central value of the culture of Italian Harlem. Described as the Italian home and family, the *domus* is closely tied to *la bella figura*. The maintenance of the *domus* is supposed to take precedence over the happiness of the individual. The difference between Orsi's argument and mine is that his is more centered on the family, while mine is more centered on the larger culture. Scorsese's work in some ways dictates such an approach, since traditional families are usually absent in his Italian American–focused movies.

41. Like Hill, Tommy DeVito (Joe Pesci) acts like a child, but unlike Henry, he kills people impulsively for trivial insults. See Mac in Dougan 135; and Bliss, *Word* 98.

42. Roger Ebert's review of the film suggests that Hill's desire for material comforts (without doing the grunt work) resonated with a culture only a few years removed from the economic boom of the 1980s ("*GoodFellas*" 321). Stern asserts that the film's form seduces viewers into the gangster lifestyle. She writes of the famed long take at the Copacabana: "[Karen is] impressed. And so are we. It's as though you can't believe this is happening and you don't want it ever to end, and when it does end so spectacularly with champagne and everyone's attention it's like pure ecstatic wish fulfillment" (9).

43. It is worth mentioning that Scorsese was very particular about the representation of Italian Americans offered in the film. He told production designer Kristi Zea that the picture "never should have been made by anyone but an Italian" and according to Sangster was clear that the "essential idea would be that there'd be no parody of the Italian lifestyle, except toward the end of the picture when Karen and Henry's house should show their garish lack of taste" (191). In an interview with Amy Taubin, after the film's release, he said, "No doubt I'll always be interested in underworld stories. But no cutesy films about mama's pasta and people getting married. I can't stand that. It's completely fake" ("Blood and Pasta" 14).

44. Henry Hill's commentary track on the *GoodFellas* DVD is interesting for the range of emotions Hill expresses. In one moment, he is remembering the good old days. In the next, he is lauding the U.S. government for offering a guy like him a second chance, and a little while later, he is melancholic about the fact that many of the characters depicted in a given scene are dead. Hill refuses to reduce his experience to a simplified narrative arc with easy conclusions, and perhaps that is the beauty of the cinematic representation of his life as well.

45. On LaMotta's commentary track on the *Raging Bull* DVD, he admits that he introduced the teenage girls to grown men. But, he says, he did not know they were underage, and he was not operating as their pimp.

46. As Roger Ebert has said, "Upward mobility for [Scorsese's] characters means moving to Vegas (*Casino*) or Miami (*Raging Bull*) and continuing to lead the same lives" (*Scorsese* 220).

47. As Casillo suggests, the shafts of light that enter the cell from above represent "awakening insight and the descent of grace" (*Gangster Priest* 257). Tomasulo has suggested that Scorsese intended for the Bible verse at the end of the film to redeem LaMotta but that the quotation cannot overcome LaMotta's actions. I agree that LaMotta is not fully redeemed at the end of the film, but the Bible verse may also be asking viewers to withhold judgment of the character. Incidentally, Scorsese inserted the Bible verse initially as a comment on his relationship with Manoogian, his NYU mentor, who died before *Raging Bull* was completed.

48. Interestingly, this laudatory treatment of the Irish is not as apparent in the Herbert Asbury book upon which the film is based. See Czitrom 303.

49. Scott's reference to state violence against citizens is an element of Scorsese's films that has started to receive more attention. See Cook 169; Palmer 331; Christie, "Manhattan" 21; and Casillo, *Gangster Priest* 323, 389.

50. For an analysis of the relationship between race and class in the film, see Palmer. Tayler, Justice, and Czitrom provide more detailed discussions of the film's oversimplified take on race. The film was also criticized, because the actual population of the Five Points was much more diverse than was shown in the movie (DiGirolamo 127).

51. In attacking the film's representation of history, Richard Oestreicher writes that Scorsese "didn't listen to historical advice readily at hand because he, his screenwriter and his set designer, among others, don't consider getting the history right to be very important" (211). In response to criticisms like this, Scorsese says, "You know, the movie is not a history book; it's mostly a personal story" (quoted in Baker 53).

52. Jacobson notes that visual imagery from movies and photography has allowed many to collapse ethnic difference into a homogenized standard (*Roots* 83).

53. Although differences obviously exist between Irish and Italian forms of Catholicism, it is clear that Scorsese sees faith-based connections. In the commentary track to the *Gangs of New York* DVD, Scorsese says he was interested in exploring the role that faith plays in community formation.

54. The representation of the Irish has taken on a new importance in the post-9/11 era. Sinéad Molony writes, "Other commentators agree that the participation of the New York fire and police departments during the 9–11 crisis have had a crucial effect on the way Irishness is deployed 'in the articulation of white, working-class male identity'" (137).

55. Scorsese currently lives on New York's Upper East Side. Of his old neighborhood, he says, "I don't belong there anymore. But I can damn well try to make sure that when I use it in a film like *GoodFellas*, I make it as truthful as possible" (quoted in DeCurtis 460).

56. In this way, Sullivan resembles characters like *Age of Innocence*'s Newland Archer (Daniel Day-Lewis). Blake writes, "[Scorsese's] heroes grow restless under the restraints of their social caste, but they cannot move into another caste. Their own tribe will not let them go and the alternate tribe will not accept them, or most tragically, as in the case of Newland Archer, they simply lack the inner strength to make the transition" (206).

57. In *Mou gaan dou* (Infernal affairs) (Lau Wai-keung and Mak Siu Fai, 2002), the

film upon which *The Departed* is based, this scene is much shorter and does not include a comparable image.

58. Costello's strategies work to consolidate whiteness. As Molony shows, "The opposition between black and Irish reinforces the whiteness of Irish America, but reminds the audience that this whiteness was earned through masculine assertions of power" (139).

59. The real-life Frank Costello refused to take the Fifth Amendment as other Mafiosi had, because he felt doing so would convict him in the minds of the public. He believed he could outsmart the committee and create the illusion that he was a legitimate businessman (Raab 98). Costello agreed to appear on one condition: that television crews not be allowed to show his face. "During three grueling days of testimony," writes Raab, "the cameras focused on his hands, with close-ups of his cuticles, his fingers drumming on the table, and his hands clasping and unclasping. The eerie combination of Costello's hands and his accented, gravel-crunching voice cast him in a more sinister and mysterious role than showing his face on television" (98).

60. See Cohen.

61. Alleva writes, "*The Departed* is like an athlete who has spent as much time in therapy as on the playing field, and, with a layer of fat he can't afford, shows as much strain as strength" (16).

62. For years, Scorsese has been planning a project titled *The Neighborhood*. The feature-length film would chart an Italian American family's progress in America across three generations. For synopses of the film, see Sangster 279; and Ehrenstein 244.

63. It is worth mentioning that later in her life, long after the release of *Italianamerican*, Catherine Scorsese moved to the more ritzy Gramercy Park area.

64. In fairness to Jacobson, the film does celebrate the Scorsese family history and may play into the conservative politics of the White Ethnic Revival even while other aspects of the film work to undermine them. Verdicchio, for example, has offered an interpretation of the film that seems to validate Jacobson's fears by framing the American story as one of ethnic uplift rather than racial oppression. *Italianamerican*, Verdicchio argues, declares "the legitimacy of Italian immigration and the installation of Italians in America as part of the hard-working, struggling masses who find in the ideals of the American republic a source of inspiration" (117).

65. Casillo's reading of *Italianamerican* suggests that Charlie and Catherine Scorsese are representative of Italian Americans as a group, and, at times, this seems to be the case (*Gangster Priest* 3–55). But the beauty of the film for me is that it finds the individual within the group and personalizes the history of an ethnic group.

66. Scorsese's father also evidences a problematic gender politics when he suggests that the kitchen is not his "line," even though he previously claimed, "It's known that a man can cook better than a woman."

67. For a discussion on the discomfort that Scorsese's movies inspire, see Dickstein 659; and Wood, "The Radicalism of Scorsese."

68. On the commentary track to *Raging Bull*, Scorsese talks about how Jake LaMotta and the film's other characters function in this way. Scorsese says that the film is really about the filmmaker's feelings toward (and identification with) the character of Jake rather than Jake LaMotta himself.

69. In his review of the film, Richard Gambino writes, "The characters in *Mean Streets* live many of the values of Italian Americans, but, like most Italian Americans, are poorly conscious of them, ignorant of their cultural roots, and are able to express and live the values only in poor, self-defeating ways" (quoted in Kelly, *First Decade* 175).

Chapter 3. Nancy Savoca: Ethnicity, Class, and Gender

1. See Sautman.

2. Savoca shares this interest with many ethnic women authors and filmmakers. See Giunta, *Writing with an Accent.*

3. Savoca's paternal grandfather worked for Mussolini's secret police and left Italy just after he got married (interview, March 17, 2008).

4. See Gardaphé, "From *The Italian American Writer.*"

5. As Gloria Nardini has shown, *True Love*'s Bronx neighborhood, much like Scorsese's Manhattan neighborhood, seems to exist as a community unto itself. Only Italians are present, and no contemporary events—political, athletic, or otherwise—are ever discussed.

6. See Nardini.

7. Because of the lack of prominent female characters in Hollywood films generally, Savoca developed a unique viewing strategy. "I learned in my childhood that you are going to be looking at these movies from a male point of view," she says, "and [by 1972] I had already learned in my head to flip that to enjoy a film" (interview, March 17, 2008).

8. Despite offering a voice-over to Karen Hill (which Martha P. Nochimson identifies as the first female voice-over in an American gangster film [63]), *GoodFellas* is no exception. At multiple points, Henry usurps Karen's narration, and the film is clearly more interested in Henry's story than Karen's.

9. At another point in the film, we see a similar scene where the Catholic Church encourages a sense of female inferiority. As Teresa's classmates question why the pope has not revealed the contents of Sister Fatima's letter as had been promised, the nun responds, "Well, if that's what the pope decided, he knows best."

10. For Vitullo and Baker, characters like Catherine and Nicky critique traditional notions of femininity and masculinity by rebelling against them in their actions. But both of these characters also reject the traditional roles ascribed to the opposite sex. Catherine's retreat from ethnic Italian culture's religious views is based on the idea that such beliefs not only marginalize women but also dictate roles for men that lead some to treat women dismissively. The same concern is evident in Scorsese's films.

11. The extent to which Catherine rejects Old World Italian culture is debatable. Whereas Baker and Vitullo suggest that she is nearly completely assimilated by the end of the film, Ruberto disagrees. "Catherine's relationship to assimilation is slightly more complex," Ruberto writes. "After Carmela dies she puts away her mother-in-law's cross, votives, and Madonna statues, yet sends her daughter, Teresa, to Catholic school; she mocks Carmela's ideas about curses and the power of the evil eye, but continues to use her recipe/incantation in order to make perfect sausages" (171).

12. What the alternate ending would have been remains a bit of a mystery. Savoca never

saw the pages but says "the executives [at Warner Bros.] disliked the ending because they felt it was 'unresolved and depressing'" (e-mail to the author, May 27, 2010).

13. The narration of the two films is slightly different. In *Dogfight*, Rose's narration is contained completely within a flashback controlled by Eddie, whereas *Household Saints'* flashback is controlled by male and female characters.

14. *Dogfight*'s most explicit reference to ethnic issues comes when Eddie first meets Rose at the diner. As the two talk, an Irish flag and an American flag are crossed on the wall above them.

15. This turn of events echoes a narrative pattern found in Pietro Di Donato's seminal Italian American novel, *Christ in Concrete* (1939).

16. At one point in the film, all of the characters are sitting around a table comparing immigrant experiences. Each insists that his or her journey was more harrowing than everybody else's. The scene is played comically, demonstrating the ridiculousness of the discussion.

17. As a result, Hollywood generally ignores the cultural differences and tensions between Chinese and Japanese cultures, for instance. Similarly, Hollywood features often disregard the diversity that exists among Mexican, El Salvadoran, Guatemalan, Puerto Rican, and other Hispanic cultures. In corresponding fashion scholarly studies of whiteness tend to homogenize and oversimplify racial identities. Under the rubric of blackness fall a number of different cultures from Dominicans to Haitians to African Americans to Afro-Cubans. What is lost here is a notion of ethnic specificity and cultural difference. The same might be said (though to a lesser degree) of the diversity within "whiteness." Here Italians, Australians, Hungarians, and others are grouped together.

18. For a discussion of the history of U.S. immigration policies, see Daniels and Steinberg.

19. Since *Dirt* was made for Showtime, a subscriber-based premium cable network, we can assume that the target audience would be middle to upper middle class.

Chapter 4. Francis Ford Coppola: Ethnic Nostalgia in the Godfather *Trilogy*

1. Peter Biskind has suggested that these scenes were filmed in Rome, but Coppola has indicated that they were filmed in Trieste. See Biskind 88; and Coppola, *Godfather Part II* DVD commentary.

2. Cook's definition of *nostalgia* is necessarily in conversation with Frederic Jameson's understanding of the term. For Jameson, *nostalgia* refers to a stylistic rather than a historical phenomenon, but one that nonetheless carries the potential for stagnation and even regression. Jameson writes, "The nostalgia film was never a matter of some old-fashioned 'representation' of historical content, but instead approached the 'past' through stylistic connotation, conveying 'pastness' by the glossy qualities of the image, and '1930s-ness' or '1950s-ness' by the attributes of fashion" (*Postmodernism* 19). Jameson argues that we have become "increasingly incapable of fashioning representations of our own current experience," and instead we have allowed art to stagnate by simply recycling the commercially profitable aesthetic innovations of the past (21).

3. Discussing the *Godfather* trilogy is complicated by the number of versions that exist. A televised version of the first films featuring additional scenes and edited into chronological order was broadcast on American television. And when *The Godfather, Part II* was screened in Chile, dictator Augusto Pinochet excised the Cuba sequence, fearing that the depiction of Castro's overthrow of Batista "might have given people ideas" (Biskind, *Godfather* 91).

4. There were also a number of immigrant-themed films that appeared around this time, including Jan Troell's Academy Award–nominated *Utvandrarna* (The Emigrants) and Joan Micklin Silver's *Hester Street* (1975). Jacobson suggests that this interest in immigrants may have been closely connected to the U.S. bicentennial. Coppola's "bicentennial film" was supposed to be *Apocalypse Now* (Schumacher 185).

5. For a general history of the production of *The Godfather,* see Biskind; Cowie, *The Godfather Book;* Gardner and Gardner; Puzo, *The Godfather Papers;* Jones; and Lebo.

6. Coppola's directorial style irked Paramount and drove the production costs to six times the initial budget. In comparing Coppola's style to his own, *Godfather* cinematographer Gordon Willis offered the following: "I like to lay a thing out and make it work, with discipline. Francis's attitude is more like, 'I'll set my clothes on fire—if I can make it to the other side of the room it'll be spectacular'" (quoted in Phillips, *Interviews* 176). However, in *The Godfather,* Coppola's direction is measured. He does not use handheld cameras or crane shots, and any camera movements are slow and discreet (Malyszko 55), giving viewers an opportunity to take in the detail of the film in a way that would not be possible with staccato editing or obtrusive camera techniques.

7. Several critics have noted the importance of Coppola's ethnic background in the making of *The Godfather.* See, for instance, Bergen 12. Coppola's own thinking on the subject was revealed in his casting. Fred Roos says, "It was Francis's theory that being Italian, if you grow up in an Italian-American community or family, there are locked-in hardwired behavioral things that are just in you that will come out in performance—without even having to be directed—and he was hoping to get that" (quoted in Jones 151).

8. See Schumacher 94; Malyszko 78; Cowie, *Coppola* 10; and Phillips, *Interviews* 171. Despite Evans's claims, it is important to note that *The Brotherhood* was written by an Italian American, Lewis John Carlino.

9. In *The Godfather Notebook,* Coppola writes of the wedding scene, "This whole thing is like when I took Emaline to Anthony's wedding. All the family was eyeing her, criticizing her, the way she was dressed, etc." (18).

10. Coppola says, "One minute we had a little bit of money, the next my father was saying he couldn't afford the mortgage. It was tempestuous" (quoted in Goodwin and Wise 18).

11. Although the Coppola family embraced their Italian roots, they also were careful to raise "their children in the mold of genuine Americans" (Cowie, *Coppola* 15). Lourdeaux writes, Coppola "experienced ethnicity not as a way of life on the streets but as a way of relating within a middle-class family" (172). Lourdeaux's words are poorly chosen here, since "relating within a middle-class family" is also "a way of life," but his assertion that ethnicity played a different role in Coppola's life than Scorsese's (or Savoca's) is an important one.

12. Coppola's self-image is also greatly influenced by his Italian cultural background. In a 1996 interview, Coppola offered the following about the state of his career: "I'm very embarrassed about my career over the last ten years. You know, an Italian family puts a lot of stock on not losing face, not making what we call 'una brutta figura,' or a bad showing. When you have people writing about you in a mocking way and making fun of your ideas and calling you a crackpot, that's a real 'brutta figura'" (quoted in Papke 15–16).

13. See Cowie, *Coppola* 41.

14. When the film's running time needed to be shortened, Coppola cut many of the songs and dance numbers performed by the film's African American actors (Phillips, *Godfather* 238).

15. See also De Stefano.

16. Other Coppola works, including *Apocalypse Now* and his script for *Patton,* also offer ambivalent viewing positions and politics. See Tomasulo, "The Politics of Ambivalence."

17. See Puzo, *The Godfather Papers* 23–64. However, whereas Puzo liked to contend that the final result was largely Coppola's, Coppola often contended it was Puzo's. See Phillips, *Interviews* 183.

18. Gardaphé is right to see a difference between Puzo's second-generation perspective and Coppola's third-generation perspective. Cowie, however, argues that Coppola grew up "enveloped in the same family values as those adumbrated by Puzo in his novels" (*Godfather* xii).

19. Coppola has said, "Oddly enough [Michael] was doing all of this to preserve his family, and he was destroying his family at the same time—and that was the central theme of that character" (*Part II* DVD commentary).

20. In an extended and stimulating discussion of Filomena (and Brasi), Michele Fazio suggests that this often forgotten but important character challenges *The Godfather*'s usual representation of women (94).

21. Fred Gardaphé and Michele Fazio suggest that the baby's mixed heritage threatens Brasi's identity. Destroying it preserves the ethnic boundaries that define his personal and professional life. See Gardaphé, *Italian Signs* 94; and Fazio 92.

22. As Thomas J. Ferraro argues, in Puzo's novel, family and business are "casually intermingled" (*Ethnic Passages* 28), whereas Coppola's films "reif[y] the distinction between the private and the corporate, home and work" (29). As a result, Ferraro suggests, "if we wish to press charges against capitalism, we must press charges against family and ethnicity, too" (38). How successful Coppola is in distinguishing between business and personal is debatable. Scholars such as Peter Bondanella suggest that the two are still somewhat intertwined. Bondanella writes, "Ultimately, in spite of what everyone says, everything is personal, not just business" (263).

23. Far from being something Puzo embraced, Italian ethnicity was something he loathed as a child. Puzo's upbringing was so deplorable that he writes, "Later in life when I was exposed to all the clichés of lovable Italians, singing Italians, happy-go-lucky Italians, I wondered where the hell the moviemakers and storywriters got all their ideas from" (*Papers* 1).

24. Critics have accused Puzo of idealizing his gangsters as well. Cowie writes, "Mario

Puzo's romantic attitude to his characters may explain this blind spot, for in practice *Mafiosi* were involved in the drug trade as early as 1935, when Serafino Mancuso was sentenced by a US court to forty years in jail for dealing in narcotics" (*Godfather* 173).

25. Several critics have shared this kind of reaction to the films. One commentator wrote, "I want to be like Michael," suggesting that "his coldness, his authority, his clarity, his sense of necessity" are respected by viewers (Thomson 60–61). Bondanella writes, "A part of every contemporary audience expresses satisfaction in the defeat of the 'system,' cheering when Don Vito or Don Michael settles the family's 'debts' at the end of each of the three films" (262). It is true that the films encourage a degree of sympathy toward the Corleones, but they also encourage us to be critical of their enterprise and their methods.

26. Despite such criticism, critics hailed the film generally.

27. As Todd Berliner says, "Michael is doing just what the movie invites us to do—remember the past with regret" (119).

28. *Peggy Sue Got Married,* as Phillips writes, "evokes the past as an innocent, more wholesome time" (*Godfather* 256). In *The Outsiders* and *Tucker,* the very style of the films creates a nostalgic mood. *The Outsiders* is bathed in a "gold-hued light" (Cowie 202), and *Tucker* is similarly envisioned in a "golden light of nostalgia" (Clarke 191).

29. In the film, the characters refer to it as the "sauce," but in many Italian American families, including my own, it is referred to as "gravy."

30. See Nochimson.

31. When *The Godfather* made its television debut, Coppola addressed the issue of stereotyping. In introducing the film, the director said, "I tried to avoid any stereotypes in the film so that the mannerisms and home life and feelings of the people are as authentic as I could remember from my own upbringing in an Italian American home even though my family was, as are the majority of Italian Americans, in a quite different business."

32. It is worth remembering Gardaphé's suggestion that "we must try not to censure art, but to enhance society's abilities to interpret it" (*Wiseguys* 213).

33. When Bonasera offers to pay the Don, Vito stands up, abruptly places the cat he has been petting on his desk, turns his back to the undertaker, looks out the window, and eventually turns to face Bonasera, his hands at waist level, palms facing up.

34. Dika cites two essays by Jameson: "Reification and Utopia in Mass Culture" and "Postmodernism and Consumer Society."

35. Todd Gitlin's 1972 review of the film acknowledged the cultural longing for ethnic representation. Gitlin wrote that the film "[tapped] a hunger for ethnicity, a desire to recrystallize out of the melting pot, to 'rediscover roots' (*somebody's* if not one's own) which can make us feel, even briefly, that we are not like the rest of those nondescript melted-down Americans" (38).

36. Bondanella asserts, "The theme of the sequel thus becomes quite literally the relationship of past and present, which are inextricably linked, as well as the power of the past over the present and even the future" (252).

37. Despite astute readings like this one, Lourdeaux's analysis of Coppola's engagement with ethnicity is often perplexing. He argues, for instance, that audiences were "repulsed only by the hypocrisy of institutional Catholicism and Italian ethnics" during the baptism scene at the end of *The Godfather* (187). Further, he writes, "*The Godfather*

triggered a second life stage in Coppola's films, revealing his deep symbolic anger against his immigrant identity, his childhood religion, and especially the successful ethnic father" (185). In Lourdeaux's reading, Coppola sides with Michael, endorsing his rejection of Old World values, and goes on to make films in which Coppola himself rejects his ethnic background. This is an odd assessment that does not seem to be supported by either the films Coppola made or his public comments about them.

38. About Coppola's plans for *Part II*, Goodwin and Wise write, "Vito's scenes would be shot in warm, nostalgic gold and sepia tones to reveal him as a Lower East Side Robin Hood. In contrast, Michael's scenes would be filmed in a cool, bright, modern style, with the character growing colder, harder, and more ruthless with every scene" (163).

39. For a discussion of how the film relates capitalism to family life, see Shadoian.

40. Many scholars have investigated the ambivalence of Hollywood texts. See Wood; Ray; and Tomasulo, "Politics." Tomasulo writes, "It is a common marketing strategy of the American cinema to attempt to deal with controversial subject matter by having it both ways, so as not to alienate segments of the mass audience who have strong feelings on one side or another of a particular issue" ("Politics" 147).

41. Martha P. Nochimson sees Michael's second-generation Americanness as a costume that the character sheds when his father is shot. But she also sees Michael's Italian self as unstable (56–57). "Michael Corleone," Nochimson writes, "set the model for the new Hollywood gangster protagonist who recognizes his ethnic background, but whose ethnic heritage becomes more elusive and powdery as he gains success" (57). Nevertheless, Michael seems to play a more active role in both constructing his Americanness and erasing his Italianness than Nochimson's perspective suggests.

42. In an earlier version of the script, Coppola had Vito kill Fanucci in front of Fanucci's three daughters. In his script notes to Coppola, Puzo balked at the idea, writing, "You cannot have Vito kill Fanucci with daughters present. To what purpose? It makes him less sympathetic. Remember these killings are business = not personal. As sheer good manners, Godfathers do not kill men in front of their wives and children" (September 26, 1973).

43. Coppola says of Vito's move into crime, "Clearly, the motivation of Vito in this film for going on the other side of the law and making a bid for power himself comes out of his feeling about his family and wanting to provide for his family" (*Part II* DVD commentary).

44. In an early script for *The Godfather, Part II*, Clemenza (who was later replaced by the character of Pentangeli) meets with Michael during Anthony's communion party. Clemenza says, "Since you've been on the West Coast . . . ever since your pop died, I mean, you're cold, Michael. Your pop, he wasn't cold—he . . . he loved people, he liked people, he liked music. You're not like your pop, Michael" (31).

45. Schumacher writes, "Michael Corleone's Lake Tahoe residence, as designed by Dean Tavoularis, could not have been more different from Vito Corleone's compound in the first movie. The elder Corleone had gathered his family around him, preserving at least a semblance of a home; Michael's place was a fortress, surrounded by walls and shielded by a lake, his isolated family virtually captive in their own house" (167).

46. Gardaphé writes, "The urban settings in Italian-American works of fiction and film become claustrophobic traps for those who live there. Often the protagonists see traveling

west as the best way out" (*Wiseguys* 112). Yet, for the Corleones, the move west becomes more of a prison.

47. In a deleted scene, Coppola showed the arrival of Fredo and his wife, Deanna, at the communion party. The couple creates a similar scene, which ends with Fredo attempting to explain to Deanna why it is so important for him to be deferential toward his younger brother.

48. Cowie has compared the violence in Coppola's work and the violence in Scorsese's. "We rarely feel obliged to turn aside in pain from Coppola's killings as we do from Scorsese's," he writes. "Instead, the spectacle absorbs us, enthralling rather than appalling" (*Godfather* 164).

49. Many of these scenes were included in the chronological rendering of the two films that was shown on network television in the 1970s, and Jenny M. Jones also includes quite a few of them in *The Annotated Godfather: The Complete Screenplay.*

50. Coppola has said, "By the end of *Godfather II* just like America in that period, Michael had become wrapped in a kind of self-righteousness and distrusts everyone and is getting more and more like a paranoid person, like a Nixon" (Werner).

51. Some critics have found ways to "save" the film's gender politics. Goodwin and Wise see the role of women as "guardians of the home" (117). Coppola has argued that the gender norms reflect historically accurate relations within Mafia families (Phillips, *Interviews* 33), and Bergen suggests that the outsider Kay becomes the character through which many understand the film (41).

52. As Ingrid Walker Fields says of the novel's Vito, "One of the major functions of Don Corleone's code as Puzo articulates it is to live life as a critique of mainstream America and its hypocrisies" (618–19).

53. In a letter to Coppola regarding *The Godfather, Part II,* Puzo wrote, "I was maybe too strong on keeping the women in the background. Maybe they should be given a little more to do. But never really calling any shots" (August 1, 1973).

54. It is interesting to note that Paramount's parent company (Gulf + Western) had become involved with Immobiliare in the early 1970s. See Cowie, *Godfather* 8.

55. Most critics judged the film harshly upon its initial release, but in recent years, several scholars have revisited the widely held belief that *Part III* was an inferior *Godfather* film. Clarke argues that "when viewed as the culmination of the trilogy the film is very satisfying, elaborating further on the theme of guilt where the second film took revenge as its driving force" (207). See also Bondanella 263–71; and De Stefano 125–31.

56. In a famous line from *Part II,* Michael tells Geary, "We're both part of the same hypocrisy, Senator." And in *Part I,* Michael tells Kay, "My father is no different than any other powerful man—any man who is responsible for other people, like a senator or a president."

57. Fred Gardaphé and Richard Gambino have argued that the inequalities that characterize Coppola's representation of Old World Italian culture are actually more the product of New World Italian American culture. See Gardaphé, *Wiseguys* 1–41; and Gambino, *Blood of My Blood* 21–42.

58. Scorsese's *GoodFellas* is often compared to the *Godfather* films and is generally judged to undermine the romanticization of the gangster found in Coppola's trilogy. See Gardaphé, *Wiseguys* 80; L. S. Friedman 171; Duncan 114; and Connelly 139.

Chapter 5. Quentin Tarantino: Ethnicity and the Postmodern

1. Tarantino's mother never asked Tony "to play the role of father" (Clarkson 14). Of his dad, Tarantino says, "I've never had any desire to get in touch with him. . . . I'm not mad at him or anything like that. . . . [I]t would just be more or less embarrassing to look at somebody who I'm supposed to feel something for, even though I don't know him at all" (quoted in Bernard 8).

2. Willis writes, "For the world of Tarantino's films is a world without history—a world where all culture is simultaneous, where movies only really watch other movies. *Pulp Fiction* is steadfast in its refusal to be assigned any specific historical moment; its very collision of styles and signs undermines any effort to stabilize it historically" (213). But rather than seeing this as a detriment, Willis sees it as an asset. "This artificial contemporaneity," she writes, "operates as a kind of utopian eternal present. In relying on these artifacts as central organizing devices, his films offer the perfect salvage operation, redeeming a past for the generation that inhabited it, but that also 'missed' it" (197–98). See also Irwin 72.

3. See James Wood in Sammells 45–46; Wood, "Slick Shtick" 65; Dowell 5; Kermode 46; A. O. Scott, "Blood Bath and Beyond"; and Mendelsohn.

4. David Denby offers a different perspective by suggesting that Tarantino is actually commenting on Scorsese's representations. See "Thugfest" 96, 99.

5. Each of the above-mentioned critics should be commended for their willingness to recognize the politics of Tarantino's work. Even "not saying anything" is a political act, and as Comolli and Narboni have shown, all films are political. See also Fried; Gormley; Rosenbaum, "Allusion Profusion"; and Alleva, "*Pulp.*" For a discussion of the perceived shallowness of Tarantino's movies, see Levine 22.

6. Dawson's answer is that *homage* essentially means not hiding the source of your reference, a definition that is admittedly "easy in literature, not so clear-cut on film" (89).

7. For similar assessments, see Barnes and Hearn 131; Hattenstone 164; Topel 185; and Peary xiii. Tom Charity counters such opinions, writing, "It's easy to caricature Tarantino as a film geek cocooned in cineliteracy—but hard to think of another art form in which knowledge of the medium would be disparaged like this" (154).

8. D. K. Holm labels Tarantino's work the "cinematic equivalent of hip-hop sampling techniques" (46).

9. See Bernard; Barnes and Hearn; and Charyn.

10. According to Charles Ramirez Berg, Tarantino's willingness to "frustrat[e] [generic] expectations by omitting obligatory scenes," his "tangential speeches" that contribute "little—if anything—to the narration of the story," and his (along with others') "new film narration," which is intended for "multiple viewings," are some of the ways in which his work has helped to advance the art of cinema (42–43).

11. See Taubin, "Critics' Commentary"; Romney 34, 36; and Charyn xxii.

12. Tarantino often allows his characters the opportunity to tell stories. See Levy, "Critics' Commentary."

13. In *Mean Streets*, the posturing belies a homosocial and perhaps homosexual attraction between characters like Charlie and Johnny Boy. In his *Cineaste* review of *Reservoir Dogs*, Robert Hilferty makes a similar argument about Tarantino's film.

14. See Botting and Wilson 107.

15. Several stepfathers were present in Tarantino's life, but most, if not all, of them disappeared when their relationships with Tarantino's mother ended (Bernard 19–22).

16. The relationship between Orange and White is not the only father-son relationship in the film. Joe Cabot (Lawrence Tierney) is Nice Guy Eddie's (Chris Penn) actual father, and he is also a kind of surrogate father for Mr. Blonde.

17. Although he is not based on Tarantino's actual father, *Jackie Brown*'s Ordell is based on the male mentors Tarantino had while growing up (*Jackie Brown* DVD Trivia Track). Additionally, *Kill Bill*'s Esteban Vihaio (Michael Parks, again) is said to be a father figure to Bill.

18. See Barnes and Hearn 15; Charyn 10, 171; and Willis 215.

19. Dawson has suggested that *True Romance* should not be treated as a Tarantino film (99). Yet the script has more autobiographical overtones than any other Tarantino screenplay.

20. Many critics have recognized the influence of *Taxi Driver* on Tarantino's movies. See Woods, *Film;* and Charyn 173.

21. Tarantino suggests that the tone of the scene mimics that of his relationship with his stepfather Kurt, even though a confrontation between the director and his stepdad never actually occurred.

22. Tarantino's use of anime in *Kill Bill: Volume 1* was preceded by his use of a cartoon in the *Natural Born Killers* script (Oliver Stone, 1994).

23. In addition to the critics cited earlier, Oliver Stone has said, "You can make fun movies, or pulpy movies, but I don't know, is there really something being said?" (Stone quoted in Bernard 99–100).

24. Giroux writes that discussions about the "realistic depiction" of violence serve "pedagogically to justify abstracting the representation of violence from the ethical responsibility of both film makers and the audience to challenge it as an established social practice" (309).

25. For a discussion of this dynamic in *Reservoir Dogs'* ear-slicing scene, see Dargis 11; Rittger 361; Rafferty 105; Jardine n.p.; Lyons 112; Taubin, "Critics' Commentary"; Hill, *Shocking Entertainment* 97; and Tarantino, *Reservoir Dogs* DVD commentary.

26. For a more detailed summary of the ways in which Tarantino can be seen as a postmodernist, see Page 19–20.

27. At least two essays have even investigated the medieval roots of *Pulp Fiction.* See Terkla; and Reed and Jewers. For one of the most exhaustive lists of Tarantino's references, see Holm 11–12.

28. I saw *Pulp Fiction* on its initial theatrical run when I was a freshman in college. The viewing experience was unlike any film I had seen before. After watching the movie, I recall having conversations about its homages and thematic concerns with high school friends over e-mail. In many ways, the experience of watching *Pulp Fiction* laid the groundwork for my interest in film study.

29. According to the *Pulp Fiction* DVD Trivia Track, Mia and Vincent share similarities with the characters in *Out of the Past* (Jacques Tourneur, 1947), Jules's Ezekiel monologue has associations with *Night of the Hunter* (Charles Laughton, 1955), and the process shot of Butch's cab ride is an homage to classic noir.

30. To acknowledge Bava's influence, Tarantino has suburban drug dealer Lance (Eric Stoltz) offer a brand of heroin to Vincent Vega that he calls "Bava."

31. Julie Salomon suggests that Keitel's Wolf also draws on his previous role as Charlie in Scorsese's *Mean Streets* (A16).

32. Tarantino often uses an actor's backstory as the backstory for a character. For a discussion of this technique in *Pulp Fiction,* see Charyn 106. For a discussion of its use in *Jackie Brown,* see Tarantino quoted in Mendolsohn 41.

33. Interestingly, Godard's *Pierrot le Fou* (1965) also includes a scene that is similar to *Pulp Fiction*'s dance-contest sequence. In *Pierrot,* a brunette dances a modified version of the twist in what looks like a café-garage hybrid.

34. Travolta's flaccid appearance, his effect on the audience and the narrative, and his smoothly awkward dance moves have been the subject of several critical assessments. See Gleiberman 10; Woods, *King* 115; Charyn 106–7; Woods, *Film* 80; and Polan 51.

35. The exchange between Vincent and Mia in which they call each other cowboy and cowgirl references previous roles for each of them. Travolta had starred in *Urban Cowboy* (James Bridges, 1980), and Thurman had starred in *Even Cowgirls Get the Blues* (Gus Van Sant, 1993).

36. Vincent may be an Italian American anyway, since "Vega" could very well be an Italian American last name.

37. In a 1994 interview with Charlie Rose, Tarantino listed Howard Hawks, Sam Fuller, Sergio Leone, Jean-Luc Godard, and Jean-Pierre Melville alongside Scorsese as some of the filmmakers who have had a strong influence on his work. In discussing *Hero* (Stephen Frears, 1992) in another interview, Tarantino said, "That would have been my Capra movie" (quoted in Hirschberg 114). His *Inglourious Basterds* script makes two references to his fellow Italian American director. The Nazi film *Lucky Kids* is labeled "Goebbels Frank Capra copy" (71) and also "the bosch Capra-corn abomination" (74). Neither reference made the final cut of the film.

38. See Carradine 281; Bernard 206; and Dawson 53.

39. For comparative analyses of *Reservoir Dogs* with *Mean Streets* and *GoodFellas,* see Woods, *King* 33; Taubin, "Critics' Commentary"; Levy, "Critics' Commentary"; Rafferty 105; and Crouch 232.

40. Not only did he have producer Rand Vossler hype him like Scorsese, but while working with Italian American filmmaker Bill Lustig, he often talked about how he and Lustig would be the next Scorsese and Paul Schrader (Bernard 67).

41. *Kill Bill: Volume 1* is not the only Tarantino film that references other Tarantino films. *Death Proof* also references previous Tarantino movies. The mustang in which Abernathy (Rosario Dawson) and her friends drive around has a sticker that reads "Lil' Pussywagon" on the back of the car—a clear reference to *Kill Bill: Volume 1.* For a discussion of Tarantino's self-quoting in *Jackie Brown,* see Holm 19–20.

42. For a more lengthy discussion of other cinematic influences in the hospital scene, see J. Smith 218.

43. Tarantino further hints at a potential sequel by literally concluding *Volume 2* with a question mark. As the names of each of the actors who played the members of the Deadly Viper Assassination Squad appear, they are crossed off in the same fashion that Kiddo crosses them off her checklist. But when Daryl Hannah's name appears, a question mark is drawn.

44. Dawson has pointed out that this technique now associated with Tarantino was first employed in a 1965 episode of *The Flintstones* entitled "No Biz Like Showbiz" (177).

Tarantino's former writing partner and friend Roger Avery also used it in *Killing Zoe* (1994) (*King* 91).

45. It should be noted that Dimmick does not use the word again, but its use is already excessive. For a discussion of the politics of Tarantino's use of the word, see Rosenbaum 177; Willis 210, 212; and Crouch 232. For Tarantino's take on his understanding and use of the word, see Bauer 6–9.

46. What may have been more upsetting than the word's appearance is Tarantino's apparent delight in using it. See Taylor in Peary 42–43; Giroux 310; and Van Peebles quoted in Barnes and Hearn 108–9.

47. More recently, Tarantino has used a different strategy to defend *True Romance*'s Sicilian speech. On the DVD commentary track to the film, Tarantino says that "Don" or "Big D," one of his mom's black friends, inspired the monologue. Big D, the director says, had told him the story and was excited to see it included in *True Romance*. Essentially, the director attempts to share the scene's authorship with a black man in order to marginalize questions of artistic responsibility. Later in the commentary, Tarantino cites *Long Ships* (a 1964 film directed by Jack Cardiff and starring Sidney Poitier as a Moorish prince who is married to Aminah, a character played by Italian actress Rosanna Schiaffino) as a film that recounts the historical events that the monologue references. This strategy works to shift the debate to questions of historical accuracy. It is not about whether Tarantino should use the word but whether "Big D," *Long Ships,* and now Tarantino have their facts straight. Ultimately, what *may* save the scene's use of the *n* word is the performative nature of Cliff's speech. Cliff delivers the monologue to anger Coccotti so much that he might evade further torture, secure a fast death for himself, and avoid the risk of confessing his son's whereabouts.

48. One such critic goes so far as to write, "There is not a better person to pass judgment on this matter than Samuel Jackson" (Scott quoted in Dawson 117), without offering any further explanation as to why Jackson would be such an unassailable authority on the matter.

49. Pat Dowell has also used the term *postracist* in regards to *Pulp Fiction,* but unlike Smith, Dowell is not convinced that it was or is possible to be postracist. He finds in *Pulp* "a kind of post–civil rights bravado" that was indicative of the political discourse surrounding the film's release in 1994. "The same kind of attitude [is] manifesting itself in discussions in Newt [Gingrich]'s Congress," Dowell wrote, "where eager young turks of the Republican Party proclaim that Affirmative Action is no longer needed as a remedy for 'past' injustices" (5). Dowell also argues that the film takes a comparable position on gender by "[following] a similar pattern of displaying stereotypes under the guise of postfeminist sensibility" (5).

50. Anthony Lane disagrees, writing, "I couldn't help glimpsing something queasy in [Samuel L. Jackson's] role; it is as if Tarantino were getting off on the idea of a character who allows him, the white screenwriter, to write the word 'nigger' with impunity as many times as possible" (84).

51. The film made significant progress not just in Tarantino's engagement with racial issues but in Hollywood's overall engagement with racial, gender, and age-based politics. See Lane 54; and Roger Ebert's review of the film on the *Siskel and Ebert* television program.

52. Although the character's name is "Brett," Jules refers to him as "Brad" during their conversation.

53. For a discussion of the label *reverse racist,* see Shohat and Stam 178–219.

54. See, for instance, the *Jackie Brown* DVD Trivia Track and "Interview with Quentin Tarantino." In some ways, Tarantino's comments mimic the industry's oversimplified understanding of racially diverse audiences. *Variety* wrote that *Jackie Brown* "looks to find its most ardent fans among cinephiles and black viewers. . . . B. O. prospects are OK in urban areas, less so elsewhere" (McCarthy 57). For a discussion of such reductive and stereotypical imaginings of the black audience, see Willis 212.

55. In 2002, Halle Berry became the first and (to date) only African American woman to be awarded an Academy Award for Best Actress.

56. Critics are divided over how much *Jackie Brown* is indebted to blaxploitation pictures. See Carson 28; and Bruzzi 40. For a discussion of blaxploitation's influence on *Pulp Fiction,* see Holm 43.

57. Gary Indiana has noted the link that Tarantino's films make between "black" and "cool." Indiana writes, "To be really, really cool becomes the spiritual equivalent of blackness, and even superior to it: there are plenty of square black people but not one square cool person. For the Tarantino of *Pulp Fiction,* blackness is a plastic holy grail, a mythic substance with real effects and its own medieval code" (65).

58. Hip-hop artists often claim that the misogynistic, homophobic, and racist lyrics of their compositions are merely a performance and that they do not really believe the things that they say. Even if this is true, the positions these media productions offer enable the racist, sexist, and homophobic views of listeners.

59. The films are also deeply concerned with comics. See Charyn 155; and Carradine 130.

60. See Shohat and Stam.

61. Page neglects to mention that Lee also played "Kato" on three episodes of the *Batman* television series between 1966 and 1967.

62. Lee was born in San Francisco, California, but acted in productions in both the United States and Hong Kong.

63. Among other roles, Lopez played Mary Fiore in *The Wedding Planner* (Adam Shankman, 2001), and Leguizamo played Vinny in *Summer of Sam* (Spike Lee, 1999).

64. Tarantino's invocation of these various national cinemas led Peter Travers to remark, "Tarantino has made the hottest mix tape in the history of cinema" (quoted in Woods, *Film* 179). *Mix tape* is a particularly adept term, since the director borrows music from Ennio Morricone, Luis Bacalov, Isaac Hayes, Quincy Jones, and Bernard Herrmann (Olsen 12). For a discussion of the film's references to Asian cinemas, see Machiyama.

65. See Rich, Schwarzacher, and Tomita.

66. For a discussion of the other themes in the *Kill Bill* films, see Gallafent 116, 119; Charyn 157; and Holm 136.

67. This would be especially true if one belonged to an ethnic group that was racially marginalized as well.

68. The film never indicates Raine's spiritual background, but on an appearance to promote the film on *The Today Show,* Tarantino claimed that Raine was "not Jewish" (August 14, 2009).

69. On the *Inglourious Basterds* DVD, Elvis Mitchell interviews Tarantino and Pitt, and Raine's backstory comes up. Neither divulges the character's history, but Pitt hints that there may be a *Basterds* prequel. Presumably, the rope burn would play a role in that film.

70. Significantly, Tarantino's comments imply a different understanding of racial boundaries than his previous films had offered.

Conclusion: Ancestral Legacies and History's Lessons

1. See Tamburri, "An Offer We Can Refuse"; and Applegate.

2. After the series finale, several cast members appeared in commercials that drew on the characters they played on the program. Tony Sirico did a series of advertisements for Denny's, while Frank Vincent appeared in spots for Miller Lite. Italian American groups protested both advertising campaigns, and both were taken off the air.

3. In 2002, AIDA attorneys entered a Chicago courtroom alleging that HBO violated a dignity clause found in the Illinois state constitution. The presiding judge later dismissed the case. See Quinn 166.

4. "Roukema" is a Dutch name, but the Italian American congresswoman's maiden name is "Scafati." In fact, Roukema has said that it was the memory of her parents, Margaret and Claude Scafati, that inspired her to introduce her resolution (Roukema L10).

5. According to Tom Avril, "The rates of searched cars with minority drivers are generally higher on the southern stretch of the [New Jersey] turnpike" (E3). Statistics indicate that the vast majority of minority motorists (seven out of ten) who were searched were not carrying illegal drugs. See also Ruderman.

6. In her letter, Roukema wrote, "If we were to be completely honest, we know that if a television show were to depict African-Americans or Hispanics with negative stereotypes, those ethnic groups would be marching in the streets, as well they should. Talk about racial profiling: This is ethnic profiling" (L10).

7. However, while serving as New York's governor, Mario Cuomo had to answer accusations that his father-in-law was Mob connected.

8. For a discussion of the ways in which Italian Americans have sometimes used other ethnic groups to leverage their own assimilation, see Roediger, *Wages;* Ignatiev; Guglielmo, *White on Arrival;* Jacobson, *Whiteness of a Different Color;* and Guglielmo and Salerno, *Are Italians White?*

9. For a longer discussion of this topic, see Cavallero, "Gangsters."

10. In October 2010, this site was no longer available. However, the campaign was covered in the press. See G. Wright.

11. *Lost in Translation's* representation of the Japanese created fears that the film would fail commercially in Japan (see Hall). Unfortunately, I was unable to find the film's Japanese box-office statistics. However, according to http://www.boxofficemojo.com, the film grossed $75,138,403 (62.8 percent) in foreign markets and $44,585,453 (37.2 percent) domestically. Hollywood films typically see slightly higher box-office revenues in foreign markets than in the United States. However, it is somewhat unusual for foreign markets to account for a percentage as high as *Lost in Translation's.* Coppola's *Marie Antoinette* earned an even higher percentage of its total revenues from the international box office. Almost 74 percent of *Marie's* $60,917,718 worldwide gross came from international markets.

12. Coppola has her defenders. Paul Julian Smith argues that the film is less interested in "foreign clichés" than "the process of translation" (15), and Stephanie Zacharek justifies the stereotypical moments by contending that Coppola "delights in all cultural differences

not just those that are politically correct" (n.p.). Todd McGowan argues that the film is not racist, because racism is based on the idea of excessive difference, whereas Coppola's film demonstrates "an absence of difference" (59). McGowan's essay is oftentimes insightful, but on this point, he seems misguided. Rather than identifying an absence of difference, the film is quick to point out as many differences as possible. Repeatedly, viewers are reminded that the Japanese speak differently, that they are shorter, and that their television personalities and programs are eccentric and strange. For an extended discussion of the stereotypes mobilized in the film, see Tomasulo, "Japan."

13. Frank P. Tomasulo rightly argues, "It appears that Coppola really wanted to say something about the United States, not about Japan" ("Japan" 154).

14. There are a number of other films that are even more vicious to Asian peoples. Films that specifically target the Japanese include (but are not limited to) *Know Your Enemy: Japan*, *Black Rain* (Ridley Scott, 1989), and *Rising Sun* (Philip Kaufman, 1993) (Tomasulo, "Japan" 155). For a critique of Cimino's film, see Marchetti. Cimino also has his defenders (see Lawton).

15. Visitors to http://www.tancredo.org are now redirected to http://www.tancredofor-governor2010.org, where he writes of "stopping illegal immigration cold" but no longer uses the word *invasion*. He was defeated in the 2010 election.

16. My disagreements with Lewis's take on the auteur theory are not indicative of my opinion of his book as a whole. In fact, I have assigned Lewis's text as required reading in one of my introductory-level classes. Lewis is not the only scholar who has described the auteur theory as fictional. During a visit to Indiana University, Jane Gaines spoke of what she called the "author fiction."

17. As Deborah Cartmell and I. Q. Hunter argue, "Although academic history has typically shown the individual dwarfed by the vast, blind and relentless machinery of historical processes, popular film and literature assert that people energetically influence history" (2).

18. The scene was actually shot in Putnam County, just to the north of New York City.

19. Springsteen makes a nod toward his Italian American family in the song. In the next-to-last verse he lists the names of immigrant families. "The McNicholas, the Posalskis, the Smiths, Zerillis too." Springsteen's mother's (Adele) maiden name is Zerilli.

Bibliography

Manuscript Collections

Capra, Frank. Collection. Wesleyan Cinema Archives, Middletown, Connecticut.
The Godfather Materials. American Zoetrope Research Library, Rutherford, California.

Books, Articles, and Media Productions

Aaron, Daniel. "The Hyphenate Writer and American Letters." *Smith Alumnae Quarterly* (July 1964): 213–17.

Affron, Mirella J. "The Italian American in American Films, 1918–1978." *Italian Americana* 3 (Spring–Summer 1977): 232–55.

Alba, Richard A. "Whiteness Just Isn't Enough." *Sociological Forum* 22, no. 2 (2007): 232–41.

Alleva, Richard. "Boston Massacre: *The Departed*." *Commonweal* 133, no. 19 (2006): 16–17.

———. "*Godfather III*." *Commonweal* 118, no. 4 (1991): 133–34.

———. "*Pulp Fiction*." *Commonweal* 121, no. 20 (1994): 30–31.

Anderson, Benedict. *Imagined Communities: Reflections on the Origin and Spread of Nationalism*. Rev. ed. New York: Verso, 1991.

Applegate, Aaron. "Politician's Flier Offends Some with Italian Roots." *Virginia Pilot*, August 27, 2008.

Avril, Tom. "Panel Slams Point Used to Fend Off Profiling Charges; State Senators Ask: If a Survey of How Likely Drivers of Different Races Are to Break the Law Is Crucial, Why Hasn't It Been Done?" *Philadelphia Inquirer*, March 25, 2001.

Bailey, Samuel L. *Immigrants in the Lands of Promise: Italians in Buenos Aires and New York City, 1870–1914*. Ithaca: Cornell University Press, 1999.

Baker, Aaron, and Juliann Vitullo. "Mysticism and the Household Saints of Everyday Life." *VIA: Voices in Italian Americana* 7, no. 2 (1996): 55–63.

Baker, Kevin. "You Have to Give a Sense of What People Wanted." *American Heritage* 52, no. 8 (2001): 50+.

Barnes, Alan, and Marcus Hearn. *Tarantino: A to Zed.* London: B. T. Batsford, 1999.

Barthes, Roland. "The Death of the Author." In *Image, Music, Text,* 142–48. New York: Hill and Wang.

Bauer, Erik. "The Mouth and the Method." *Sight and Sound* 8, no. 3 (1998): 6–9.

Bazin, André. "On Why We Fight: History, Documentation, and the Newsreel (1946)." Trans. Bert Cardullo. *Film and History* 31, no. 1 (2001): 60–62.

Beck, Henry Cabot. "Quentin Bloody Quentin." *New York Daily News,* October 5, 2003. Reprinted in *Quentin Tarantino: The Film Geek Files,* ed. Paul A. Woods, 167–69. London: Plexus, 2005.

Behar, Henri. "Bringing It All Back Home." *Empire* (November 1990). Reprinted in *Scorsese: A Journey through the American Psyche,* ed. Paul A. Woods, 184–89. London: Plexus, 2005.

Berg, Charles Ramírez. "A Taxonomy of Alternative Plots in Recent Films: Classifying the 'Tarantino Effect.'" *Film Criticism* 31, nos. 1–2 (2006): 5–61.

Bergan, Ronald. *Francis Coppola, Close Up: The Making of His Movies.* New York: Thunder's Mouth Press, 1998.

Berliner, Todd. "The Pleasures of Disappointment: Sequels and *The Godfather, Part II.*" *Journal of Film and Video* 53, nos. 2–3 (2001): 107–23.

Bernard, Jami. *Quentin Tarantino: The Man and His Movies.* New York: HarperPerennial, 1995.

Bertellini, Giorgio. *Italy in Early American Cinema: Race, Landscape, and the Picturesque.* Bloomington: Indiana University Press, 2009.

Biderman, Shai. "The Roar and the Rampage: A Tale of Revenge in *Kill Bill, Volumes 1 and 2.*" In *Movies and the Meaning of Life: Philosophers Take on Hollywood,* ed. Kimberly Ann Blessing and Paul J. Tudico. La Salle, Ill.: Open Court, 2005.

Bidwell, Duane R. "'Let's Get into Character': A Narrative/Constructionist Psychology of Conversion in Quentin Tarantino's *Pulp Fiction.*" *Pastoral Psychology* 49, no. 5 (2001): 327–40.

Biskind, Peter. *The "Godfather" Companion: Everything You Ever Wanted to Know about All Three.* New York: HarperPerennial, 1990.

Blake, Richard A. "Redeemed in Blood: The Sacramental Universe of Martin Scorsese." *Journal of Popular Film and Television* 24, no. 1 (1996): 2–9.

———. *Street Smart: The New York of Lumet, Allen, Scorsese, and Lee.* Lexington: University Press of Kentucky, 2005.

Blakefield, William J. "An Enemy Within: The Making of *Know Your Enemy: Japan.*" *Sight and Sound* 52, no. 2 (1983): 128–33.

Bliss, Michael. *Martin Scorsese and Michael Cimino.* Metuchen, N.J.: Scarecrow Press, 1985.

———. *The Word Made Flesh: Catholicism and Conflict in the Films of Martin Scorsese.* Filmmakers, vol. 45. Lanham, Md.: Scarecrow Press, 1995.

Bliven, Bruce. "Boston's Civil War." *New Republic,* June 29, 1927. Reprinted in *Sacco and Vanzetti,* ed. John Davis, 65–71. Rebel Lives Series. New York: Ocean Press, 2004.

Boehnel, William. "Capra Excels Himself in the *Mr. Smith* Film." *New York World-Telegram,* October 20, 1939.

Bohn, Thomas William. *An Historical and Descriptive Analysis of the "Why We Fight" Series.* New York: Arno Press, 1977.

Bona, Mary Jo. *Claiming a Tradition: Italian American Women Writers.* Carbondale: Southern Illinois University Press, 1999.

Bondanella, Peter. *Hollywood Italians: Dagos, Palookas, Romeos, Wise Guys, and Sopranos.* New York: Continuum, 2004.

Bordewich, Fergus M. "Manhattan Mayhem: Martin Scorsese's Realistic Portrayal of Pre–Civil War Strife—*Gangs of New York* —Re-creates the Brutal Street Warfare Waged between Immigrant Groups." *Smithsonian,* December 2002, 44+.

Bordwell, David, Janet Staiger, and Kristin Thompson. *The Classical Hollywood Cinema: Film Style and Mode of Production to 1960.* New York: Columbia University Press, 1985.

Bosley, Rachael K. "Native Sons." *American Cinematographer* 84, no. 1 (2003): 36–49.

Botting, Fred, and Scott Wilson. "By Accident: The Tarantinian Ethics." *Theory, Culture, and Society* 15, no. 2 (1998): 89–113.

———. *The Tarantinian Ethics.* London: Sage, 2001.

Bowser, Kenneth, dir. *Frank Capra's American Dream.* 1997. ZM Productions, Frank Capra Productions, Columbia TriStar Television, and American Movie Classics.

Brintnall, Kent. "Tarantino's Incarnational Theology: *Reservoir Dogs,* Crucifixions, and Spectacular Violence." *Currents* 54, no. 1 (2004): 66–75.

Browne, Nick. "The Politics of Narrative Form: Capra's *Mr. Smith Goes to Washington.*" *Wide Angle* 3, no. 3 (1980): 4–11.

Brunette, Peter. "Sofia Coppola's Overly Subtle *Lost in Translation.*" 2004. http://www.indiewire.com/movies/movies_030917lost.html. Accessed May 30, 2007.

Bruzzi, Stella. "*Jackie Brown.*" *Sight and Sound* 8, no. 4 (1998): 39–40.

Burke, Frank. "Reason and Unreason in Federico Fellini's *I Vitelloni.*" *Literature/Film Quarterly* 8, no. 2 (1980): 116–24.

Busch, Noel F. "Joe DiMaggio: Baseball's Most Sensational Big-League Star Starts What Should Be His Best Year So Far." *Life,* May 1, 1939.

Cahan, Abraham. *The Rise of David Levinsky.* 1917. Reprint, New York: Harper and Row, 1960.

"Campaign: No Votes for *Lost in Translation.*" 2003–4. http://www.lost-in-racism.org/. Accessed June 29, 2007.

Capra, Frank. "Fun in a Sicily Madhouse by, of, and for the Inmates." *Philadelphia Daily News,* December 31, 1972.

———. "Letter to Dominic Candeloro." October 22, 1978. http://h-net.msu.edu/cgi-bin/logbrowse.pl?trx=vx&list=h-itam&month=0107&week=c&msg=H15KQxxZVNw14vc42EzIRQ&user=&pw. Accessed September 20, 2010.

———. *The Name above the Title: An Autobiography.* New York: Macmillan, 1971.

Carducci, Mark. "Martin Scorsese." *Millimeter* (May 1975). Reprinted in *Scorsese: A Journey through the American Psyche,* ed. Paul A. Woods, 48–55. London: Plexus, 2005.

Carney, Ray. *American Vision: The Films of Frank Capra.* 1986. Reprint, Hanover, N.H.: Wesleyan University Press, 1996.

Carradine, David. *The "Kill Bill" Diary: The Making of a Tarantino Classic as Seen through the Eyes of a Screen Legend.* New York: Harper Paperbacks, 2006.

Carson, Tom. "Painting with Blood: No, Quentin Tarantino's *Kill Bill* Isn't the Most Violent Movie Ever Made. It's Just the Bloodiest Love Story." *Esquire,* February 2004, 26–28.

Cartmell, Deborah, and I. Q. Hunter. "Pulping Fictions: Consuming Culture across the Literature/Media Divide." Introduction to *Pulping Fictions: Consuming Culture across the English/Media Divide,* ed. Deborah Cartmell, I. Q. Hunter, Heidi Haye, and Imelda Whelehan, 1–10. New York: Pluto Press, 1996.

Casillo, Robert. *Gangster Priest: The Italian American Cinema of Martin Scorsese.* Toronto: University of Toronto Press, 2006.

———. "Moments in Italian-American Cinema: From *Little Caesar* to Coppola and Scorsese." In *From the Margin: Writings in Italian Americana,* ed. Anthony Julian Tamburri, Paolo A. Giordano, and Fred L. Gardaphé, 394–416. Rev. ed. West Lafayette, Ind.: Purdue University Press, 2000.

Cavallero, Jonathan J. *"Forbidden." Quarterly Review of Film and Video* 29, no. 5 (2010): 399–401.

———. "Gangsters, *Fessos,* Tricksters, and Sopranos: The Historical Roots of Italian American Stereotype Anxiety." *Journal of Popular Film and Television* 32, no. 2 (2004): 50–63.

———. "'Maybe Because You're Italian': The Depiction of Italian and Italian American Characters in the Films of Frank Capra." *VIA: Voices in Italian Americana* 14, no. 1 (2003): 15–34.

Chaillet, Jean-Paul, and Elizabeth Vincent. *Francis Ford Coppola.* Trans. Denise Raab Jacobs. New York: St. Martin's Press, 1984.

Charity, Tom. "Big in Japan: Face to Face Bill Murray and Sofia Coppola." *Time Out,* January 7, 2004, 18–19.

———. "Fun Lovin' Criminals." *Time Out,* March 25, 1998. Reprinted in *Quentin Tarantino: The Film Geek Files,* ed. Paul A. Woods, 152–59. London: Plexus, 2005.

Charyn, Jerome. *Raised by Wolves: The Turbulent Art and Times of Quentin Tarantino.* New York: Thunder's Mouth Press, 2006.

Christie, Ian. "Manhattan Asylum." *Sight and Sound* 13, no. 1 (2003): 20–23.

———. "Scorsese: Faith under Pressure." *Sight and Sound* 16, no. 11 (2006): 14–17.

Chumo, Peter N., II. "The Next Best Thing to a Time Machine: Quentin Tarantino's *Pulp Fiction." Post Script* (Summer 1996). Reprinted in *Quentin Tarantino: The Film Geek Files,* ed. Paul A. Woods, 75–88. London: Plexus, 2005.

Ciment, Michael, and Hubert Niogret. "Interview at Cannes." *Positif* 379 (1992): 28–35. Reprinted in *Quentin Tarantino: Interviews,* ed. Gerald Peary, 9–26. Jackson: University Press of Mississippi, 1998.

Clarke, James. *Coppola.* London: Virgin Books, 2003.

Clarkson, Wensley. *Quentin Tarantino: Shooting from the Hip.* Woodstock, N.Y.: Overlook Press, 1995.

Cohen, Paula Marantz. "Underworld with an Overbite: The Corrupting Effects of Martin Scorsese's Late Epic Style." *TLS: Times Literary Supplement,* October 20, 2006, 18.

"Columbia's Gem." *Time,* August 8, 1938, 35–38.

"Commentary Track." *Reservoir Dogs.* 10th Anniversary DVD. Miramax Home Video, 2002.

Comolli, Jean-Luc, and Jean Narboni. "Cinema/Ideology/Criticism." In *Film Theory and Criticism: Introductory Readings,* ed. Leo Braudy and Marshall Cohen, 752–59. New York: Oxford University Press, 1999.

Connelly, Marie Katheryn. *Martin Scorsese: An Analysis of His Feature Films, with a Filmography of His Entire Directorial Career.* Jefferson, N.C.: McFarland, 1993.

"A Conversation with Quentin Tarantino." *Newsweek,* December 26, 1994, 119.

Cook, Pam. "Portrait of a Lady: Sofia Coppola." *Sight and Sound* 16, no. 11 (2006): 36–40.

———. *Screening the Past: Memory and Nostalgia in Cinema.* London: Routledge, 2005.

Coppola, Francis Ford. "Director's Commentary." *The Godfather, Part II.* DVD. Paramount Home Video, 2001.

———. "Director's Commentary." *The Godfather, Part III.* DVD. Paramount Home Video, 2001.

Corliss, Richard. "Adding Kick to the Chic." *Time,* November 16, 1992, 95+.

———. "A Blast to the Heart." *Time,* October 10, 1994, 76+.

———. "A Victory for Lonely Hearts." *Time,* September 15, 2003.

Cortés, Carlos. "Italian-Americans in Film: From Immigrants to Icons." *MELUS* 14, nos. 3–4 (1987): 107–26.

Cowie, Peter. *Coppola.* New York: Charles Scribner's Sons, 1990.

——— *The "Godfather" Book.* Boston: Faber and Faber, 1997.

Cramer, Richard Ben. *Joe DiMaggio: The Hero's Life.* New York: Simon and Schuster, 2000.

Cripps, Thomas. "Racial Ambiguities in American Propaganda Movies." In *Film and Radio Propaganda in World War II,* ed. K. R. M. Short, 125–45. Knoxville: University of Tennessee Press, 1986.

Crouch, Stanley. *The All-American Skin Game; or, The Decoy of Race: The Long and the Short of It, 1990–1994.* New York: Pantheon Books, 1995.

Culbert, David. *Films and Propaganda in America: A Documentary History.* Vol. 2, pt. 1. New York: Greenwood Press, 1990.

———. "Why We Fight: Social Engineering for a Democratic Society at War." In *Film and Radio Propaganda in World War II,* ed. K. R. M. Short, 173–91. Knoxville: University of Tennessee Press, 1986.

Cullen, Jim. *The American Dream: A Short History of an Idea That Shaped a Nation.* New York: Oxford University Press, 2003.

Czitrom, Daniel. "*Gangs of New York.*" *Labor History* 44, no. 3 (2003): 301+.

D'Acierno, Pellegrino. "Cinema Paradiso: The Italian American Presence in American Cinema." In *The Italian American Heritage: A Companion to Literature and Arts,* ed. Pellegrino D'Acierno, 563–690. Garland Reference Library of the Humanities, vol. 1473. New York: Garland Publishing, 1999.

———. "Cultural Lexicon: Italian American Key Terms." In *The Italian American Heritage: A Companion to Literature and Arts,* ed. Pellegrino D'Acierno, 703–66. Garland Reference Library of the Humanities, vol. 1473. New York: Garland Publishing, 1999.

Daniels, Roger. *Guarding the Golden Door: American Immigration Policy and Immigrants since 1882.* New York: Hill and Wang 2004.

Dargis, Manohla. "*Reservoir Dogs.*" *Artforum* 31, no. 3 (1992): 11.

Daugherty, Frank. "He Has the Common Touch." *Christian Science Monitor,* November 9, 1938. Reprinted in *Frank Capra Interviews,* ed. Leland Poague, 19–22. Jackson: University Press of Mississippi, 2004.

Davis, John, ed. *Sacco and Vanzetti.* New York: Ocean Press, 2004.

Dawson, Jeff. *Quentin Tarantino: The Cinema of Cool.* New York: Applause, 1995.

DeCurtis, Anthony. "What the Streets Mean: An Interview with Martin Scorsese." *South Atlantic Quarterly* 91, no. 2 (1992): 427+.

Denby, David. "Dead Reckoning." *New Yorker,* October 13, 2003, 112+.

———. "*Mean Streets:* The Sweetness of Hell." *Sight and Sound* (Winter 1973–74). Reprinted in *Scorsese: A Journey through the American Psyche,* ed. Paul A. Woods, 35–40. London: Plexus, 2005.

———. "A Thugfest." *New York,* October 3, 1994, 96–99.

Denning, Michael. *The Culture Front: The Laboring of American Culture in the Twentieth Century.* New York: Verso, 1996.

De Stefano, George. *An Offer We Can't Refuse: The Mafia in the Mind of America.* New York: Faber and Faber, 2007.

Dickstein, Morris. "Self-Tormentors." *Partisan Review* 61, no. 4 (1994): 658–64.

di Donato, Pietro. *Christ in Concrete.* 1939. Reprint, New York: New American Library, 1993.

DiGirolamo, Vincent. "Such, Such Were the B'hoys . . ." *Radical History Review* 90 (Fall 2004): 123–41.

Dika, Vera. "The Representation of Ethnicity in *The Godfather.*" In *Francis Ford Coppola's "The Godfather" Trilogy,* ed. Nick Browne, 76–108. Cambridge Film Handbooks. New York: Cambridge University Press, 2000.

Di Stasi, Lawrence, ed. "*Una Storia Segreta*": *The Secret History of Italian American Evacuation and Internment during World War II.* Berkeley: Heyday Books, 2001.

Doherty, Thomas. *Projections of War: Hollywood, American Culture, and World War II.* Film and Culture. New York: Columbia University Press, 1993.

Donatelli, Cindy, and Sharon Alward. "'I Dread You'? Married to the Mob in *The Godfather, GoodFellas,* and *The Sopranos.*" In *This Thing of Ours: Investigating "The Sopranos,"* ed. David Lavery. New York: Columbia University Press, 2002.

Dougan, Andy. *Martin Scorsese: Close Up.* New York: Thunder's Mouth Press, 1998.

Dowell, Pat. "Two Shots at Quentin Tarantino's *Pulp Fiction.*" *Cineaste* 21, no. 3 (1995): 4+.

Dower, John W. *War without Mercy: Race and Power in the Pacific War.* New York: Pantheon Books, 1986.

"Drive for Law to Deport 6,000,000 Aliens Will Be Organized All over the Country." *New York Times,* June 23, 1935, sec. 1, p. 1.

Duncan, Paul. *Martin Scorsese.* Harpenden, England: Pocket Essentials, 2004.

Durgnat, Raymond. "Martin Scorsese: Between God and the Goodfellas." *Sight and Sound* 5, no. 6 (1995): 22+.

Ebert, Roger. "*Goodfellas.*" In *Roger Ebert's Video Companion,* 320–21. 1997. Reprint, Kansas City, Mo.: Andrews McMeel, 1998.

———. *Scorsese by Ebert.* Chicago: University of Chicago Press, 2008.

———. "Young Manhood on a More Truthful Level?" *Chicago Sun-Times,* March 17, 1969. Reprinted in *Martin Scorsese: The First Decade,* ed. Mary Pat Kelly, 159–60. Pleasantville, N.Y.: Redgrave, 1980.

Ehrenstein, David. *The Scorsese Picture: The Art and Life of Martin Scorsese.* New York: Birch Lane Press, 1992.

Elsaesser, Thomas. "The Pathos of Failure: American Films in the '70s." *Monogram* 6 (1975): 13–19.

Everts, Desiree E. "Martin Scorsese and His Young 'Girl': Female Objectification in *Who's That Knocking at My Door.*" *VIA: Voices in Italian Americana* 8, no. 1 (1997): 159–65.

Ewing, Charles Burgess. *An Analysis of Frank Capra's War Rhetoric in the "Why We Fight" Films.* Ann Arbor: University Microfilms International, 1986.

"Extract from 'Martin Scorsese Seminar' at the American Film Institute's Center for Advanced Film Studies, 12 February 1975." From *Dialogues on Film* (1975). Reprinted in *Scorsese: A Journey through the American Psyche,* ed. Paul A. Woods, 25–34. London: Plexus, 2005.

"Fact Sheet on the Internment of Italian Americans during World War II." http//scottoline. com/site/books/internment.html. Accessed November 8, 2010.

Fausty, Joshua, and Edvige Giunta. "An Interview with Nancy Savoca." *VIA: Voices in Italian Americana* 12, no. 2 (2001): 47–57.

———. "Quentin Tarantino: An Ethnic Enigma." In *Screening Ethnicity: Cinematographic Representations of Italian Americans in the United States,* ed. Anna Camaiti Hostert and Anthony Julian Tamburri, 210–21. Boca Raton: Bordighera Press, 2002.

Fazio, Michelle. "The Power of Storytelling in Mario Puzo's *The Godfather*: A Midwife's Tale." *VIA: Voices in Italian Americana* 19, no. 2 (2008): 81–96.

Ferraro, Thomas J. *Ethnic Passages: Literary Immigrants in Twentieth-Century America.* Chicago: University of Chicago Press, 1993.

———. *Feeling Italian: The Art of Ethnicity in America.* New York: New York University Press, 2005.

"Film Noir Web." *Reservoir Dogs.* DVD. 10th Anniversary ed. Miramax Home Video, 2002.

Fischler, Steven, dir. *Beyond Wiseguys: Italian Americans and the Movies.* Beachcomber Films and Pacific Street Films, 2008.

Foucault, Michel. "What Is an Author?" Trans. Donald F. Bouchard and Sherry Simon. In *Language, Counter-Memory, Practice: Selected Essays and Interviews,* ed. Donald F. Bouchard, 113–38. Ithaca: Cornell University Press, 1977.

Fried, John. "Two Shots at Quentin Tarantino's *Pulp Fiction.*" *Cineaste* 21, no. 3 (1995): 4+.

Friedman, Lawrence S. *The Cinema of Martin Scorsese.* New York: Continuum, 1998.

Friedman, Lester D. "Celluloid Palimpsests: An Overview of Ethnicity and the American Film." In *Unspeakable Images: Ethnicity and the American Cinema,* ed. Lester D. Friedman, 11–35. Chicago: University of Chicago Press, 1991.

Fuller, Graham. "Answers First, Questions Later." In *Projections 3: Filmmakers on Filmmaking,* 174–95. London: Faber and Faber, 1994. Reprinted in *Quentin Tarantino: Interviews,* ed. Gerald Peary, 49–65. Jackson: University Press of Mississippi, 1998.

Fulton, Valerie. "The Meaning of Violence in Quentin Tarantino's *Pulp Fiction*: Annotated Version." In *Society for the Interdisciplinary Study of Social Imagery Conference (5th: 1995: Colorado Springs, CO): The Image of Violence in Literature, the Media, and Society; Selected Papers [from the] 1995 Conference [of the] Society,* 178–82. Pueblo, Colo.: Society for the Interdisciplinary Study of Social Imagery, 1995.

Gallafent, Edward. *Quentin Tarantino.* New York: Pearson Education, 2006.

Gallman, J. Matthew. "*Gangs of New York.*" *Journal of American History* 90, no. 3 (2003): 1124–26.

Gambino, Richard. *Blood of My Blood: The Dilemma of the Italian-Americans.* 2nd ed. Picas Series. 1974. Reprint, Buffalo: Guernica, 1996.

———. "Despair, Italian Style." *Village Voice,* May 23, 1974. Reprinted in *Martin Scorsese: The First Decade,* ed. Mary Pat Kelly, 174–76. Pleasantville, N.Y.: Redgrave, 1980.

———. *Vendetta: The True Story of the Largest Lynching in U.S. History.* Picas Series. 1977. Reprint, Montreal: Guernica, 2000.

Gardaphé, Fred. "A Class Act: Understanding the Italian/American Gangster." In *Screening Ethnicity: Cinematographic Representations of Italian Americans in the United States,* ed. Anthony Julian Tamburri and Anna Camaiti Hostert, 48–68. Boca Raton: Bordighera Press, 2002.

———. "From *The Italian-American Writer: An Essay and an Annotated Checklist.*" In *Don't Tell Mama! The Penguin Book of Italian American Writing,* ed. Regina Barreca, 221–28. New York: Penguin Books, 2002.

———. *From Wiseguys to Wise Men: The Gangster and Italian American Masculinities.* New York: Routledge, 2006.

———. *Italian Signs, American Streets: The Evolution of Italian American Narrative.* Durham: Duke University Press, 1996.

Gardner, Gerald, and Harriet Modell Gardner. *The "Godfather" Movies: A Pictorial History.* New York: Wings Books, 1993.

Garrett, Greg. "It's Everybody's War: Racism and the World War Two Documentary." *Journal of Popular Film and Television* 22, no. 2 (1994): 70–78.

German, Kathleen M. "Frank Capra's 'Why We Fight' Series and the American Audience." *Western Journal of Speech Communication* 54, no. 2 (1990): 237–48.

Gilbey, Ryan. "*Lost in Translation.*" *Sight and Sound* 14, no. 1 (2004): 52.

Giles, Paul. "The Intertextual Politics of Cultural Catholicism: Tiepolo, Madonna, and Scorsese." In *Catholic Lives, Contemporary America,* ed. Thomas J. Ferraro, 120–40. Durham: Duke University Press, 1997.

Gilroy, Paul. *Against Race: Imagining Political Culture beyond the Color Line.* Cambridge: Harvard University Press, 2000.

Giovannini, Joseph. "Tarantino's Los Angeles: Roadside Noir." *New York Times,* December 30, 1997, B1.

Giroux, Henry A. "*Pulp Fiction* and the Culture of Violence." *Harvard Educational Review* 65, no. 1 (1995): 299–315.

Gitlin, Todd. "On the Popularity of *The Godfather.*" *Performance* 4 (September–October 1972): 37–40.

Giunta, Edvige. "Narratives of Loss: Voices of Ethnicity in Agnes Rossi and Nancy Savoca." *Canadian Journal of Italian Studies* 19, no. 53 (1996): 164–83.

———. "The Quest for True Love: Ethnicity in Nancy Savoca's Domestic Film Comedy." In *Screening Ethnicity: Cinematographic Representations of Italian Americans in the United States,* ed. Anna Camaiti Hostert and Anthony Julian Tamburri, 259–74. Boca Raton: Bordighera Press, 2002.

———. *Writing with an Accent: Contemporary Italian American Women Authors.* New York: Palgrave, 2002.

Glibereman, Owen. "Knockout Bunch." *Entertainment Weekly,* October 7, 1994. Reprinted in *Pulp Fiction* insert, 10–11. DVD. Miramax Home Video, 2002.

Golden, Daniel Sembroff. "The Fate of *La Famiglia:* Italian Images in American Film." In *The Kaleidoscopic Lens: How Hollywood Views Ethnic Groups,* ed. Randall M. Miller, 73–97. Englewood, N.J.: Jerome S. Ozer, 1980.

Goodwin, Michael, and Naomi Wise. *On the Edge: The Life and Times of Francis Coppola.* New York: William Morrow, 1989.

Gorin, Jean-Pierre. "Dramatis Personae." *Film Comment* 42, no. 6 (2006): 30–33.

Gormley, Paul. "The Affective City: Urban Black Bodies and Milieu in *Menace II Society* and *Pulp Fiction.*" In *Screening the City,* ed. Mark Shiel and Tony Fitzmaurice, 180–99. New York: Verso, 2003.

———. "Trashing Whiteness: *Pulp Fiction, Se7en, Strange Days,* and Articulating Affect." *Journal of the Theoretical Humanities* 6, no. 1 (2001): 155–71.

Graham, David John. "Redeeming Violence in the Films of Martin Scorsese." In *Explorations in Theology and Film: Movies and Meaning,* ed. Clive Marsh and Gaye Ortiz. Malden, Mass.: Blackwell, 1998.

Greene, Ray. "Grace Period." In *Boxoffice, 1997.* Reprinted in *Scorsese: A Journey through the American Psyche,* ed. Paul A. Woods, 232–36. London: Plexus, 2005.

Grist, Leighton. *The Films of Martin Scorsese, 1963–77.* New York: St. Martin's Press, 2000.

Guerrero, Ed. *Framing Blackness: The African American Image in Film.* Philadelphia: Temple University Press, 1993.

Guglielmo, Jennifer, and Salvatore Salerno, eds. *Are Italians White? How Race Is Made in America.* New York: Routledge, 2003.

Guglielmo, Thomas A. *White on Arrival: Italians, Race, Color, and Power in Chicago, 1890–1945.* New York: Oxford University Press, 2003.

Hall, Kenji. "Months before *Lost in Translation* Debut in Tokyo, Net Chat Sites in Japan Abuzz with Reviews." *Associated Press,* February 25, 2004.

Handzo, Stephen. "Under Capracorn." *Film Comment* 8 (1972): 8–14. Reprinted in *Frank Capra: The Man and His Films,* ed. Richard Glatzer and John Raeburn, 164–76. Ann Arbor: University of Michigan Press, 1975.

Harris, David A. "Ethnic Profiling by Police in Europe: Policing Practice; Case Study: Confronting Ethnic Profiling in the United States." 2007. http://www.soros.org/initiatives/justice/focus/equality_citizenship/articles_publications/publications/jutice-init_20050610. Accessed June 29, 2007.

Harrison, Paula. "The Master of the Human Touch." *Motion Picture* (July 1935): 55, 76. Reprinted in *Frank Capra Interviews,* ed. Leland Poague, 15–18. Jackson: University Press of Mississippi, 2004.

Hartley, Heather, dir. *"Linciati": Lynchings of Italians in America.* Distributed by National Film Network, 2004.

Haskell, Molly. "World of *The Godfather:* No Place for Women." *New York Times,* March 23, 1997, 17, 24.

Hattenstone, Simon. "I, Quentin." *Guardian,* February 27, 1998. Reprinted in *Quentin Tarantino: The Film Geek Files,* ed. Paul A. Woods, 160–65. London: Plexus, 2005.

Hellman, Geoffrey. "Thinker in Hollywood." *New Yorker,* February 24, 1940, 23–28. Reprinted in *Frank Capra: The Man and His Films,* ed. Richard Glatzer and John Raeburn, 3–13. Ann Arbor: University of Michigan Press, 1975.

Henkin, David. "*Gangs of New York.*" *American Historical Review* 108, no. 2 (2003): 620–22.

Hernandez, Raymond. "Congresswoman Takes a Whack at *The Sopranos* Stereotype." *New York Times,* May 24, 2001, B2.

Hilferty, Robert. "*Reservoir Dogs.*" *Cineaste* 19, no. 4 (1992): 79+.

Hill, Annette. *Shocking Entertainment: Viewer Response to Violent Movies.* Bedfordshire, UK: University of Luton Press, 1997.

Hill, Henry, and Edward McDonald. "Commentary Track." *GoodFellas.* DVD. Warner Bros. Home Video, 2004.

Holm, D. K. *Quentin Tarantino.* Harpenden, England: Pocket Essentials, 2004.

hooks, bell. "Cool Tool." In "Pulp the Hype: On the Q.T." *Artforum International* 33 (March 1995): 62+.

Hull, Stephanie, and Maurizio Viano. "The Image of Blacks in the Work of Coppola, De Palma, and Scorsese." In *Beyond the Margin: Readings in Italian Americana,* ed. Paolo A. Giordano and Anthony Julian Tamburri, 169–97. Madison, N.J.: Fairleigh Dickinson University Press, 1998.

Ignatiev, Noel. *How the Irish Became White.* New York: Routledge, 1995.

I'm an American! Radio broadcast, March 23, 1941. United States Department of Justice and NBC Blue Network.

Indiana, Gary. "Geek Chic." In "Pulp the Hype: On the Q.T." *Artforum International* 33 (March 1995): 62+.

"Interview with Charlie Rose." *Pulp Fiction.* DVD. Miramax Home Video, 2002.

"Interview with Quentin Tarantino." *Jackie Brown.* DVD. Miramax Home Video, 2002.

Italians in America. Greystone Communications and the A&E Network, 1998.

Jacobson, Matthew Frye. *Roots Too: White Ethnic Revival in Post–Civil Rights America.* Cambridge: Harvard University Press, 2006.

———. *Whiteness of a Different Color: European Immigrants and the Alchemy of Race.* Cambridge: Harvard University Press, 1998.

Jameson, Frederic. *Postmodernism; or, The Cultural Logic of Late Capitalism.* Durham: Duke University Press, 1991.

———. "Postmodernism and Consumer Society." In *The Anti-Aesthetic,* ed. Hal Foster, 11–25. Port Townsend, Wash.: Bay Press, 1983.

———. "Reification and Utopia in Mass Culture." In *Signatures of the Visible.* New York: Routledge, 1990.

Jardine, Dan. "The Killing Fields (on *Reservoir Dogs*)." *Film Journal* 1, no. 10. http://www.thefilmjournal.com/issue10/reservoirdogs.html. Accessed November 8, 2010.

Jewers, Caroline. "Heroes and Heroin: From True Romance to Pulp Fiction." *Journal of Popular Culture* 33, no. 4 (2000): 39–61.

Johnson, Brian D. "*Pulp Fiction.*" *Maclean's,* October 24, 1994, 57+.

Johnson, James Weldon. *The Autobiography of an Ex-Coloured Man.* 1927. Reprint, New York: Vintage Books, 1989.

Jolly, Mark. "A Terrible Beauty." *Guardian,* December 11, 1999. Reprinted in *Scorsese: A Journey through the American Psyche,* ed. Paul A. Woods, 241–50. London: Plexus, 2005.

Jones, Jenny M. *The Annotated "Godfather": The Complete Screenplay.* New York: Black Dog and Leventhal, 2007.

Jones, Kent. "A Critic's Heart Is an Ocean of Longing." *Film Comment* 34 (March–April 1998): 20–25.

Justice, Benjamin. "Historical Fiction to Historical Fact: *Gangs of New York* and the Whitewashing of History." *Social Education* 67, no. 4 (2003): 213–14.

Kael, Pauline. "Alchemy." *New Yorker,* March 18, 1972, 132+.

Kamiya, Gary. "He Got Game." Salon.com, April 30, 1998. http://www.salon.com/entertainment/movies/review/1998/04/30/game/index.html. Accessed November 8, 2010.

Kaplan, James. "The Outsider." *New York,* March 4, 1996, 32+.

Kapsis, Robert E. *Hitchcock: The Making of a Reputation.* Chicago: University of Chicago Press, 1992.

Kelly, Mary Pat. *Martin Scorsese: The First Decade.* Pleasantville, N.Y.: Redgrave, 1980.

———. *Martin Scorsese: A Journey.* New York: Thunder's Mouth Press, 1991.

Kennedy, Lisa. "Natural Born Filmmaker." *Village Voice,* October 25, 1994, 29–32.

Keough, Peter, transcriber. "Quentin Tarantino: Press Conference on *Jackie Brown.*" In *Quentin Tarantino: Interviews,* ed. Gerald Peary, 198–203. Jackson: University Press of Mississippi, 1997.

Kermode, Mark. "Teenage Kicks: Tarantino's Follow-up Is Neither Trashy nor Truthful—Just Adolescent." *New Statesman,* April 26, 2004, 46.

Keyser, Les. *Martin Scorsese.* Twayne's Filmmakers. New York: Twayne Publishers, 1992.

Kinney, Monica Yant. "In Any Language, It's Ugly." *Philadelphia Inquirer,* October 3, 2007, B1.

Kolker, Robert Phillip. *A Cinema of Loneliness: Penn, Kubrick, Scorsese, Spielberg, Altman.* 2nd ed. 1980. Reprint, New York: Oxford University Press, 1988.

Koppes, Clayton R., and Gregory D. Black. *Hollywood Goes to War: How Politics, Profits, and Propaganda Shaped World War II Movies.* London: Tauris Parke Paperbacks, 1988.

Kruth, Patricia. "The Color of New York: Places and Spaces in the Films of Martin Scorsese and Woody Allen." In *Cinema and Architecture: Méliès, Mallet-Stevens, Multimedia,* ed. François Pens and Maureen Thomas, 70–83. London: British Film Institute, 1997.

Kubek, Elizabeth. "'Spent for Us': Capra's Technologies of Mastery in *Lady for a Day.*" *Journal of Film and Video* 50, no. 2 (1998): 40–57.

LaGumina, Salvatore. *Wop! A Documentary History of Anti-Italian Discrimination in the United States.* 1973. Reprint, Buffalo: Guernica, 1999.

Lane, Anthony. "*Jackie Brown.*" *New Yorker,* January 12, 1998, 83–84.

Latimer, Jonathan P. "*The Godfather:* Metaphor and Microcosm." *Journal of Popular Film* 2, no. 2 (1973): 204–8.

Laurino, Maria. *Were You Always an Italian? Ancestors and Other Icons of Italian America.* New York: W. W. Norton, 2000.

Lawton, Ben. "America through Italian/American Eyes: Dream or Nightmare?" In *From the Margin: Writings in Italian Americana,* ed. Paolo A. Giordano, Anthony Julian Tamburri, and Fred L. Gardaphé, 417–49. Rev. ed. West Lafayette, Ind.: Purdue University Press, 2000.

Lebo, Harlan. *The "Godfather" Legacy.* 1997. Reprint, New York: Fireside, 2005.

LeCain, Maximilian. "Tarantino and the Vengeful Ghosts of Cinema." http://archive. sensesofcinema.com/contents/04/32/tarantino.html. Accessed September 20, 2010.

Lee, Nathan. "Pretty Vacant: The Radical Frivolity of Sofia Coppola's *Marie Antoinette*." *Film Comment* 42, no. 5 (2006): 24–26.

Levine, David. *"Pulp Fiction." New York Review of Books,* April 6, 1995, 22+.

Levy, Emanuel. "Critics' Commentary." *Reservoir Dogs.* 10th Anniversary DVD. Miramax Home Video, 2002.

Lewis, Jon. *American Film: A History.* New York: W. W. Norton, 2007.

———. *Whom God Wishes to Destroy . . . Francis Coppola and the New Hollywood.* Durham: Duke University Press, 1995.

Lindsey, Robert. "Promises to Keep." *New York Times Magazine,* July 24, 1988. Reprinted in *Francis Ford Coppola: Interviews,* ed. Gene D. Phillips and Rodney Hill, 132–42. Jackson: University Press of Mississippi, 2004.

Linn, Travis. "Media Methods That Lead to Stereotypes." In *Images That Injure: Pictorial Stereotypes in the Media,* ed. Paul Martin Lester and Susan Dente Ross. 2nd ed. Westport, Conn.: Praeger, 2003.

Lipman, Amanda. *"Pulp Fiction." Sight and Sound* 4, no. 11 (1994): 50–51.

Lipsitz, George. *The Possessive Investment in Whiteness: How White People Profit from Identity Politics.* Philadelphia: Temple University Press, 1998.

LoBrutto, Vincent. *Martin Scorsese: A Biography.* Westport, Conn.: Praeger, 2008.

Lourdeaux, Lee. *Italian and Irish Filmmakers in America: Ford, Capra, Coppola, and Scorsese.* Philadelphia: Temple University Press, 1990.

Luconi, Stefano. "Frank L. Rizzo and the Whitening of Italian Americans in Philadelphia." In *Are Italians White? How Race Is Made in America,* ed. Salvatore Salerno and Jennifer Guglielmo, 177–91. New York: Routledge, 2003.

Lyons, Donald. *Independent Visions: A Critical Introduction to Recent Independent American Film.* New York: Ballantine Books, 1994.

Maas, Peter. *The Valachi Papers.* 1968. Reprint, New York: Bantam Books, 1969.

———. "Why We Love the Mafia in the Movies." *New York Times,* September 9, 1990, 23, 45.

Mac. *"Goodfellas." Variety,* September 10, 1990. Reprinted in *Martin Scorsese: Close Up,* ed. Andy Dougan, 134–36. New York: Thunder's Mouth Press, 1998.

MacDougall, Robert. "Red, Brown, and Yellow Perils: Images of the American Enemy in the 1940s and 1950s." *Journal of Popular Culture* 32, no. 4 (1999): 59–75.

MacFarquhar, Larissa. "The Movie Lover: In Quentin Tarantino's Mind, the Projector Never Stops Running." *New Yorker,* Fall 2003, 146–59.

Machiyama, Tomohiro. "Quentin Tarantino Reveals Almost Everything That Inspired *Kill Bill*." Japattack.com, 2003. Reprinted in *Quentin Tarantino: The Film Geek Files,* ed. Paul A. Woods, 172–78. London: Plexus, 2005.

Magid, Ron. *"Mean Streets." American Cinematographer* 84, no. 1 (2003): 50–59.

Makarushka, Irena. "Tracing the Other in *Household Saints.*" *Literature and Theology* 12, no. 1 (1998): 82–92.

Maland, Charles J. "Capra and the Abyss: Self-Interest versus the Common Good in Depression America." In *Frank Capra: Authorship and the Studio System,* ed. Robert Sklar and Vito Zagarrio, 95–129. Philadelphia: Temple University Press, 1996.

———. *Frank Capra.* 1980. Reprint, New York: Twayne Publishers, 1995.

Malyszko, William. *The Godfather.* London: York Press, 2001.

Mangione, Jerre, and Ben Morreale. *"La Storia": Five Centuries of the Italian American Experience.* New York: HarperPerennial, 1992.

Marchetti, Gina. "Ethnicity, the Cinema, and Cultural Studies." In *Unspeakable Images: Ethnicity and the American Cinema,* ed. Lester D. Friedman, 277–307. Urbana: University of Illinois Press, 1991.

Martin, Mardik, Paul Schrader, Jason Lustig, and Jake LaMotta. "Storyteller's Commentary." *Raging Bull.* DVD. Warner Bros. Home Video, 2005.

"Martin Scorsese on *La Strada.*" *La Strada.* DVD. Criterion Collection, 2003.

Maslin, Janet. *"Pulp Fiction." New York Times,* September 23, 1994, C1.

Maxfield, James F. "'The Worst Part': Martin Scorsese's *Mean Streets.*" *Literature/Film Quarterly* 23, no. 4 (1995): 279–86.

McBride, Joseph. *Frank Capra: The Catastrophe of Success.* New York: Simon and Schuster, 1992.

McCarthy, Todd. *"Jackie Brown." Variety,* December 22, 1997, 57+.

McDonald, William. "Thicker than Water, and Spilled by the Mob." *New York Times,* May 21, 1995, 11, 20.

McGowan, Todd. "There Is Nothing Lost in Translation." *Quarterly Review of Film and Video* 24, no. 1 (2007): 53–63.

McLellan, Jim. "Tarantino on the Run." *Observer,* July 3, 1994. Reprinted in *Quentin Tarantino: The Film Geek Files,* ed. Paul A. Woods, 53–60. London: Plexus, 2005.

Mendelsohn, Daniel. "It's Only a Movie." *New York Review of Books,* December 18, 2003, 38+.

Meyer, Nicholas, dir. *Vendetta.* Home Box Office, 1999.

"Michael Imperioli's Mob Scene: Emmy-Winning Actor Talks to Russ Mitchell about *The Sopranos.*" *CBS Sunday Morning,* September 26, 2004.

Miklitsch, Robert. "Audiophilia: Audiovisual Pleasure and Narrative Cinema in *Jackie Brown.*" *Screen* 45, no. 4 (2004): 287–304.

Miller, Jonathan. "Walken v. Hopper in *True Romance.*" *Creative Screenwriting* 5, no. 1 (1998). Reprinted in *Quentin Tarantino: The Film Geek Files,* ed. Paul A. Woods, 43–47. London: Plexus, 2005.

Minganti, Franco. "The Hero with a Thousand and Three Faces: Michele, Mike, Michael Corleone." *Rivista di Studi Angel-American* 3, nos. 4–5 (1984–85): 257–68.

Molony, Sinéad. "'The Blood Stays on the Blade': An Analysis of Irish-American Masculinities in the Films of Martin Scorsese." *Irish Feminist Review* 3 (December 2007): 137+.

Mooney, Joshua. "Interview with Quentin Tarantino." *Movieline,* August 1994, 51–90. Reprinted in *Quentin Tarantino: Interviews,* ed. Gerald Peary, 70–79. Jackson: University Press of Mississippi, 1998.

Mormino, Gary. "World War II: Consequences." American Italian Historical Association

Thirty-fifth Annual Conference, "The Impact of World War II on Italian Americans, 1935–Present." Loyola University, Chicago, 2002.

Morris, Wesley. "*Kill Bill: Volume 1.*" *Boston Globe*, October 10, 2003. Reprinted in *Quentin Tarantino: The Film Geek Files*, ed. Paul A. Woods, 170–71. London: Plexus, 2005.

Munby, Jonathan. *Public Enemies, Public Heroes: Screening the Gangster from "Little Caesar" to "Touch of Evil."* Chicago: University of Chicago Press, 1999.

Murf. "*Finian's Rainbow.*" *Variety*, October 9, 1968. Reprinted in *Francis Coppola: Close Up*, by Ronald Bergen, 105–7. New York: Thunder's Mouth Press, 1998.

Muscio, Giuliana. "From the Lower East Side to Fifth Avenue, and Back: Frank Capra's *The Younger Generation.*" *European Contributions to American Studies* 53 (2004): 313–22.

———. "Roosevelt, Arnold, and Capra; or, The Federalist-Populist Paradox." In *Frank Capra: Authorship and the Studio System,* ed. Robert Sklar and Vito Zagarrio, 164–89. Philadelphia: Temple University Press, 1998.

Nardini, Gloria. "*Che Bella Figura!*": The Power of Performance in an Italian Ladies' Club in Chicago. Albany: SUNY Press, 1999.

———. "Is It *True Love*? Or Not? Patterns of Ethnicity and Gender in Nancy Savoca." *VIA: Voices in Italian Americana* 2, no. 1 (1991): 9–17.

Naremore, James. "Authorship." In *A Companion to Film Theory,* ed. Robert Stam and Toby Miller, 9–24. Oxford: Blackwell Publishers, 1999.

———. "Authorship and the Cultural Politics of Film Criticism." *Film Quarterly* 44, no. 1 (1990): 14–22.

Newman, Kim. "Day of the Women." *Sight and Sound* 14, no. 6 (2004): 24–27, 63–64.

———. "*Kill Bill, Vol. 1.*" *Sight and Sound* 13, no. 12 (2003): 39–42.

Nochimson, Martha P. *Dying to Belong: Gangster Movies in Hollywood and Hong Kong.* Malden, Mass.: Blackwell, 2007.

Novak, Michael. *The Rise of the Unmeltable Ethnics: Politics and Culture in the Seventies.* New York: Macmillan, 1971.

Oestreicher, Richard. "How Should Historians Think about *The Gangs of New York*?" *History Workshop Journal* 56, no. 1 (2003): 210–16.

O'Hagen, Sean. "X Offender." *Times Magazine,* October 15, 1994. Reprinted in *Quentin Tarantino: The Film Geek Files,* ed. Paul A. Woods, 61–66. London: Plexus, 2005.

Olsen, Mark. "Turning on a Dime." *Sight and Sound* 13, no. 10 (2003): 12–15.

Orsi, Robert Anthony. *The Madonna of 115th Street: Faith and Community in Italian Harlem, 1880–1950.* New Haven: Yale University Press, 1985.

Page, Edwin. *Quintessential Tarantino.* New York: Marion Boyars, 2005.

Palmer, B. D. "The Hands That Built America: A Class-Politics Appreciation of Martin Scorsese's *The Gangs of New York.*" *Historical Materialism* 11, no. 4 (2003): 317–45.

Papke, David Ray. "Myth and Meaning: Francis Ford Coppola and Popular Response to the *Godfather* Trilogy." In *Legal Realism: Movies as Legal Texts,* ed. John Denvir, 1–22. Urbana: University of Illinois Press, 2006.

Peary, Gerald. "A Talk with Quentin Tarantino." In *Quentin Tarantino: Interviews,* ed. Gerald Peary, 27–29. Jackson: University Press of Mississippi, 1992.

Penman, Ian. "Don't Try This at Home." In *Vital Signs: Music, Movies, and Other Manias.* Reprinted in *Quentin Tarantino: The Film Geek Files,* ed. Paul A. Woods, 124–27. London: Plexus, 2005.

Phillips, Gene D. *Godfather: The Intimate Francis Ford Coppola.* Lexington: University Press of Kentucky, 2004.

Phillips, Gene D., and Rodney Hill, eds. *Francis Ford Coppola: Interviews.* Jackson: University Press of Mississippi, 2004.

Platten, David. "Private Spectacle, Public Voice: Two Sides to Contemporary Cinema in France and the USA." In *Making Connections: Essays in French Culture and Society in Honour of Philip Thody,* ed. James Dolamore, 255–69. New York: Peter Lang, 1999.

Poague, Leland A. *Another Frank Capra.* New York: Cambridge University Press, 1994.

———. *The Cinema of Frank Capra: An Approach to Film Comedy.* New York: A. S. Barnes, 1975.

———, ed. *Frank Capra: Interviews.* Jackson: University Press of Mississippi, 2004.

Polan, Dana. *Pulp Fiction.* BFI Modern Classics. 2000. Reprint, London: BFI Publishing, 2004.

Poon, Phoebe. "The Tragedy of Michael Corleone in *The Godfather: Part III.*" *Literature/ Film Quarterly* 34, no. 1 (2006): 64–70.

"*Pulp Fiction:* The Facts." *Pulp Fiction.* DVD. Miramax Home Video, 2002.

Puzo, Mario. *The Fortunate Pilgrim.* 1964. Reprint, New York: Ballantine, 1997.

———. *The Godfather.* 30th Anniversary ed. 1969. Reprint, New York: New American Library, 1999.

———. "The Making of *The Godfather.*" In *The "Godfather" Papers and Other Confessions.* New York: G. P. Putnam's Sons, 1972.

Quart, Leonard, and Paul Rabinow. "The Ethos of *Mean Streets.*" *Film and History* (1975). Reprinted in *Scorsese: A Journey through the American Psyche,* ed. Paul A. Woods, 42–45. London: Plexus, 2005.

"Quentin Tarantino on *Pulp Fiction.*" *Pulp Fiction.* DVD. Miramax Home Video, 2002.

Quinn, Roseanne Giannini. "Mothers, Molls, and Misogynists: Resisting Italian American Womanhood in *The Sopranos.*" *Journal of American Culture* 27, no. 2 (2004): 166–74.

Raab, Selwyn. *Five Families: The Rise, Decline, and Resurgence of America's Most Powerful Mafia Empires.* New York: Thomas Dunne Books, 2006.

Rafferty, Terrence. "*Reservoir Dogs.*" *New Yorker,* October 19, 1992, 105+.

Rapf, Joanna E. "Doing Nothing: Harry Langdon and the Performance of Absence." *Film Quarterly* 59, no. 1 (2005): 27–35.

Ray, Robert. *A Certain Tendency of the Hollywood Cinema.* Princeton: Princeton University Press, 1985.

Rheuban, Joyce. *Harry Langdon: The Comedian as Metteur-en-Scène.* Rutherford, N.J.: Fairleigh Dickinson University Press, 1983.

Rich, Motoko, Lukas Schwarzacher, and Fumie Tomita. "Land of the Rising Cliche." *New York Times,* January 4, 2004, sec. 2, p. 1.

Richards, Jeffrey. "Frank Capra and the Cinema of Populism." In *Movies and Methods,* ed. Bill Nichols, 1:65–77. Berkeley and Los Angeles: University of California Press, 1976.

Ritter, Kelly. "Postmodern Dialogics in *Pulp Fiction:* Jules, Ezekiel, and Double-Voiced Discourse." In *The Terministic Screen: Rhetorical Perspectives on Film,* ed. David Blakesley, 286–302. Carbondale: Southern Illinois University Press, 2003.

Rittger, Guy C. "The Regime of the Exploding Body and the Erotics of Film Violence: Penn,

Peckinpah, Tarantino, and Beyond." In *Society for the Interdisciplinary Study of Social Imagery. Conference (5th: 1995: Colorado Springs, CO): The Image of Violence in Literature, the Media, and Society; Selected Papers [from the] 1995 Conference [of the] Society for the Interdisciplinary Study of Social Imagery*, ed. Will Wright and Steven Kaplan, 357–62. Pueblo, Colo.: Society for the Interdisciplinary Study of Social Imagery, 1995.

Rochlin, Margy. "Twenty Questions with Quentin Tarantino." *Playboy*, November 1994, 32–33, 166–70.

Roediger, David R. *The Wages of Whiteness: Race and the Making of the American Working Class*. Rev. ed. 1991. Reprint, New York: Verso, 1999.

———. *Working towards Whiteness: How America's Immigrants Became White; The Strange Journey from Ellis Island to the Suburbs*. New York: Basic Books, 2005.

Rogin, Michael. *Blackface, White Noise: Jewish Immigrants in the Hollywood Melting Pot*. Berkeley and Los Angeles: University of California Press, 1996.

Rollins, Peter C. "Birth of a Film Genre." *The World and I* 10, no. 6 (1995): 64–73.

———. "Frank Capra's 'Why We Fight' Film Series and Our American Dream." *Journal of American Culture* 19, no. 4 (1996): 81–86.

Romney, Jonathan. "*Reservoir Dogs*." *New Statesman and Society* (January 8, 1993): 34+.

Rosenbaum, Jonathan. "Allusion Profusion: *Ed Wood, Pulp Fiction*." In *Movies as Politics*, 171–78. Berkeley and Los Angeles: University of California Press, 1997.

Rothstein, Edward. "Chilling Balance of Love and Evil." *New York Times*, March 23, 1997, 17, 26.

Roukema, Marge. "Roukema Defends *Sopranos* Critique." *Bergen County Record*, May 16, 2001, L10.

"Roundtable Discussion with Quentin Tarantino, Brad Pitt, and Elvis Mitchell." *Inglourious Basterds*. DVD. Universal Studios, 2010.

Ruberto, Laura E. "Where Did the Goodfellas Learn to Cook? Gender, Labor, and the Italian American Experience." *Italian Americana* 21, no. 2 (2003): 164–76.

Ruderman, Wendy. "Profiling Was Used in War on Drugs: Papers Show Troopers Labeled Ethnic Groups." *Bergen County Record*, November 28, 2000, A1.

Russo, John Paul. "An Unacknowledged Masterpiece: Capra's Italian American Film." In *Screening Ethnicity: Cinematographic Representations of Italian Americans in the United States*, ed. Anna Camaiti Hostert and Anthony Julian Tamburri, 291–321. Boca Raton: Bordighera Press, 2002.

Salomon, Julie. "*Pulp Fiction*." *Wall Street Journal*, October 18, 1994, A16.

Saltzman, Joe. *Frank Capra and the Image of the Journalist in American Film*. Los Angeles: Image of the Journalist in Popular Culture, 2002.

Sammells, Neil. "Pulp Fictions: Oscar Wilde and Quentin Tarantino." *Irish Studies Review* 11 (1995): 39–46.

San Filippo, Maria. "*Lost in Translation*." *Cineaste* 31, no. 2 (2003): 26–28.

Sangster, Jim. *Scorsese*. London: Virgin, 2002.

Sarris, Andrew. *The American Cinema: Directors and Directions, 1929–1968*. 1968. Reprint, Chicago: Da Capo Press, 1996.

Sautman, Francesca Canadé. "Women of the Shadows: Italian American Women, Ethnicity, and Racism in American Cinema." *Differentia: Review of Italian Thought* 6–7 (1994): 219–46.

Savoca, Nancy. "Conversation with Edvige Giunta." American Italian Historical Association Thirty-sixth Annual Conference, "Italian Americans in the Arts and Culture." Florida Atlantic University, Boca Raton, 2003.

Scarpaci, Vincenza. "Walking the Color Line: Italian Immigrants in Rural Louisiana, 1880–1910." In *Are Italians White? How Race Is Made in America,* ed. Jennifer Guglielmo and Salvatore Salerno, 60–76. New York: Routledge, 2003.

Schatz, Thomas. "The New Hollywood." In *Film Theory Goes to the Movies,* ed. Jim Collins, Hilary Radner, and Ava Preacher Collins, 8–36. New York: Routledge, 1993.

Schelly, William. *Harry Langdon.* Filmmakers Series. Metuchen, N.J.: Scarecrow Press, 1982.

Scherini, Rose D. "When Italian Americans Were Enemy Aliens." In *"Una Storia Segreta": The Secret History of Italian American Evacuation and Internment during World War II,* ed. Lawrence Di Stasi, 10–31. Berkeley: Heyday Books, 2001.

Scherle, Victor, and William Turner Levy. *The Complete Films of Frank Capra.* 1977. Reprint, New York: Carol Publishing Group, 1992.

Scheuer, Philip K. "*State of the Union* to Pace Election." *Los Angeles Times,* September 28, 1947, sec. 2, pp. 1–2. Reprinted in *Frank Capra Interviews,* ed. Leland Poague, 31–33. Jackson: University Press of Mississippi, 2004.

Schmidt, Paul H. "Charming Pigs and Mimetic Desire in Quentin Tarantino's *Pulp Fiction.*" *University of Dayton Review* 24, no. 1 (1996): 43–53.

Schumacher, Michael. *Francis Ford Coppola: A Filmmaker's Life.* New York: Three Rivers Press, 1999.

Sciorra, Joseph. "'Italians against Racism': The Murder of Yusuf Hawkins (R.I.P.) and My March on Bensonhurst." In *Are Italians White? How Race Is Made in America,* ed. Salvatore Salerno and Jennifer Guglielmo, 192–209. New York: Routledge, 2003.

Scorsese, Martin. "Commentary." *Gangs of New York.* DVD. Warner Bros. Home Video, 2003.

Scott, A. O. "Blood Bath and Beyond." *New York Times,* October 10, 2003, E1.

———. "To Feel a City Seethe." *New York Times,* December 20, 2002, E1, 35.

Scott, Ian. *In Capra's Shadow: The Life and Career of Screenwriter Robert Riskin.* Lexington: University Press of Kentucky, 2006.

Scottoline, Lisa. *Killer Smile.* New York: HarperCollins, 2004.

———. "An Open Secret about the Italian American Internment." http://scottoline.com/Site/Italians/. Accessed June 26, 2008.

Sennett, Mack. *King of Comedy.* Garden City, N.Y.: Doubleday, 1954.

Shadoian, Jack. *Dreams and Dead Ends: The American Gangster Film.* 2nd ed. New York: Oxford University Press, 2003.

Shohat, Ella, and Robert Stam. *Unthinking Eurocentrism: Multiculturalism and the Media.* New York: Routledge, 2000.

Sklar, Robert. "The Imagination of Stability: The Depression Films of Frank Capra." In *Frank Capra: The Man and His Films,* ed. Richard Glatzer and John Raeburn, 121–38. Ann Arbor: University of Michigan Press, 1975.

———. "A Leap in the Void: Frank Capra's Apprenticeship to Ideology." In *Frank Capra: Authorship and the Studio System,* ed. Robert Sklar and Vito Zagarrio, 37–63. Philadelphia: Temple University Press, 1998.

Slotkin, Richard. *Gunfighter Nation: The Myth of the Frontier in Twentieth-Century America.* New York: HarperCollins, 1992.

Smith, Gavin. "The Art of Vision: Martin Scorsese's *Kundun*." *Film Comment* (January–February 1998). Reprinted in *Martin Scorsese: Interviews*, ed. Peter Brunette, 236–56. Jackson: University Press of Mississippi, 1999.

———. "Martin Scorsese Interviewed." *Film Comment* (November–December 1993). Reprinted in *Martin Scorsese: Interviews*, ed. Peter Brunette, 200–219. Jackson: University Press of Mississippi, 1999.

———. "When You Know You're in Good Hands." *Film Comment* (1994): 32–43. Reprinted in *Quentin Tarantino: Interviews*, ed. Gerald Peary, 97–114. Jackson: University Press of Mississippi, 1998.

Smith, Jim. *Tarantino*. London: Virgin Books, 2005.

Smith, Paul Julian. "Tokyo Drifters." *Sight and Sound* 14, no. 1 (2004): 12–16.

Smoodin, Eric. *Regarding Frank Capra: Audience, Celebrity, and American Film Studies, 1930–1960*. Durham: Duke University Press, 2004.

Sobchack, Vivian. "Postmodern Modes of Ethnicity." In *Unspeakable Images: Ethnicity and the American Cinema*, ed. Lester D. Friedman, 329–52. Urbana: University of Illinois Press, 1991.

Sollors, Werner. *Beyond Ethnicity: Consent and Descent in American Culture*. New York: Oxford University Press, 1986.

Sragow, Michael. "Twenty-five Years Later, Francis Ford Coppola Thinks It's a Mixed Blessing." *New Yorker*, March 24, 1997, 44+.

Staiger, Janet. "Authorship Approaches." In *Authorship and Film*, ed. David A. Gerstner and Janet Staiger, 27–57. New York: Routledge, 2003.

Steele, Richard W. "'The Greatest Gangster Movie Ever Filmed': *Prelude to War*." *Prologue* 11, no. 4 (1979): 220–35.

Steinberg, Stephen. *The Ethnic Myth: Race, Ethnicity, and Class in America*. 3rd ed. Boston: Beacon Press, 2001.

Stern, Lesley. *The Scorsese Connection*. Bloomington: Indiana University Press, 1995.

Stewart, Jacqueline. *Migrating to the Movies: Cinema and Black Urban Modernity*. Berkeley and Los Angeles: University of California Press, 2005.

Steyn, Mark. "Comic-Book Spirit." *Spectator*, April 24, 2004, 61+.

Stuart, John. "Fine Italian Hand." *Collier's*, August 17, 1935.

Studlar, Gaylyn. *This Mad Masquerade: Stardom and Masculinity in the Jazz Age*. New York: Columbia University Press, 1996.

Tamburri, Anthony Julian. "An Offer We Can Refuse." September 11, 2008. http://www.i-italy.org/bloggers/4232/offer-we-can-refuse. Accessed September 20, 2010.

———. "To Hyphenate or Not to Hyphenate: The Italian/American Writer and *Italianitá*." *Italian Journal* 3, no. 5 (1989): 37–42.

Tancredo, Tom. "Tom's Quest." http://www.tancredo.org/. Accessed September 20, 2010.

Tarantino, Quentin. "Commentary Track." *True Romance*. Two-Disc Special Edition. Warner Bros. Home Video, 2002.

———. *Inglorious Basterds*. Blue revised script. 2008.

———. Interview on *The Today Show*. NBC, August 14, 2009.

Tarantino Connection. Hip-O Records, 1997.

Taubin, Amy. "Blood and Pasta." *New Statesman and Society* (November 9, 1990): 12+.

———. "Critics' Commentary." *Reservoir Dogs*. 10th Anniversary DVD. Miramax Home Video, 2002.

———. "The Men's Room." *Sight and Sound* (1992). Reprinted in *Quentin Tarantino: The Film Geek Files,* ed. Paul A. Woods, 26–29. London: Plexus, 2005.

Tayler, Christopher. "Old Knives Tale." *TLS: Times Literary Supplement,* January 24, 2003, 19.

Taylor, Ella. "Quentin Tarantino's *Reservoir Dogs* and the Thrill of Excess." *L.A. Weekly,* October 16, 1992, 18–25. Reprinted in *Quentin Tarantino: Interviews,* ed. Gerald Peary, 41–48. Jackson: University Press of Mississippi, 1998.

Terkla, Dan, and Thomas L. Reed Jr. "'I'm Gonna Git Medieval on Your Ass': *Pulp Fiction* for the '90s—the 1190s." *Studies in Popular Culture* 20, no. 1 (1997): 39–52.

Thompson, David, and Ian Christie, eds. *Scorsese on Scorsese.* 1989. Reprint, Boston: Faber and Faber, 1996.

Thompson, Frank. "Harry Langdon: The Fourth Genius?" *Film Comment* 33, no. 3 (1997): 77–80.

Thomson, David. "Michael Corleone, Role Model." *Esquire,* March 1997, 60–61.

Tomasulo, Frank P. "Italian-Americans in the Hollywood Cinema: Filmmakers, Characters, Audiences." *VIA: Voices in Italian Americana* 7, no. 1 (1996): 65–72.

———. "Japan through Others' Lenses: *Hiroshima Mon Amour* (1959) and *Lost in Translation* (2003)." *Japan Studies Review* 11 (2007): 143–56.

———. "The Politics of Ambivalence: *Apocalypse Now* as Postwar and Antiwar Film." In *From Hanoi to Hollywood: The Vietnam War in American Film,* ed. Linda Dittmar and Gene Michaud, 145–58. New Brunswick: Rutgers University Press, 1990.

———. "Raging Bully: Postmodern Violence and Masculinity in *Raging Bull.*" In *Mythologies of Violence in Postmodern Media,* ed. Christopher Sharrett, 175–97. Detroit: Wayne State University Press, 1999.

Topel, Fred. "Tarantino Talks *Kill Bill: Vol. 2.*" *Screenwriters Monthly* (February 2004). Reprinted in *Quentin Tarantino: The Film Geek Files,* ed. Paul A. Woods, 181–85. London: Plexus, 2005.

Travers, Peter. "Critics' Commentary." *Reservoir Dogs.* 10th Anniversary DVD. Miramax Home Video, 2002.

———. "*Kill Bill: Volume 2.*" *Rolling Stone,* April 29, 2004. Reprinted in *Quentin Tarantino: The Film Geek Files,* ed. Paul A. Woods, 179–80. London: Plexus, 2005.

"Trivia Track." *Jackie Brown.* DVD. Miramax Home Video, 2002.

"Trivia Track." *Pulp Fiction.* DVD. Miramax Home Video, 2002.

Truman, James. "Interview with Martin Scorsese." *Face,* no. 82 (February 1987). Reprinted in *Scorsese: A Journey through the American Psyche,* ed. Paul A. Woods, 13–15. London: Plexus, 2005.

Verdicchio, Pasquale. "Return Voyages: Rossellini, Scorsese, and the Identity of National Cinema." In *'Merica: A Conference on the Culture and Literature of Italians in North America,* ed. Aldo Bove and Giuseppe Massarra. Stony Brook, N.Y.: Forum Italicum Publishing, 2006.

Walker Fields, Ingrid. "Family Values and Feudal Code: The Social Politics of America's Twenty-first Century Gangster." *Journal of Popular Culture* 37, no. 4 (2004): 611–33.

Werner, Jeff, dir. *The "Godfather" Family: A Look Inside.* Paramount Pictures and Zoetrope Studios, 1990.

West, Rebecca. "Scorsese's *Who's That Knocking at My Door:* Night Thoughts on Italian Studies in the United States." In *Romance Languages Annual,* ed. Jeanette Beer, Charles

Ganelin, and Anthony Julian Tamburri, 3:331–38. West Lafayette, Ind.: Purdue Research Foundation, 1992.

Wiener, Thomas. "Martin Scorsese Fights Back." *American Film* (November 1980). Reprinted in *Scorsese: A Journey through the American Psyche,* ed. Paul A. Woods, 116–23. London: Plexus, 2005.

Willis, Sharon. "The Fathers Watch the Boy's Room." *Camera Obscura* 32 (June 1995): 40–73.

Wolfe, Charles. *Frank Capra: A Guide to References and Resources.* Boston: G. K. Hall, 1987.

———. "*Mr. Smith Goes to Washington:* Democratic Forums and Representations Forms." In *Frank Capra: Authorship and the Studio System,* ed. Robert Sklar and Vito Zagarrio, 190–221. Philadelphia: Temple University Press, 1998.

Wood, Robin. "Ideology, Genre, Auteur." In *Film Theory and Criticism: Introductory Readings,* ed. Leo Braudy and Marshall Cohen, 668–78. 5th ed. New York: Oxford University Press, 1999.

———. "Slick Shtick." In "Pulp the Hype: On the Q.T." *Artforum International* 33 (March 1995): 62+.

Woods, Paul A. *King Pulp: The Wild World of Quentin Tarantino.* New York: Thunder's Mouth Press, 1996.

———, ed. *Quentin Tarantino: The Film Geek Files.* London: Plexus, 2005.

"World Opinion on Sacco and Vanzetti." *Nation,* August 1927. Reprinted in *Sacco and Vanzetti,* ed. John Davis, 72–75. Rebel Lives Series. New York: Ocean Press, 2004.

Wright, Evan. "Quentin's Kung-Fu Grip." *Rolling Stone,* October 30, 2003, 42+.

Wright, George. "Hit Film Gets Lost in Racism Row." *Guardian,* February 27, 2004. http://www.guardian.co.uk/world/2004/feb/27/oscars2004.usa. Accessed November 8, 2010.

Young, Toby. "All Bark and No Bite." *Modern Review* 1, no. 17 (1994): 13.

Zacharek, Stephanie. "*Lost in Translation.*" Salon.com, September 12, 2003. http://www.salon.com/entertainment/movies/review/2003/09/12/translation. Accessed November 8, 2010.

Zagarrio, Vito. "It Is (Not) a Wonderful Life: For a Counter-Reading to Ideology." In *Frank Capra: Authorship and the Studio System,* ed. Vito Zagarrio and Robert Sklar, 64–94. Philadelphia: Temple University Press, 1998.

Index

JONATHAN J. CAVALLERO is an assistant
professor of communication at the University
of Arkansas.

The University of Illinois Press
is a founding member of the
Association of American University Presses.

———————————————————

Composed in 10.5/13 Adobe Minion Pro
at the University of Illinois Press
Manufactured by Cushing-Malloy, Inc.

University of Illinois Press
1325 South Oak Street
Champaign, IL 61820-6903
www.press.uillinois.edu